Fashion | Sense

Also Available from Bloomsbury

It's Not Personal: Post 60s Body Art and Performance
Susan Best
Gaga Aesthetics: Art, Fashion, Popular Culture, and the Up-Ending of Tradition
Adam Geczy and Vicki Karaminas
Adornment: What Self-Decoration Tells Us about Who We Are
Stephen Davies
Aesthetics of Ugliness: A Critical Edition
Karl Rosenkranz, trans. by Andrei Pop and Mechtild Widrich

Fashion | Sense

On Philosophy and Fashion

Gwenda-lin Grewal

BLOOMSBURY ACADEMIC
LONDON • NEW YORK • OXFORD • NEW DELHI • SYDNEY

BLOOMSBURY ACADEMIC
Bloomsbury Publishing Plc
50 Bedford Square, London, WC1B 3DP, UK
1385 Broadway, New York, NY 10018, USA
29 Earlsfort Terrace, Dublin 2, Ireland

BLOOMSBURY, BLOOMSBURY ACADEMIC and the Diana logo
are trademarks of Bloomsbury Publishing Plc

First published in Great Britain 2022

Copyright © Gwenda-lin Grewal, 2022

Gwenda-lin Grewal has asserted her right under the Copyright, Designs and
Patents Act, 1988, to be identified as Author of this work.

"The Truest Poetry is the Most Feigning," copyright 1954 by W. H. Auden and © renewed
1982 by The Estate of W. H. Auden; from COLLECTED POEMS by W. H. Auden,
edited by Edward Mendelson. Used by permission of Random House,
an imprint and division of Penguin Random House LLC. All rights reserved.

You're So Vain
Words and Music by Carly Simon
Copyright © 1972 C'EST MUSIC
Copyright Renewed
All Rights Administered by UNIVERSAL MUSIC CORP.
All Rights Reserved Used by Permission
Reprinted by Permission of Hal Leonard LLC

Girl's Talk
Words and Music by Elvis Costello
Copyright © 1980 by Universal Music Publishing MGB Ltd.
All Rights in the United States Administered by Universal Music - MGB Songs
International Copyright Secured All Rights Reserved
Reprinted by Permission of Hal Leonard LLC

For legal purposes the Acknowledgments on pp. ix–x constitute an
extension of this copyright page.

Cover design: Ben Anslow
Cover image: *Bubbles* @Sevenarts Ltd.

All rights reserved. No part of this publication may be reproduced or
transmitted in any form or by any means, electronic or mechanical,
including photocopying, recording, or any information storage or
retrieval system, without prior permission in writing from the publishers.

Bloomsbury Publishing Plc does not have any control over, or responsibility
for, any third-party websites referred to or in this book. All internet addresses
given in this book were correct at the time of going to press. The author and
publisher regret any inconvenience caused if addresses have changed or sites
have ceased to exist, but can accept no responsibility for any such changes.

A catalogue record for this book is available from the British Library.

A catalog record for this book is available from the Library of Congress.

ISBN: HB: 978-1-3502-0145-3
       PB: 978-1-3502-0146-0
       ePDF: 978-1-3502-0147-7
       eBook: 978-1-3502-0148-4

Typeset by Integra Software Services Pvt. Ltd.

To find out more about our authors and books visit www.bloomsbury.com
and sign up for our newsletters.

μνᾶμ' ἀνέθηκα τόδε σοι

Contents

Acknowledgments	ix
nota bene	xi
Note to the Reader	xii
Preface: The "Other" Ancient Quarrel	**xv**
Fashion's Poetry and Philosophy's Disapproval	xvi
"The Truest Poetry Is the Most Feigning"	xviii
The Soul	xxi
Fashion Is Not Modern	xxiii
1 Fashion Sense	**1**
Touch of Clothes and Sense of Self	3
The Nude Abides: Origins of Words and Clothes	7
Utilitarian Narcissism	11
"Real" Clothes and Buried Selves	21
Profanity and Disinvested Vestment	25
2 Phantom Selves	**29**
Euripides' *Bacchae*: The Tragedy of Punk and Prep	30
Bacchic Leisurewear	37
Euripides' *Helen*: Greek Expectations and Trojan Clotheshorses	41
Normcore's Mean: Democracy and Tyranny	51
Seeing without Being Seen: Gyges, Sweatpants, and World Domination	56
3 The Dead	**63**
Fashion and Philosophy in Their Prime	65
Sophocles' *Antigone*: Anti-aging Goth	76
The Plot to Bury/Kill	79
Clothes as Poetic Dust	83
Blood and Armor	85
What Is Not: Hair	90
4 The Dandy	**99**
To Wit	101

	Political Interlude	109
	Dandy Demagoguery	113
	Athleisure	115
	The Rational Dress Society	116
	The Carnival	122
	Sound ft. Vision	124
5	**Divine Tailoring**	**131**
	Sartor Resartus: Divine Nonsense	133
	Clotho	138
	Hephaestus	142
6	**The Beauty of Ugliness**	**147**
	Bernie's Mittens	148
	Hippias of Elis	151
	Conceptual Cash	154
	Partial Wholes and Evil Twinning	157
	Apparent Beauty	162
	You	168
	Looking Bad	171
7	**The Question of Fashion's Beginning**	**179**
	Notes	187
	Bibliography	204
	Index	213

Acknowledgments

These Acknowledgments must begin with a special thanks to my first and perhaps most unsuspecting audience: in 2011, I was an Andrew W. Mellon postdoctoral fellow in Humanities at Yale University, where I gave a cheeky talk on fashion and philosophy during the fellows' lunch hour. I was then a recent PhD, and had become fascinated by the strange way in which academics seem to both condemn and live by the rules of fashion. I am grateful to the Whitney Humanities Center for the opportunity to give that talk, and especially to the support of Norma Thompson.

I also owe a profound debt to the thoughts and contributions of my students over the last decade. Their voices are present throughout the pages. I taught seminars on fashion and philosophy under various guises at the University of Dallas with John Macready (2013), Sarah Lawrence College (2016 and 2017), Vassar College (2019 and 2020), and, as I was in the process of finalizing the manuscript, The New School for Social Research (2021). I am grateful to John for our initial conversations, which were integral to imagining what could be.

I met Nickolas Pappas at a *kairon* point during the manuscript's evolution, and its current form owes a great deal to our ongoing conversations, as well as to Nick's steadfast advice and comments. A more singular reader would be hard to come by, especially one who could quote both Herodotus and Elvis Costello (the epigraph of Chapter 7 is thanks to Nick).

For their tireless cheering and confidence, I am grateful to Nathaniel ("Natty") Adams, Selin and Anthony Barrow, Michael Davis (after twenty years of reading books together, I'm much better dressed), Benjamin Hale, Marshall Kibbey, Syrie Moskowitz, and Salman Rushdie. Travis Qualls was a good luck charm who kept me away from dangerous rabbit holes and put up with all my complaining.

Conversations with Antoine Picon (materiality) and Jonas Rosenbrück (smell) contributed important pieces to my argument. Carolyn Dewald, Leonard Muellner, Gregory Nagy, and Laura Slatkin were immediately supportive of the significance of fashion as an ancient phenomenon. Other specific contributions are acknowledged in notes in the text, but for their support and inspiration at pivotal moments, thank you to Seemee Ali, Abraham Anderson, Akeel Bilgrami, Ronna Burger, Rachel Friedman, Anthony Gottlieb, Susan Hiner, Harvey C. Mansfield,

Mitchell Miller, Toni Nagy, Shirly and Orlando Palacios, Nalin Ranasinghe (dearly missed), Valerie Steele, David Sweet, Richard Velkley, and last only alphabetically, Péter Zilahy. To my new friends at the New School—especially, Cinzia Arruzza, Simon Critchley, Preeti Gopinath, and Daniel Rodríguez-Navas—your conversation and encouragement mean so much.

I had a great deal of difficulty composing these acknowledgments, because I have constantly rethought this book from many angles as I reopen its questions with new and old friends, colleagues, and students. Each conversation has made a difference to how I have thought to phrase things or what references I have thought to include. So, to the many friends mentioned here and to the many who are not, I'm lucky to know you, and the dedication of this book is an homage *to you* each.

I finished the manuscript with generous funding from the Onassis Foundation, typing the last pages in their offices overlooking St. Patrick's Cathedral, in the same building where the designer Halston once had his studio. Thanks to Emre Turkolmez for beautifying the bibliography and preparing the index. And to the wonderful editors at Bloomsbury, Lisa Goodrum and Liza Thompson—thank you for understanding the book's meaning from the start and for your care and thoughtfulness at every stage.

Finally, to my parents, much gratitude for everything. I am certain of one thing at least: on my mother, no pun will be lost.

nota bene: All translations of foreign text are my own, unless otherwise noted.

Where I have transliterated Greek words, the reader will find that I have sometimes used *c*, sometimes *k,* for kappa, and sometimes *u*, sometimes *y,* for upsilon. This is partly guided by my hope that the reader will notice the kindred looks in these words of English and other languages.

Note to the Reader

When you die you will lie;
no memory of you
will there be—not once nor
later—for you do not
have a share of the roses
from Pieria. But unseen
you'll frequent Hades' house,
flying with dim corpses.

—Sappho, Fragment 55[1]

Dear reader, in this book I dare to trace fashion back to ancient Greece. This is not a fashionable view. Antiquity seems far away from us, and especially far away from that always new-fangled term "modernity" with which fashion is a conceptual bedfellow. I won't say that the ancient Greeks are essential to an understanding of fashion or philosophy as we imagine them now, since that would be a kind of scholarly suicide. Rather, Greek antiquity, especially Athens in the fifth and fourth century BC, is what Brian Eno calls a place of "scenius." Scenius, not the same as genius, ties individual prowess to a pregnant set of circumstances, when and where sparks are keener to fly. Plato was one such spark; Greek tragedy another.

Scenius sets the scene for chance interactions that make us privy to some sort of portal, where the cave opens up more distinctively than it does during other periods. Voice and audience are able to find each other then and there in unforgettable ways. Pierian roses bloom. Pieria, just below Mount Olympus, is the birthplace and haunt of the Muses, and roses are Sappho's peculiar connection to them. The addressee of Sappho's lines either doesn't have or doesn't deserve from Sappho's poem a portion of roses. Roses seem to stand for the perennial possibility of poetic inspiration. But the very same roses are endangered the moment they pop up, their petals tinged with desire and envy. "A little learning is a dangerous thing / Drink deep or taste not the Pierian spring"—so wrote Alexander Pope.

I stand on a tightrope, daring as I do to critique academic style as anything but rosy, and to do so with necromantic zest. While fashion resurrects the dead quite regularly, I am traveling back to a time when fashion thinking and thinking fashion were more fluid, when fashion could more easily be imagined as mode or manner, and philosophy was not yet a card-carrying profession, but readable as something like "thinking." Once upon a time, the tone of academic fearfulness was not crushed by moral guilt or decked out in citational armor. But there was a fearfulness that is recognizable to us in another form: the fear of looking *weird* (or, to borrow Simon Critchley's look, being "bald"), and it comes perilously close to the fear of looking *wrong*. The word in Greek would be *atopos*: "out-of-place," "extraordinary," "odd."

The Academy, under the watchful eyes of peers, is no place for wild roses. Not for any lack of protection either; it was at first a stabilizing greenhouse, and only grew into an insider's club for outsiders. Maybe that growth was inevitable, but the academic fear of the intellectual wilderness is visible, too, in the more ordinary fear of being misunderstood—a fear that is fanned by fashion's suggestion that "looks matter." As if to mock this sentiment as vulgar, where fashion is allowed into the lecture hall, academics deem it a light reprieve from weightier topics. Fashion sounds fun and talking about it seriously looks funny—which is to say, strange. Intellectual horticulture gets in the habit of weeding out or branding strangers. It combs through and absorbs outliers into the fold with a domestication of thinking done up as understanding. This, in turn, requires that thinking turn fashionable, and so that it conceal the conditions under which the Academy sprouts.

I regret to report that it doesn't spring up from leisurely conversation, but something more like the death of Socrates. Nickolas Pappas has written a captivating book, *The Philosopher's New Clothes: The Theaetetus, the Academy, and Philosophy's Turn against Fashion*, about the emergence of the Academy as a problematic home for the Everyman misfit that is the philosopher. It is a place that does not solve the tensions of Socrates' death but shows them in the process of being redressed. Maybe it is still the safest place to take cover, even amidst the shortage of blooms. But I wonder about the status of Greek antiquity in an inquiry into fashion and philosophy more generally. Are the Greeks only a contingently remarkable entry point into something that is available more or less through any clothes? Or is there something essential in their particular outfit?

I can pinpoint the trouble more exactly. There seems to be a tension in both philosophy and fashion between being fashionable and being interesting. Behind that tension is the longing to become intelligible to others without becoming utterly the same. That longing is entangled in the very thought of fashion, and it is at work in powerful ways in ancient Greek authors. Partly this is the vantage point of time, about which I will say more in the Preface; but partly it is the Greeks themselves. The Greeks are special, which is not to say they are special because they are Greeks.

So, reader beware—however vital the Greeks might begin to seem to my pages, the condition they are standing in for is this: philosophy seems to have to appear as "fashion" before it can think of itself as "philosophy." Its looks are as peculiar as its modes, and some of them more fruitful than others to the intelligent gaze. This does not quite mean that thinking takes on the traits of the threads in and through which you catch its glimpse. In other words, philosophy is not Greek and it is not fashion. But fashion might be philosophy's most important and underestimated doppelgänger—for fashion is the seed of the surface without which roses cannot bloom and yet which demands that they learn how to thrive in the shade.

Preface:
The "Other" Ancient Quarrel

Be subtle, various, ornamental, clever,
And do not listen to those critics ever
Whose crude provincial gullets crave in books
Plain cooking made still plainer by plain cooks
As though the Muse preferred her half-wit sons:
Good poets have a weakness for bad puns.
—W. H. Auden, from "The Truest Poetry Is the Most Feigning"

Before there was virtual reality, there was poetry. In the *Republic*, Plato alludes to an already ancient quarrel between philosophy and poetry.[2] While philosophy undresses the world to try to get at the naked truth, poetry overdresses reality, concealing it in display. Poetry's apparent "lies" are therefore the target of philosophy's defrocking. But identities become blurred as philosophy's disassembling draws near to poetic nudity and poetry's dress up appears to reveal more than it covers. In this context, poetry means something quite broad: it means fashioning a version of the world that is deceptive or that lures viewers into believing in fakes. By unleashing "fantasy" worlds that compete with or outshine the "existing" world, poetry stimulates rebels and nourishes lemmings with a simple change of hats. You might call this the power of fashioning in general.

This book is designed to explode "fashioning," and with it, the usual connotations of the word, "fashion." In the broader sense, "fashion" means "style" or "mode." Fashion is not only costumes but also customs,[3] not only habits but also *habits*. Fashion is italics: a poetic or rhetorical flourish on the plain, a punctuation mark, which is already suggestive of some grammatical corset. Fashion is anything that adorns or adds flair. It is the air of certainty with which someone delivers an argument; the snoot of erudition that makes another feel foolish; the turn of phrase that solidifies conviction, the tilt of a hat, the point of a hot poker. Fashion is not the outfit but it can make the outfit, just as rhetoric is not the argument but can make the argument. But this is part of the worry about fashion. Its force seems somehow illegitimate, entering "in," as it seems to do, from the outside and affecting the whole ensemble, like an adverb permeates an entire sentence.

Fashion occupies a variety of angles from elegant to vulgar, while always remaining somehow peripheral to the subject, as a popped collar is to a jacket is to a shirt is to a …? Fashion is an infinite regress of ruffles that seems to postulate some underlying thing modified. Yet it is precisely in the emergence of fashion as a subject in its own right that one finds philosophy's suspicions aroused. Clotheshorses are lumped in with poets and sophists for their unabashed vanity—for treating the surface as if it were the main event. Yet even where fashion takes its designated seat at the back of the room, it continues to speak, whether by a casual look of obscurity or perfumed silhouette. Fashion affects us, maybe even rules us, and its effect is especially marked when it is ignored or dismissed as *merely* superficial.

Fashion's Poetry and Philosophy's Disapproval

Tailors at least do not underestimate fashion's power, since their profession bears witness to a dialogue between bodies and garments. Tailors must understand life's patterns. They must study how human beings move in order to make appropriate measurements, stitches, and alterations. At the same time, a tailor's modifications might change the fashion in which one walks or sits. In this way, tailoring confronts some of the same issues as philosophy, since philosophy, too, must be wary of its own unwitting poetry. This may hint at a motive for philosophy's disapproval of fashion. Fashion revels in the collision of perception with reality. In its uncanny ability to shapeshift and forge identities, it summons a poetic—nearly divine—power that would be the envy of every political ruler and the nemesis of every truth-seeker. The Greek word *kosmos* means not only "fashion" or "adornment," but also "order," "world," or "universe"; it gives us the adjectives "cosmic" and "cosmetic."[4] Perhaps, then, philosophers hate fashion because they fear it?[5]

Philosophers, now ungirded from *philosophy*, wouldn't like the thought, especially not "professional philosophers." The phrase is almost an oxymoron, like high-end sneakers, an extraordinary display of ordinary fashion, already present in the pretentiously bare words, "philosopher" and "philosophy." So Nickolas Pappas writes that "philosophy is and understands itself to be either continuously, or at important junctures, doing the kind of thing that all people do. Professionals do more when they philosophize than others do, with the expertise that comes of long practice—but not as if they had a spectrophotometer while everyone else saw colors" (2016: 2). Pappas traces the philosopher's distinctively indistinctive looks back to Plato's Academy and the *Theaetetus*, wherein philosophy starts to become an activity reserved for members only.[6] In contrast to the modern-day University (thusly named as if it were the whole world), philosophizing in Plato's Academy was naked and free. Only sophists charged money and wore cloaks.[7] The mode differed, too; philosophy occurred in live dialogue.

And Plato's written dialogues were replete with drama, character, and wordplay. By comparison, philosophy's later incarnations look somber and scholarly, insistently nonpoetic, nowadays heavily footnoted with a rolodex of honorable mentions. Philosophy, perhaps even academia more generally, cultivates a look that says, "I am good at looking," or "Look at me, I'm a looker." *scholê*, which originally meant "leisure," now means "school." The tendency is toward prose. Poetic speech, on the other hand, caters to *hoi polloi*—those sheepish humans who need honey-coated parables to stomach medicinal reality.[8]

Nietzsche, a self-styled poet who despised so-called philosophers, may be, like Plato, an exception, but he is far from being a staple in the closet of high-end philosophical jetsetters. There are, of course, Parmenides, Empedocles, and Lucretius, all of whom write in dactylic hexameter (the meter of the epic poets, Homer and Hesiod). But Epicurus, as early as the fourth century BC, reprimands: wise men do not write in poetry.[9] Does this mean that stripped speech, pared down to unadorned formulae, brings us closer to the naked truth? Or, is "the unadorned" an outfit of formality that has lost touch with its original purpose, like the medieval hood of a graduation gown or the costume of the Vatican Swiss guards? Is barren prose, in fact, its own sort of poetry?[10] What if contemporary philosophers, despite their sober appearances, have adopted their *mode* as whimsically, as poetically, as fashionistas? Maybe poetry, wit, and embellishment bring us closer to the "real" even while seeming to obfuscate, distract, or conceal it? At the very least, the wish for precision without artifice sheds an initial ray of light on why philosophers are so dismissive—sometimes casually, sometimes viscerally—of fashion.

But perhaps there is a more obvious reason for philosophy's dirty looks. Classically, philosophers are ugly. Socrates, for example, was so ugly that Aristotle used his snub nose as an example of the concave and convex.[11] He was so ugly that when the clouds looked at him they formed the shape of monsters and animals. That is to say, his ugliness could not even be seen on the surface. An appeal to the poetry of the clouds had to be made in order to capture it.[12] Ugliness is here a metaphor for Socratic style—the Socratic method. Rather than don cosmetics and clothes, Socrates was interested in what makes up and fashions the cosmos. He was interested in stripping and exfoliating to expose the foundation of reality—unless reality, like waterproof mascara, remains stubborn, unwilling to admit philosophical astringent.

In the *Phaedo*, Socrates recounts turning to look at "things" in the mirror of speeches, lest he be blinded by trying to gaze upon them directly (99e). Hans-Georg Gadamer, too, advised truth-seekers thus: "The important thing is to be aware of one's own bias, so that the text can present itself in all its otherness and thus assert its own truth against one's own fore-meanings" (1960/2013: 271–2). But it is precisely this awareness of bias that proves problematic to both fashion and philosophy, as if in a single stroke. Fashion is courageously skewed and its neutral palette no exception—for disinvested vestment is investment nonetheless, a methodical minimalism all too visible in philosophy's expository shroud. Philosophy's disapproval of fashion, then, seems the sign not of a simple disinterest in a certain subject, but rather, of an inevitable failure to perceive the peculiarity of its own perception. Simply fashioned, fashion makes philosophy look bad.

In the *Theaetetus* and the *Charmides*, philosophy is connected to stripping, "as if the philosophizing required the stripping; as if practicing philosophy any other way would be a fashion misstep" (Pappas 2016: 112). In the *Republic*, Socrates proposes that everyone, not just philosophers, should get naked.[13] But the more common stereotype is the disheveled, absent-minded look of the Cynic. Thales, sometimes called the "first" philosopher—a moniker as ludicrous as "trendsetter"—looked like such an airhead that, while he was walking around staring at the heavens, he fell into a well, only to discover that everything was water, much to the amusement of a nearby Thracian servant girl. His wondering precluded a certain reflection on the ground, and this led to both his downfall and his discovery.[14]

Not that all philosophers are space cadets. Intellectuals at large are *supposed* to know that the surface is a locus of vanity. *Supposedly*, it is what is on the inside that counts. Meanwhile, the word "fashion" threatens depth with its mere proximity and capricious transience. The difficulty is that our strongest notion of the inside comes by way of the outside. The very possibility of seeing more deeply depends on an intrigue provoked by the opacity of the surface. To be a good looker—or, to be good at looking—you must look at your own looking, since it is the way or fashion in which depth appears from the vantage point of surface that catches philosophy's eye. Besides, if you could see the inside without the outside, it would only appear as another outside. Even ideas are surfaces through which we "see" into the "reality" of things. Reality, in this case, must also be an idea.

"The Truest Poetry Is the Most Feigning"

Auden's words and title (quoted above) are especially auspicious now that reality has become trendy. Maybe it all began when Reality TV made public defrocking fashionable, so much so that a Reality TV star became President of the United States. American fashion is dominated by a complicated cocktail of normality and uniqueness, which seems a playful idealization of democracy, or style that liberates you from any particular style: we are all wearing different types of jeans. While jeans at first seem a *"fantasy of nakedness,"*[15] they hardly win the distinction of being the one and only *faux naturel*. Athleisure leggings and yoga pants are quickly replacing them, and "comfort" has become one of the reigning doctrines for both clothing and thinking.

Comfortable styles have moved from "next-door" to "vanilla" to "basic,"[16] all of which foreshadowed "normcore," which, because so perfectly normal, was easily forgotten. "Looking natural" has been poached by so many marketing schemes that the word itself seems entirely conventional. In its effortlessness, the "natural look" mimics ordinary humans in the wild, as if their default state would be casual clothes, nude hues and dewy highlights, an application with the effect of nothing applied. The more "100% organic" this look becomes, the more we ourselves seem to be given the opportunity to become whole and free from additives (read: society's chains?). Maybe with our natural looks, we will become "100% Human" (an actual sales pitch used by the brand Everlane). Maybe with concealer, we can reveal who we truly are.[17]

Style tribes achieve the same end with the opposite fashion. They busy themselves with defied expectations and cult combinations: the ever-mutating species of genera such as hipster, Harajuku, and goth (the latest guilds include, respectively, grandmacore, angelcore, and goblincore). Think street-style-subculture-takeover; its greatest hits end up in Urban Outfitters; its best insights occur on the streets of Tokyo. This is the accident of design, playing god with chance to give off an air of indigenous authenticity: another version of the "natural" captured not by the glossy, whitened smile of cosmetic dentistry but the misshapen, yellowed teeth that Gucci used in its 2019 ad campaign to sell lipstick. On the one hand, the natural is variegated, pock-marked, time-stricken; on the other hand, it is unadulterated, monochrome, and ageless. Both looks are an attempt to approximate nonidentity or perfectly flawed identity, which is our notion of the generically and specifically human.

The difference between "fashion" and "style" is typically thought to be of similar ilk: timely versus timeless. But this distinction itself is born from a tension already present in fashion, perhaps emanating from its underdetermined beginnings. Where fashions are recycled or given a longevity that catapults them into the "classics," we might begin to think of them as styles. But style becomes an accessory possessable by anyone only when fashion becomes a profession of the few. Style is devised, according to Alexander Nagel, as "an antidote to fashion, and so it is little surprise that the cure should taste of the poison" (2004: 34). The poison is fashion's incessant recycling—"The category, 'the new,' seems, despite everything, to belong to the past" (Svensden 2006: 32). Models who sign a deal with the dubiously titled agency, *Next*, may soon find themselves afterthoughts. And yet, there is Heraclitus' consolation—that "you can't step in the same river twice" is something that can be uttered only by those who believe there is a river.

Here, philosophy and fashion discover a most unexpected kinship. Fashion aims to capture the fleeting—that moment which, once trapped in a trend, is lost to the world, and yet all the same has inspired the world. Whatever may be the inner working of fashion's pineal gland, it is not located in any particular fashion. Like thinking, fashion arrives on the scene contingently and only afterwards admits itself to questions of causation. When fashion rolls up the sleeves on a shirt, it is already in the process of reinventing the shirt, just as thinking "poses" its questions only when the stitches of a thought are already beginning to come loose. This seems to be the thing we take for granted the more comfortable we are in our clothes. That is, we cease to recall the presence of ourselves in distinction from the way we are outfitted, like a story we tell so often we have forgotten why we were originally moved to tell it. We speak of times in our lives when we were more comfortable in our own skin, as if aging involved the unwilling adoption of a variety of bodily outfits to clothe the moving target of the self. In this, fashion unwittingly, almost accidentally, posits a self that is alienated from its fabricated clutches. This self must be either once not clothed-in-time or progressing toward some timeless look. The timeless look, another oxymoron, would have to mean an outfit for every occasion or an outfit that defies age, appearance, and eventually, altogether all specificity.

Take the person who wears the same outfit everyday: the proverbial jeans and hoodie. The regularity of it seems to border on uniform; its nondescript character proclaims either "don't look at me" or "don't look at my look." It is either a protest or a disappearing act, but what it cannot be is not a choice. Even among hoodies there are countless variations—some of us are drawn to some cuts, others to others; our free will is limited, to be sure, since we can't all be our own designers, but there are a plethora of options. What is more, the possibility of concealment, even in the most basic style, paves the way for a certain empowerment, which subliminally embraces the wearer like a Supreme t-shirt.

Apart from beauty brands such as "The Ordinary" and "In Common," which use the specialness of the mundane to sell products, the power of clothes to harness the human bubbled up into the mainstream when "normcore" defied the odds and became popular (almost an embarrassment to the very movement, yet somehow not unwelcome). Normcore got its wings from the burial of the self in common threads. While its essence aimed at unaffected normalcy, many of its looks were slightly backdated, just old enough to provide a subtle differentiation from the crowd, as if normal people are always in need of renovation. By definition a style extinct, normcore remained ruthless: it seduced humble bagginess, borrowed from the meek, and sported mediocre looks that were hyperbolically typical—polar fleece, baseball caps, and artisanally scuffed sneakers (successor of those sparkling white kicks that announce their untrodden footsteps like uncalloused hands). Its ascended descent was almost like that of a philosopher returning to darkness, an enlightened soul living in the garb of the brainwashed, the genuflected clothing of angels.

The Soul

On this note, it is worth wondering about the relationship between fashion and death. It is strange that philosophers should be so uninterested in the attempts of clothing to shield the self from dangers (both real and imagined) or to greet what is to come with some defense, whether it is the cold, an interview, or a funeral. Fashion is no less a stranger to this than a diary. There are even fashion victims, fashion police, and fashion disasters. Fashion inhabits its own peculiar metropolis, with special dialects, laws, and rulers, as well as rebels and train wrecks. While the danger is mostly mock—except where the garments are enforced by governments, religions, or middle school royalty—it is concealing something grave. Like tombstones, clothes bury bodies in an attempt to liberate our persons from their mortal coil. In this way, clothes are not exactly material; they are as substantially immaterial as thoughts.

"Substantially immaterial": the relationship of fashion to material is not a simple one, and it is tied to weightier questions about fashion and the soul. For the ancient Greeks, "soul" meant "principle of life"—that which animates and without which an entity is dead. Without soul, particularity fades into the predictable. So the soul carries some of the contemporary connotations of "identity" and "self." Lucretius imagines that the soul is made up of very fine particles (so fine and flexible that they defy our notions of usual materiality).[18] Were you to cut any limb off the body, you wouldn't be able to access the soul's fabric. It would flex, alter itself, and elude. Fashion's material manifestations are likewise essential and elusive. But material grips us in immaterial ways, only because there is some underlying substance that drives fashion's motion. Clothes are standing in for the problem of knowledge of that underlying "fabric." As an overlying image of the underlying, they provoke the question of our superfluity in our mortal outfit. That literal clothes can become so closely related to "us" crowns them with a special status over other, more distant objects. Indeed, they are so close to us that they can nearly dissolve our being into them.

Think of Gandhi's iconic fashion "statement": the handspun *dhoti*. Though simple, this piece of *khadi* cloth embodied the guts of Gandhi's life and work. So much did it signify the spirit and inner fabric of Gandhi himself that, if one were to see the garment, one would think immediately of the man. We leave our impression on clothes to the point that they can remind us of us more than our bodily persons do. They hold memories like photographs or journals, but with the visible impressions of the weight of the person, not the body but the body's demeanor, an utterance of the self in its absence. Department and thrift stores are graveyards occupied by ghost personalities, each hung up on one statement or another—a veritable Hades, where Er had his choice of life patterns, to be woven into his being by the Fate, Clotho, from *clôthein*, "to spin," which gives us the word, "clothing." For full autonomy, Er would have had to spin his own clothes, like Gandhi. Gandhi's legacy left him looking like anything but a dandy, though during his earlier life, as a student in London, he wrote about his preoccupation with the look of the British gentlemen, his love of neckties, and his having succumbed to the "fashion goddess."[19] His choice to use a garment as an icon does not seem to have been an accident. He wore his flag, the symbol of a spinning wheel, which became for a time the symbol on India's flag.

Rather than make us less vulnerable, then, clothes seem to reveal our vulnerabilities and beliefs. They say "look" even when they say "don't look." They can nip, tuck, or conceal. Or they can deliberately point to the necessity of deterioration with a raw hem, exposed stitch, or blush—a meta-concealment that pulls a loose thread to reveal one's control over flaws and imperfections. But hidden behind the desire to look a little carefree, and so a little careless, are glimmers of a longing for perfect self-reflection. We have a notion that genuine, authentic selves wouldn't appear concerned with appearances—maybe wouldn't even be conventionally beautiful. Invisibility has become a coveted beauty mark, and leisurewear the unmanned drone from which we judge and criticize its presence. It is hard to even pinpoint the standards by which we judge whether something looks beautiful or not, but judge we do.

The strange thing is that, while the gap widens between the beautiful and the real, when we encounter something true, it strikes us just like beauty: genuine conviction is a bombshell or a knockout. We hunt for beauty in a world full of specters, yet our hidden motive remains the pursuit of a solid truth. Being concerned with how one looks seems to be critical to motivating us to push beyond the surface, even so far as to reject the surface as vain.

But it is through the surface that we feel this need to push beyond. Concern for appearances is our fashion of facing the unknown depths of others and ourselves, and in this way, a thinking cap and a baseball cap are hardly old hat clichés.

Fashion Is Not Modern

One final remark on what is to come: most or at any rate many scholars claim that fashion belongs to modernity.[20] Apparently, only in the modern age does "fashion" wrest itself from being embedded in clothes to emerge as an object of pursuit apart from them. But fashion's overt looks shirk from easy tethering. "Fashion," wrote Walter Benjamin, "is a tiger's leap into the past"; not a whimsical, aimless leap, but a leap that is on the hunt. What is fashion hunting? Benjamin says fashion is "keeping to the scent of the 'now' in the thicket of the once" (1942/1980: 701). He is echoing an earlier remark made by Karl Marx about revolution conjuring up past spirits and costumes. Fashion moves ideas across time in a way that seems to smirk at historical context. Every moment in fashion, writes Nagel, is an "anachronic time-bomb", a.k.a. a blast from the past (2004: 33).

Just when you thought shoulder pads and side parts were gone forever, here they come again with a new swagger. More ancient styles return looking utterly estranged, like the paleo diet or the Greek line from Plato's *Symposium* in Lil Nas X's "Montero" music video. Being hip is like being a revolutionary, bringing what is "out" back "in" at a critical time. But since the now must be borrowed from an understanding of the now as now past, it looks as if fashion's being in the now might be not optionally but necessarily retro. Indeed, the more obsolete or out-of-style something is, the riper it is for a renaissance. Fashion's easy time-travel hastens along a non-linear path with a metaphysical nonchalance that threatens our understanding of the progression of both history and time. If we are so shaped by our historical moment, what of wearing a vintage hat? Does vintage costume mock the progressiveness of modern custom?

In this regard, fashion is caught up in the same problems that translation faces in trying to make dated text read as if it were current. To speak of fashion as in the process of translating suggests that it was originally other than it presents itself as being. Is it possible to strip off fashion from clothing to reveal clothes as naked of fashion or—and I suspect these questions might be the same—can we think back to a time when clothes were simply clothes? This would be a problem of thinking. And what is at stake in asking the question is the relationship between fashion and thinking. Just as thoughts do not appear to follow the same temporal speeds as the time in which they are unwillingly immersed, so fashion's contingency begins to suggest that time is no longer of the essence. Whether we can imagine a fashionless past or a fashionless future will have implications for what we take to be the plausible genesis of human nature. If there was a faultless, unfashioned origin, perhaps there can be a future cured of humanity's failed fashions?

The conclusion, which I can only now anticipate, may be that fashion and philosophy magnetize and repel each other in ways that make it difficult to call one superficial and the other deep. As the revelation of concealment and the concealment of revelation, they are like twins separated at birth. Birth: this is the issue, swaddled in thoughts of soul and material. While philosophy begins with a question that renders its beginning unthinkable, the same could be said of fashion's beginning, whenever that beginning can be said to be or if it can be said to be at all.

But again, dear reader, beware of judging my looks too quickly. I am not writing a "philosophy *of* fashion," but rather, illustrating a parallel between "philosophy *and* fashion." Philosophy has missed something in its sidelining of fashion—that conspicuous nothing, that egregious idling, that poetic power in which philosophy itself also partakes. Fashion is no small lacuna in philosophy's wheelhouse, nor is it merely a meaningless member of a larger set. The plot of this book is driven by the thought that our coverings reveal truths about ourselves and the cosmos we inhabit—not only our clothes, but also our thoughts and the fashion in which we style them. Fashion is somehow everything.

1

Fashion Sense

φύσις κρύπτεσθαι φιλεῖ[1]
—Heraclitus, Fragment B123 DK

It is time to come out of the closet. This is not an academic book in the traditional sense. It is written by an academic who is interested in the question: is there an academic "look," particularly for so-called philosophers? Is there a look that says, "I'm good at looking?" And is it the only look with which one can address the truth?

The question is partly motivated by another question: Why do most philosophers hate clothes—or rather, hate *fashion*? The majority rule seems to be to treat the outer surface with either ritual formality or complete derision, as if the less you comb your hair the closer you are to truth. For a philosopher in search of reality, any sort of keeping up appearances looks laced with madness. Those who appear interested in making fashion statements run the risk of being accused of wasting time on shallow things, and so, being slipshod thinkers. Smart people *know* you can't judge a book by its cover. Things are not always what they seem. Caring about fashion for its own sake—or appearance for appearance's sake—is surely the greatest of all sophistry. It is superficial, shallow, vain. But isn't it strange to live a life of careful observation—you could say, a life that treats the world with kid gloves—and yet, to have no care for what you wear? Maybe it is simply that, in their longing not to be particular about being, philosophers hate putting themselves together. The very word "philosopher" is almost an insult—as if you could identify the person who is busy identifying everything else. Philosophers are anonymous, their appearances out of fashion.[2]

But philosophers are not alone in fearing being seen with too many flounces and frills. Many people swear by fashion's insignificance: it is *too* contrived, *too* arbitrary, *too* much a sign of vanity. Fashion is excess, for changeability alone does not condemn it, but a surplus of changeability beyond perceived necessity. Fashion flits about after shiny things, like a magpie or jackdaw adorning a nest. At the same time, it teeters perilously close to extremes, unsure if one more pleat won't push it over the edge from tasteful to trendy. But this reveals another feature of fashion. Installed within its very compass is the "sense" that to appear too preoccupied with itself would be unfashionable. Fashion is about judgment. Its gavel comes down with bristly adjectives: looking "good," looking "right," even looking "just right."

So strong is the impulse of sartorial morality that it is difficult in praising clothes not to use such adjectives as "right," "good," "correct," "unimpeachable," or "faultless," which belong properly to the discussion of conduct, while in discussing moral shortcomings we tend very naturally to fall into the language of dress and speak of a person's behaviour as being shabby, shoddy, threadbare, down at heel, botched, or slipshod.

(Bell 1948: 14)

Fashion operates according to weather and essence. It speaks of seasons, occasions, essentials, and basics, as if the cogent wearer would be a master of contingency or a conqueror of fortune.[3] Still, if the variety or number of clothes *in excess* is all we mean when we utter the word "fashion" in its profane sense, why do we persist in keeping our options open when we dress ourselves? Are philosophers, in their scorn for the endless permutations that fashion represents, resistant to freedom? Or is it the specific sort of freedom that fashion's excessive options signify, over and against the tasteful refinement of the literary elite? Is fashion too vulgar, too demotic for the thoughtful? But again, fashion itself is compelled not to transgress certain unwritten limits. Firstly, everything cannot be worn at once. In the distinction between fast fashion and haute couture or runway and ready-to-wear lies the equivalent of those distinctions in philosophy between philosophy and political philosophy or metaphysics and physics.

Yet, what if, regardless of social or economic status, regardless of political or professional affiliation, regardless of cultural background, religion, or identity—what if something powerful lurks in the experience of taking off and putting on clothes? I do not yet mean to enter or exit Eden. I mean by "clothes" something that may well prove evanescent—something more or less like an awareness of our presence in some skin—signified, too, by body paint, piercings, tattoos, haircuts, or even simple gestures. The flourish of a pen fashions as does the tip of a finger pointing. When these flourishes—these clothes—touch us with even the slightest bit of excess, we are made aware of our "bodies" as a surface, and by extension, of the appearance of our "selves." The self, understood as an appearance, like an ill-fitting word or split seam, comes along with an awareness of being in space and time. And so, I hesitate to say, fashion and philosophy enter the scene at the same moment. Clothes, insofar as they make us aware of our appearances, are requisite for the experience of self-examination. They are an alienated contact with the self, gained through the strange shell of fabricated "not-us" that gives birth to the Cartesian doubt that "we" are other than it. But the question of this book, which will remain in between the lines for some time, is how this experience of ourselves as contingently clothed, and so necessarily present, begins.

Touch of Clothes and Sense of Self

In Aristotle's *De Anima*, flesh emerges as the medium through which the sense of touch produces its effect.[4] Touch is in a way the most confused of the senses, and so, emblematic of the source of "feeling" which is present in them all. Aristotle immediately encounters the difficulty of wresting the medium of touch from the sense of touch. When we touch an object, we not only seem to touch it, but we also feel the touch of ourselves touching.[5] The object presses back on us at the same time as the feeling of the otherness of our own touch touching us, as if from the outside. We "grasp" the thought of our own perception through the act of touching; "grasp" is as ambiguous in English as it is in Greek.[6] In a similar account in *De Rerum Natura*, Lucretius describes a link between touch and sight. For touch, he uses the Latin word *tangere*, which has the double sense of physical and psychical contact: you can touch something literally or be "touched" by it or "touch" on it figuratively. For Lucretius, the seeming immediacy of touch already implies a longing to "see" inside an object, and so a desire to know. He uses as an example reaching out to touch something even in the dark, where we imagine we are peering into its interior.[7] So, too, we touch the pages of a book to go beyond just feeling their outer edges. In touching the pages, we feel both the pages themselves and our own curiosity about their insides.

The analogue to clothes might be that when they are on us and when they touch us, we experience the "touch" of ourselves. Perhaps this is as simple as putting on a bathrobe or brushing your teeth—dressing and addressing yourself in even a minimal way so as to make yourself feel as if you are "in" the world. Does this ritual illustrate the whimsy or the tyranny of clothes as convention? Or in confronting the image of the self, do we confront a reflection on its absence from the image, and so, the thought of its presence?

Still, we put our faces on, then forget we did. We want to be and to look "comfortable." In American fashion, "comfort" indicates not only *feeling* that clothes do not constrain, bind, or provoke us, but also not *seeing* clothes as manifestly constraining, binding, or provoking. And if to feel is in some way to see, it will be difficult to separate how we experience ourselves in clothes and how we experience others experiencing ourselves in clothes. Beauty is associated with vanity and pain, even in the form of an imagined empathy for a person whose clothes look uncomfortable. Comfort must be executed properly, lest it make others around you squirm. American comfort looks elegant only to a point, stopping short of attractiveness: athleisure and sweatpants perhaps, or soft, flowing garments.[8] Comfort is a non-triggering safe space in which to enter freely into an experience of other clothed selves—not appearing to have been chained by those antiquated legislators of girdles and corsets (or more recently, Spanx), which sell the look of control. We comfortable people let go of the need for control. Yet the constraints on comfort's visage tell onlookers that even this novel freedom is governed by Draconian laws, defined as what appears appropriate or comfortable to others.

> This uniform is designed to telegraph to others what to see so that they will not be made uncomfortable and probably hostile by being forced to look on another human being. The uniform must suggest a certain setting and it must dictate a certain air and it must also convey, however subtly, a dormant aggressiveness, like the power of a sleeping lion. It is necessary to make anyone on the streets think twice before attempting to vent his despair on you.
>
> (Baldwin 1964/2008: 57)

The uniform of which James Baldwin speaks is being able to pass among others by being perceived to be one of them, and so subtly suggesting to the same others, *don't look*. "Dormant aggressiveness" seems to lurk in clothing by default, while behind it glimmers the possibility of getting personal, as if clothes were at once the image of a window to the soul, like the eyes, and also a set of drapes to prevent unwanted peeping.

The appearance of comfort, of course, varies, and a new dialect of comfort must be learned in different settings in order to continually go unnoticed. Working from both the outside in and the inside out, the ultimate goal is a state in which clothes no longer seem to exert their impression on you. Because the more effortlessly you can forget the "feeling" of clothes, the more you can cast away the outer image of yourself grating on you. Thanks to clothes, you can then be free not to care about clothes. We enter the comfort zone, wrapped in a security blanket of ineffectual clothing. The lure of this zone seems to be the meshing of clothes with persons. Clothing functions almost as if a second skin, and in the absence of other information, it leads to assumptions about who people are on the basis of how they look.

This is one way in which we find clothes uncomfortable: they are connected to biases and stereotypes. Such fraudulent signals are not felt or sensed to belong on the person. We say: we are so much more than our looks. We are not solely aesthetic objects. And yet, the desire for comfortable clothes suggests that the experience of the binding of the body in clothes is a metaphor for how we experience the feeling of our "selves" more generally. We forget the question of ourselves in comfortable clothes, as we do in comfortable patterns of thought. Is it the mere presence of clothes that discomforts us? To imagine a time when there was no thought of fashion would be like a time in which time ceases to exert a visible effect. Perhaps a desire to distance yourself from fashion—to be comfortable—is also a longing to stop the clock?

But what if assumptions—really, prejudices—have to be worn in order to be overturned? The democratic ideal within the Western fashion stereotype hopes for a liberation from such authoritarian constraints. The plethora of options is a new nudity, in which we are apparently now able to express ourselves without needing to do so as an act of defense. Comfort seems to be the illusion of—the desire for—nature's clothes. This may be the dream implicit in all clothing. But its fruition would be a world of phantoms. On one level, having freedom in fashion seems to mean having a diversity of options from a diversity of designers, where there is no conventional backdrop against which "standard" persons are defined. Yet the image for this is a line-up of designs and individuals that once depicted can only become stereotypes—let's call them "models."[9] How does one liberate oneself not just from the assumptions of clothes but from their inability to sufficiently express our individuality? Is the only route to display the self to build into clothes our very imperfection: a frayed hem, a sweep of blush, "distressed" fabric?

In *Se questo è un uomo* (*If This Is a Man*), Primo Levi describes his experience in Auschwitz during the Second World War. His clothes are stripped, his body shaved, and all of his possessions are taken away. The meaning is clear: Levi's freedom and identity have been removed. His clothes are then replaced with dehumanizing clothes: a striped uniform (for the Jewish people, sewn with a yellow Star of David) and a pair of wooden shoes. "Death begins with the shoes," writes Levi, for they become instruments of torture in the camp (1947/2008: 24). They are designed not to fit the foot, so as to more quickly cause injury, and with it, infection, which is left untreated and leads to death. The shoes predict and deliver Levi's fate. The Nazis used this dress code to divide prisoners into those who would live and those who would die.

> Imagine now a man who is deprived of everyone he loves, and at the same time of his house, his habits, his clothes, in short, of everything he possesses: he will be a hollow man, reduced to suffering and needs, forgetful of dignity and restraint, for he who loses all often easily loses

himself. He will be a man whose life or death can be lightly decided with no sense of human affinity, in the most fortunate of cases, on the basis of a pure judgment of utility. It is in this way that one can understand the double sense of the term "extermination camp," and it is now clear what we seek to express with the phrase: "to lie on the bottom."

(15–6)

Levi is stripped and redefined. This is the first meaning of "extermination," as the privation of life's signifiers. In having his clothes taken away and replaced is the thought of his life being taken away and his lot recast. Clothes seem capable of both expressing the freedom to define who you are and also compromising agency, when they cease to give you the "room" to be who you are, and so, constrain you by explicit or implicit compulsion. The complexity of comfortable fashion is already in the term itself, for fashion is not just about an abundance of surface but the *fitting* surface. In this, the life of the individual is at stake.

If we throw our clothes aside and say, this is *not* me, we again notice our discomfort in and with clothes. This seems to be the thing we must take for granted the more comfortable we are; that is, we cease to recall the presence of ourselves in distinction from the way we are outfitted. And if comfort is not merely some belated reaction to rib-crushing corsets, it may be the mere presence of clothes that seems to rub us the wrong way. After a long day, the body rebels against material limits. Now increasingly uncomfortable, we gravitate toward a less literal comfort: a trusty shirt that feels or looks good to us, or a favorite pair of slippers, which, though worn, seem familiar, as if an afterlife of a more comfortable self. Our skin too, unwillingly worn, seems an outfit in which we can feel more or less at ease, so that even in the thinnest cloth, if we begin to focus on the touch of the fabric on the body, we begin to feel estranged.

What shroud is this within which I am ensconced? By comparison to me, clothes seem profoundly surface level, and yet, through them it is possible to experience the depth of the self, whether in its rejection or liberation. Is the body, too, a shroud? Nudity seems insufficient after experiencing the touch of clothes. You would have to be flayed to experience the skin from all sides—the "supernudity"[10] that reveals the body as somehow not quite what we thought body was, because touch blurs the lines between self and other. We launder the surface of our skin as if it were fabric, as if personal hygiene were an outfit needed for admission into the world. On entering into a jacket by Sonia Rykiel, Hélène Cixous remarks, "I go inside, eyes closed. With my hands, with my eyes in my hands, with my eyes groping like hands, I see— touch the body hidden in the body" (1994: 96).

Do we only know of body's estrangement because of our estrangement in clothes? What if what we feel when we experience the touch of ourselves by way of clothes is really something like our own act of becoming aware of ourselves? Through clothes we experience blind self-reflection, for the touch of clothes allows us to experience their fabrication, and this is connected to our feeling of a "reality" beyond them.[11] We long to be ourselves in clothes (as if to approximate a perfectly naked selfhood, or at least not to have to worry so much about the surface self), and yet we sense ourselves in clothes precisely because our clothes are *not* us.

The reader may object here. Couldn't one sense the "self" in a similar fashion, and maybe more powerfully, through another human's touch, as one sees recognition in another's eyes?[12] But clothes touch us the whole day. If we live naked, our skin folds on itself as if a garment; if we sleep naked, the fabric of sheets touches us at night. Gravity makes it impossible for us not to be touching the *surface* of a ground. And clothes embellish that experience—they enrobe us, and cause us to feel our existing in a world all the more potently. It is not that we must be aware of our literal clothes to be aware of ourselves; it is more that the "inevitability" of clothes already points to the presence of self-awareness. Fashion may seem to reject such self-awareness, preferring to conceal rather than to translate the self into common terms. But suppose there is no perfect translation through which the self will ever appear as itself? You could say that fashion, like language, is the sign of both the translatability of the self and the impossibility of its complete rendering, for clothes are like foreign terms. The sacrifice we make for the possibility of interpretation is the unthinkable yet undeniable fantasy of the original.

The Nude Abides: Origins of Words and Clothes

Genesis is the most fashionable of proto-fashion statements. There, clothes were originally supposed to armor us against the shame of being naked, a trend we picked up last fall, but they do so by laying bare our personality types, which are often a much greater point of vulnerability. In Genesis 3, clothes are connected to Eve having eaten the forbidden fruit, and then tempting Adam to eat it, too. But it is not until Adam and Eve succumb to that temptation that they even realize they are naked. They then sew together fig leaves as coverings.[13] "God," writes Karen Hanson, "must have approved of this adornment, for even as he curses the couple, he pauses—at Genesis 3:21—to make them 'coats of skins,' to clothe them" (1990: 111). God's original template was already a likeness; and regardless of what one makes of it, insofar as Eve is capable of deceiving, and Adam capable of being deceived, both were already capable of covering themselves up, whether with metaphorical or literal fig leaves. Even in Eden, nudity and clothing are hard to pull apart. The Hebrew word, *arum*, is used to refer to both the nudity of Adam and Eve and to the shrewdness of the serpent.[14] Fig leaves entomb the body in order to elevate the soul, but they thereby reproduce temptation by way of omission. Or perhaps nudity was already a form of omission, and this was the problem. Wearing fig leaves is like the blacking out of a curse word or the closing of a bedroom door. It means privacy as opposed to transparency. After the fall out of the Garden, clothing suggests that we are no longer in a so-called state of nature, but are now in self-conscious society. How human beings emerge from the state of nature is very mysterious, but once emerged, it is impossible to think back to a world without self-reflection, because, of course, this would require reflection. The first clothes are as unwearable as the first words are unutterable. Both seem to require the prior existence of clothes or expressions. And both require some form of weaving—a metaphor for both deception and civilization.

According to Lucretius, while we now need "different garments for different seasons," once upon a time we fended off wind and rain by hiding in shrubbery and "wrapping" ourselves in "leaves and foliage" (5.231; 972). Earlier, Lucretius describes nonhuman entities as if they are clothed in likenesses: wood gives off smoke as its *simulacrum*, and fire heat, while cicadas shed their "round tunics," newborn calves their "membranes," and snakes their outer "vestment (*vestis*)" (4.54–62). These phantom clothes hit our eyes and make possible our perception of things. As for literal clothes, the wearing of animal skins "fell into contempt" among human beings (5.1418). It was replaced first by plaiting, then by woven garments (which followed the discovery of iron, because they required a shuttle).[15] Lucretius makes early transformations of clothing seem a matter of fashion; but perception itself is only possible through the natural clothing that radiates off of the surfaces of things. And if things in the world shed their *simulacra* as if outer vestments, human clothes seem to be *simulacra* of *simulacra*, and their rejection as well as our perceptual awareness implies the presence of fashion. It is not at all clear that the first skins were not human skins (or perceived as such), for not only do they spark envy in others, but they result in the ambush and death of the first person who wears them. "Then it was skins (*pelles*), now gold and purple, that exercise the life of human beings with worry and wear them out with war" (5.1423–4). Lucretius refers to his own verses, too, as woven and adorned. Is the time before plaited clothing a time before speech? Is it possible to think a time when clothes were just clothes?

For Rousseau, when humans begin to think of others as well as themselves, they begin to worry about weaving together a public image. In his *Discours sur les sciences et arts* (*Discourse on the Sciences and Arts*, also called the *First Discourse*), Rousseau stands before the Academy of Dijon to be judged in an essay contest. Rousseau writes anonymously, as "Citizen of Geneva." The question is this: "Has the restoration of the sciences and arts tended to purify morals (*les moeurs*)?"[16] Rousseau's answer is a resounding "no." The sciences and arts have made human beings more, not less barbaric. Under the auspices of a supposed "enlightenment," human beings have entered more deeply into darkness. This woke barbarism takes the form of "nondescript scientific jargon, even more despicable than ignorance," which has usurped the name of knowledge (*le nom du savoir*) (1750/1969: 35). In other words, modern scholars are all fashion and no content. Their "affected language" puts flowered garlands on our iron chains, and makes us think we have been liberated. But, "how pleasant it would be to live among us if exterior appearance always matched the heart's disposition." A human being in this sort of state would be akin to "an athlete who likes to compete in the nude.[17] He disdains all those vile ornaments which would hamper the use of his strength, most of which were invented only to hide some deformity" (37). These "vile ornaments" are intellectual jargon, back-patting citations, and a longing to gain the approval of one's peers (in an essay contest?) rather than to face one's ignorance.

Rousseau anticipates universal disapproval for this contribution. Presumably, this would be the overwhelming sign of his superiority. Jealousy is the disease as well as the stamp of approval, and Rousseau's essay wins the contest. He subsequently makes two additions, which he expects will alienate the few individuals in the Academy who thought he was praiseworthy, thus assuring a more complete disapproval. Still, his antinomian behavior, however self-canceling and "anonymous," requires the arts for its rejection of them. Rousseau seems to know this; it will not be the last time he writes an ironic discourse. What, then, is his point? And what does it have to do with fashion?

We could start by asking some preliminary questions: is it possible to separate knowledge from the wish to display it, and so, to separate the desire to know from the look of wisdom? Is there any knowledge that is not "affected"? Or, if human beings were to find themselves thus in a state of nature, in which exterior appearance matched the interior, would they know it? Adam and Eve seem to be already clothed when they clothe themselves, while Rousseau's dismissal of scholarly affect can only happen because he has been affected.

On the frontispiece of the *First Discourse* is the image of Prometheus, who stole fire from the gods to bring human beings the sciences and arts (in Plato's *Protagoras*, this move brings with it clothing). For this, Prometheus did not win a prize, but a punishment from Zeus. Rousseau elaborates on the frontispiece in a note in the second part, in which he quotes Plutarch, but edits out the degree to which fire was beneficial to human beings.[18] He also mentions Thoth, as if Thoth were equivalent to Prometheus; but, of course, Prometheus did not *invent* fire—he stole it. Thoth, on the other hand, is said to have invented writing. But when Thoth told Thamus it would make the Egyptians wiser and improve their memories, Thamus replied that it would actually make them more forgetful, because they would trust in it rather than in their memories (an early intimation of the virtual hivemind). Thoth and Prometheus are both vain; Thoth thinks he is giving a gift to humankind and Prometheus thinks he can best Zeus. The downfall of the sciences and arts seems to be an arrogance that does not understand itself to be arrogant, but rather, imagines itself as the bearer of a divine gift. The printing press only compounds the trouble by making possible the dissemination of knowledge. It thereby becomes possible, avers Rousseau, to confuse literacy with wisdom, and so, celebrity with truth.

On the title page, Rousseau places a quote from Ovid's *Tristia*: *barbarus hic ego sum / quia non intelligor illis* (5.10.37). "Here I am a barbarian, because I am not understood by those." When Ovid speaks these words, he has been exiled from Rome for unknown reasons. He finds himself a foreigner in another city, where he does not speak the language. "Those people who do not understand" has a deeper meaning of unintelligibility. Rousseau thus compares himself to an exiled poet, anonymous by position, doomed not to be understood by the very Academy that subsequently honors him. It is somehow a consequence of civilization to mistake ignorance for knowledge. But Rousseau has knowledge of ignorance: "Among us, it is true, Socrates would not have drunk the hemlock; but he would have drunk from an even more bitter cup: insulting ridicule and a scorn a hundred times worse than death" (46). Such ridicule is not only what Rousseau expects, but what he writes of in other places. In the posthumously published *Les rêveries du Promeneur Solitaire* (*The Reveries of a Solitary Walker*), Rousseau finds himself "killed," isolated, and yet also freed, by society's scorn. The result is not a state of nature that looks anything like a garden. Instead, the perspective of the *barbarus* is of having been cast out or excluded from society. Being an exile from society within society seems to involve a certain excellence. It is the acknowledgment that civilization is nothing but a brute's wish to be a god. But it is nonetheless civilization that makes its own rejection possible. Human beings can be brutes only because they are civilized.

In the *Reveries* Rousseau claims to experience the "sentiment of existence" by way of the surfaces of plants, which he refers to as "the attire and clothing of the earth" (1782/1992: 91). He tries to turn away from the intents and purposes one finds when observing human behavior. Yet in his study of botany, he unhappily discovers remedies and poisons. As he weeds out his awareness of himself as other, his mind wanders back to itself. Perhaps Descartes' experience of his own reality by way of doubt would provide another way of undermining the sense of self that leads to vanity. Through this lens, clothes function as a medium of "doubt" or a "not-the-self" that in turn provokes a "sense-of-self."

Nudity would be akin to a state completely lacking in self-awareness, where you could be perfectly "comfortable," in fabric that "breathes" like a transparent sentence that does not cause the reader to think too much about the words themselves. But self-awareness and clothing go together. Clothes emerge as vehicles of self-expression from our having become aware of ourselves as selves in clothes—being there, being alive, being a "reality." The presence of clothes leads us to imagine the presence of the self, and this implicates the epistemological problem of knowing the self, since our awareness comes not from a revelation of what we are but of what we are not—that disposition, that *fashion* of clothes, bodies, and words.

Fashion, now somehow akin to Rousseau's vile ornamentation, falls prey to the same irony. The moment human beings put on clothes—even the moment they perceive things by means of a Lucretian shedding of perceptual clothing—they speak in an affected tone. They communicate with an eye to another's recognition, perhaps out of decency or because it is more alluring to imagine what isn't visible. Clothing makes both deceit and temptation possible by implying nudity, and by dividing "uncivilized" from "civilized." It is only because we speak in different languages and wear clothes different from our skins that we can imagine a state of pure apprehension and primordial honesty. The nostalgia for this faux Eden arises from our longing to know ourselves, the success of which would leave us beyond recognition. Understood in this way, clothes are the only nature we know; their fraudulence is not essential, but grows out of their foreignness and concealment. Concealment of what? We can only guess at the innuendo.

Utilitarian Narcissism

Clothes grow from whatever lurks in hair, too. Hair is freakish—Lucretius uses the same word for "pelt," *pellis*, also, "skin," and the peach fuzz of a budding beard, which he describes as "clothing" (*vestis*, 5.673). Hair is thought to be natural, and clothing is made out of interwoven hairs or plant fibers (flax; linen), as paper from papyrus, text from textile.[19] Initially, it appears that we wear clothes to amplify our natural coat with a conventional one, when we need warmth or protection. But warmth already seems to be an effect of clothing that is out of our control, as when a smell takes us over without our consent. Clothes do not automatically generate our desired temperature; in fact, they more regularly produce an excess or a deficiency of heat. They are related to fire in this way; and in certain accounts of the Prometheus myth, they arrive together with it.

No matter for those advocates of function over form: that clothes happen to be also fashionable seems superfluous to their overall utility. This is a pair of rose-colored glasses we would opt out of if we could. So, Kant says fashion obeys a "law of imitation" in which little or no regard to "utility" is paid. Fashion is all novelty—a vanity project that belongs to the "style of courtiers, especially ladies" (7:245–6).[20] For Kant, clothing must be in its basic function utilitarian, lest it be only impractical, femme frippery: no cargo pockets and epaulets (the marks of commercialized "utilitarian" style), but only unadorned practicality, or perhaps, suggests Kant unexpectedly, taste, understood as beauty, or, in certain special cases, pomp.

The real utilitarian was Kant's contemporary, Jeremy Bentham, who reduced individuals to units of usefulness to the common good. Bentham's utilitarianism makes no distinctions among different personalities or styles; it homogenizes human beings so as to achieve a fair distribution of goods. The more humans are benefited, the better an action is. But if one delves further into the lives of both Bentham and Kant (parenthetically, I note Thomas Jefferson's agrarian-revival look because of its bewildering return in the form of Brooklyn hipsters fleeing to the fields of upstate New York; Jefferson, by the way, died in debt, a cottagecore dandy), things begin to look really weird.

In his proposal for a prison called the "Panopticon," Bentham outlines what prisoners ought to wear and spends the majority of the chapter on shoes. With an air of certainty, Bentham says that prisoners should wear wooden shoes to prevent unwanted escapes and because they are a symbol of servitude. He assures the reader that wooden shoes aren't *that* uncomfortable, since "fashion apart," poor people have worn them for centuries in Ireland. The only time fashion should enter into prison life is on Sundays, when the wooden shoes have to be exchanged for house slippers so that the prisoners don't disgust chapel visitors with their clogs (1791/2011: 2.7). It is strange that a proponent of a utilitarian view also links the quality of footwear to humility before society and God. Footwear is here clearly not utilitarian, but a symbol of enslavement—an exertion of control over the lives of the prisoners by manipulating their outer dress.

One thinks, too, of Van Gogh's painting of peasant shoes, where the shoes themselves seem to complain of the distress of use. Martin Heidegger uses this painting as an example of how a work of art does not merely reproduce what is seen in the world but somehow displays its essence.[21] Literal shoes do this, too. They are not merely utilitarian indicators of some necessity for foot covering, but windows into a whole world, the seeing of which requires seeing the shoes as Van Gogh, or perhaps as a fashion designer, might see them.[22] It could be argued that we cannot see the utility of the shoes until we see the shoes as fashion. The insight of their utility already buffets them into fashion's lair, since to design a pair of shoes is not to first use them but to imagine the image of their use—"Cloth and grain are ordinary, and yet when we're cold they warm us and when we are hungry they feed us. How strange is that! The new and strange are precisely within the ordinary" (Zhi 1602/2016: 47).[23]

Kant's life, on the other hand, reveals an obsession with socks. In Thomas de Quincey's *Last Days of Immanuel Kant*, we learn a bizarre fact about Kant's stockings:

> [F]or fear of obstructing the circulation of the blood ... [Kant] never would wear garters; yet, as he found it difficult to keep up his stockings without them, he had invented for himself a most elaborate substitute ... In a little pocket, somewhat similar to a watch-pocket ... there was placed a small box, something like a watch-case, but smaller; into this box was introduced a watch-spring in a wheel, round about which wheel was wound an elastic cord, for regulating the force of which there was a separate contrivance. To the two ends of this cord were attached hooks, which hooks were carried through a small aperture in the pockets, and so, passing down the inner and the outer side of the thing, caught hold of two loops which were fixed on the off side and the near side of each stocking. As might be expected, so complex an apparatus was liable, like the Ptolemaic system of the heavens, to occasional derangements.
>
> (1827/1873: 119)

Kant's Ptolemaic system of garters seems anything but designed for economy. Rather, it is an elaborate, nonutilitarian way to avoid ordinary garters, but for the sake of a somewhat utilitarian concern (not obstructing the blood flow). One thinks, too, of the Königsburg housewives setting their clocks by Kant's daily walks (save the day he lost track of time while reading Rousseau's *Emile*), of the fact that Kant never traveled more than seventy miles from this city, of the lone portrait of Rousseau hanging in his otherwise empty study. Is the look of rationality hatched from a slight insanity?

Philosophy can be a stressful endeavor. Great attention to composure is required. The origins of frazzled academic unkemptness may well be the portrait of Diogenes the Cynic, whose raggedy appearance haughtily said rejected, not approved: a double cloak (worn as if it were a lion skin of Heracles), leather pouch, and walking stick.[24] A chip on the shoulder, too? Is the philosophical head so far in the clouds that it has forgotten to tie its own shoelaces? Is there a Ptolemaic system for tying them?

Again, Thales is the vintage example of the absent-minded professor. His theory that "Everything is water" is said to have come to him one day when he was walking around contemplating the stars, and accidentally fell into a well. In Plato's version of the story, "Some gracefully witty Thracian servant girl is said to have jeered at him—that he was so eager to know the things in heaven, he forgot the things in front of him and at his feet" (174a4–b1). Thales is totally clueless, and apparently not a very good looker. He doesn't watch where he's going. In fact, the more deeply he looks into what is beyond him, the less aware he is of his own looks. He proclaims everything is water at the very moment his own existence takes a spill. That he cannot walk on water doesn't look good for his grasp on reality. You could say he solidifies the universe as a liquid, only to be himself liquefied, since he is part of the universe.

For a person who desires knowledge, then, the self is both an advantage and a hurdle, which may be why philosophers so often find themselves estranged from their looks. To be a neutral voyeur of truth, you must forget your looking; but to look at everything without discrimination, you must also look at your own look, or rather, watch your step. So, Genesis 3 first looks anti-philosophical, because it seems to move from nudity to clothes. But nudity now appears a phantom. The closeness of the bikini to lingerie suggests that it is not the greater presence or absence of clothes that broadcasts erotic hints. Nudity at once presumes the intelligibility of a wild human or a transcendent self. Does revealing the secrets of nature require stripping both your own vision and the object of your looks—that is, kicking the habit of habits?[25]

Cicero describes Caesar's speeches as, "nude, right and charming, with every ornament of oration stripped off as if a vestment" (*Brutus* 75.262).[26] In 1528, Count Baldessar interprets this as *sprezzatura*. True art would appear as no art,

> nor to anything must we give greater care than to conceal art, for if it is discovered, it quite destroys our credit and brings us into small esteem. And I remember having once read that there were several very excellent orators of antiquity, who among their other devices strove to make everyone believe that they had no knowledge of letters; and hiding their knowledge they pretended that their orations were composed

very simply and as if springing rather from nature and truth than from study and art.

(Castiglione 1901: 35)

There is an anecdote about G.E.M. Anscombe: once at a restaurant she was told that women were not admitted in trousers; so, she took her pants off. Anscombe also had a monocle, like the Cyclops, which she would strategically let slip from her face into her bosom during class.[27] If you are committed to plain Jane reality, you cannot be ashamed of the base. Philosophy would be at home in a nudist colony or a Catholic primary school, as long as reality has been treated in uniform. It is not its fashion to marvel at things in glasses—monocles maybe, but certainly not bifocals (that sort of double vision would be called relativism). A ruler, for example, appears bent in a glass of water when it is in reality quite straight. Philosophy doesn't like this. Philosophers are not satisfied by mere appearances. They don't window shop. Better to buy things wholesale—to see them either standardized or apart from their optical corsets altogether.

Against all odds, however, Socrates preferred the mirror. Knowledge—or at least knowledge of ignorance—requires not mistaking appearance for reality, but rather, looking at reality through its reflections in speeches.[28] So, too, Lucretius bids Memmius to "perceive" why "an image seems beyond the mirror," an injunction not only to look at mirrors but to look at Lucretius' looking (4.269–70). Mirror is the Latin word *speculum*, a diminutive that means either, "a little thing which one looks at" or "which enables one to look at things." A mirror, like touch, must be both, and when we have sensed the mirror itself, says Lucretius, the image appears suddenly distant, when before it looked as if it were close (283–90). We thus see the image of our own seeing when we look in the mirror. While the mirror-image is a reversed reality, as if poetically glossed, Lucretius notices that "It happens also that an image (*imago*) is passed from mirror to mirror so that even five or six *simulacra* can often be produced. ... Thus, the image is reflected from mirror to mirror" (302–10). It now returns the correct likeness—but, to which mirror? It seems to be the mirror of the onlooker. The words follow suit, for "image (*imago*)" is singular, and referred to as if independent of mirrors, while, when it echoes itself, it becomes "reflections" or "likenesses (*simulacra*)." The slightly askew mirror between the two words rights our reflection.

We know Socrates primarily through the written mirror of Plato (he makes a cameo in Xenophon, too), though in the *Phaedrus*, Socrates is depicted arguing against the transmission of philosophy in writing.[29] Philosophy needs the context of live conversation; it is resistant to ink.[30] Yet since Plato wrote this dialogue in which Socrates critiques writing, there seems to be a crucial difference between author and character—or, for fashion's purposes, designer and muse. Socrates was notoriously ugly and only once portrayed in shoes in the *Symposium*, a wardrobe upgrade that Plato designs.[31] It need not be a conspicuous flashiness, but may be the sign that Socrates wasn't barefoot as a rule (though Aristodemus seems to presume this in his imitation of him). Barefoot Socrates was only made into a "look" by his having been once dressed. Plato tells his readers in the Second Letter that the Socrates of his dialogues is a Socrates "become beautiful and young" (314c3). Socrates is attractive in his paradigmatic ugliness. He has followers and corrupts innocents, and Plato makes this style sexy. He puts together truth and beauty on Socrates' behalf, revealer and concealer, cosmology and cosmetics. Plato is not afraid to dress up the truth; he is not just a philosopher but also a poet. In contrast to his character Socrates, then, Plato found a means to transmit philosophy in writing by imagining dialogues in which a beautified Socrates plays an unsightly midwife. This is certainly not the standard look of wisdom.

Following Epicurus' lead, we might say that its usual garb is a dead European prose-writing male—and now, let's update it with a pipe, a thick tweed blazer, elbow patches, no tie, Clark Kent glasses, a neutral-colored sweater (Oxford blue shirt underneath), a leather messenger bag revealing sorted books and papers. Gangs of graduate students imitate this guise (replacing the pipe with a cigarette), including imagined hand gestures and facial tics, as if a replica of wisdom's look would create an osmosis of it straight to the brain. Why doesn't wisdom instead look like the child of Nietzsche's third metamorphosis? Why doesn't it laugh with the air of freedom and whimsy that you would expect from the unbridled truth?

And what is with the tweed? To be sure, it carries the power of crumpling without wrinkling, a look of durable importance, the solid academic article, neither too shabby nor too flashy. In a 1991 essay, ceremoniously entitled "The F-Word," Valerie Steele wrote this about tweed's pedigree—"Gospel, according to the traditional upper-class Englishman, has it that a good Donegal tweed jacket lasts forever. If it gets a bit frayed, all the better. American academics have simply copied this shabby-genteel look, so today the tenured sons of Russian, Italian, Polish, and Irish immigrants all look like rural Church of England vicars."

In "Reflections of an Academic Dandy," an article published in *GQ* (on the academic periphery) in 1985, Joseph Epstein took issue with the budding trend of informality in professorial garb; looking too much like your students might be seen as "unprofessional" in all the wrong ways (incompetent, flirty, careless). But Epstein noted that anyone who is even slightly dressed up stands out like "a flamingo strutting in a bowling alley." Meanwhile, Steele commented on the "tyranny of earth tones" among academic females. "Femininity is out," she wrote. It still seems to be, and the occasional hard femme look only serves to underline the point. It doesn't help that graduate school can occupy some critically formative years; while their peers are busy buying houses and having kids, doctoral students continue to cling to their alma mater, until they are suddenly delivered into adulthood stunted in their sartorial growth by penny-pinching and all-nighters. Either that or for some reason they look as if they were always mysteriously middle-aged, as if they had worn that same Donegal jacket since elementary school.

Like high-brow neologisms or a sprinkle of abstract theory, the "look" of philosophers seems especially dependent on their thoughts. Sleek, black turtlenecks must be paired with a cigarette burning a hole through the page. "Wearing a black turtleneck," writes Shahidha Bari, "of course condemns you to existential crisis, being, as it is, so beloved of pained writers and French philosophers. Part of its allure is pragmatic insofar as it circumnavigates the stuffiness of a shirt and tie, whilst not quite degrading the wearer to the slovenly blasphemy of a T-shirt" (2017). See Audrey Hepburn in *Funny Face*. Meanwhile, the German idealists appear absolutely manicured. Feminists generally aren't caught making broad statements. There are various degrees of eccentricity ranging from people who look like they got dressed at the lost-and-found to those who look like they were transported here in a time machine, but no matter where you look everyone wears their heart on their sleeve. The obsession with dressing up your resume in intellectual products of all colors and styles is right up there with collecting shoes—a fetish to which Hannah Arendt admitted, especially for Ferragamo. Heidegger was for a time her illicit lover and he too had certain stylistic preferences. While giving a lecture on skiing, Heidegger wore a ski suit; at other times he wore what Gadamer referred to as his "existential suit":

> Naturally, he did not always run around in a ski suit, but he was never to be seen in a black jacket. He had his own suit—we called it his *existential suit*. It had been designed by the painter Otto Ubbelohde and belonged to a new sort of men's clothing that vaguely resembled farmer's garb. In this clothing Heidegger certainly did have something of the unassuming splendor of a farmer dressed for Sunday.
>
> (1987/1994: 115)

One needs to look smart. Not to mention the androgyny of academic prose. It all began with the use of "he/she" in place of "he." But many scholars—especially self-identified men—now emphatically adopt a "she" in order to call attention to just how fashionably neutral they are. As to the dissolution of gender distinction with "they," I suspect this arises not from political correctness but out of deference to fashion. For many eons it has been unseemly to use the informal "you," which now so swiftly offers itself as the most viable solution. "You" defies gender and plurality without sounding grammatically dubious. It is the universal particular. But it will require the resurrection of its equally unfashionable soulmate, "I." Philosophers do not like to get personal.

They don't pray to Gandhi's "fashion goddess" either. Icons and imitations seem second or third from the truth, and faith in them even more of a sheepish attribute. It is a lesser-known fact about Gandhi that in his law school days in London he dressed like Beau Brummell. At twenty, Gandhi was, according to Sachchidanand Sinha, "a nut, a masher, a blood—a student more interested in fashion and frivolities than his studies" (Nanda 1996: 27–8). It is also rumored that Aristotle was a snappy dresser, distinctive for his beady eyes, cropped hair and rings.[32] Maybe we only have to look at his literary style. After all, if you can't judge a book by its cover, how will you know what to check out? Whether you say a book looks good or a person has good looks, this is a judgment made based on an idea of content, not on content. "Good" in this case implies an image of the good, a beautified good. This is a superficial premise without which no inquiry into reality can occur. So, while aesthetic beauty may give the appearance that it is about mere surfaces, the conviction with which it can really strike us is always connected to some truth. Maybe this is a truth about how we seek truth—namely, it has to be convincing and striking—rather than about the content of the truth we find.

But let's return for a moment to the idea of clothes as utilitarian. The idea is parallel to the philosophical distinction between useful or practical truths and abstract or theoretical truths. Useful truths are ready-to-wear. Abstract truths require more imagination. They leisurely parade across the runway of the mind with no clear direction. Practical, utilitarian clothes, on the other hand, are directed by season. But what qualifies them for what season? Is it wearing long underwear in winter to keep warm or not wearing white after Labor Day?

It is not clear that stylistic variations according to cultural custom were even a "thing" until the late Middle Ages or early Renaissance.[33] In 1420, the archbishop Symeon critiqued the replacement of "painted hair and garments" with "human hair and clothes"; in 1450, St. Antonius worried that paintings invoking secular time would not "excite devotion, but laughter and vanity, such as monkeys and dogs, and the like, or vain adornments of clothing" (Nagel 2004: 35, 48).[34] Fashion in painting apparently ushers in or is coeval to the ushering in of art history, which is to say, a notion of art being aware of itself as distinct from iconography. Nagel, along with his co-author Christopher Wood, finds it uncertain whether this attitude existed in antiquity (2010: 92). Perhaps this is simply a hazard of the moderns having used the ancients as a foil for their own modernity? At any rate, something similar could be said of the ancients in their understanding of their own time. If clothing is the "seismograph of history" (2004: 50), and its expression in painting more soaked in time than sculpture (2010: 71), it would be hard to deny that such an awareness existed among ancient authors. Indeed, it would be hard to deny that clothes, in being worn on bodies, do not thereby suggest sculpture and painting, at least insofar as humans are clothes-conscious. In Anne Hollander's *Seeing Through Clothes*, she finds the depictions of human beings in art carry implications of their relationship with and styles of clothing as early as the draping of Greek antiquity. But for Hollander, too, Greek fashion is not yet fashion. It can at least be said that, once fashion has come into being, it is unthinkable to unthink it.

In a later conversation with Sheila Heti, Nagel describes the apex of style (by which he can only mean good style) as a symbiosis of instrument and movement. Style is

> all about agency, about marking the world in a certain way. But there is also a receptive moment in style. Style is the way we let the world move through us. Think of a surfer. The surfboard is a stylus, cutting a path through the wave. The surfer finds an individual path—no two surfers will find the same path through the swell and curl. And the surfer is nothing without the wave. Without that energy, that force, the surfer can't carve her path.
>
> (2014: 187)

Nagel goes on to say that some "waves"—which is to say, some moments in history—are better for style than others. No doubt the late Medieval period is one such wave. Classical Greece may well be another. I have a bee in my bonnet about this, but for the moment, suffice it to say that self-styled "moderns" wouldn't paint a Greek in medieval garb; modern painters keep up with the trends. They are fashion-conscious, which is to say aware of time's effect on art. But each age, writes Baudelaire, has its own modernity; the mod *flaneur* simply has the more refined style of making human beings look of their time.[35]

Strangely, as clothes show themselves more prominently as "historical costumes," they also appear inseparable from existence.[36] No one will bat an eyelash if you cover yourself in green paint on St. Patrick's Day, or if you wear bunny ears on Easter. You can don a toga in mid-July, provided that you've suddenly found yourself at a fraternity hazing ritual. In December, the New York subways are crawling with imitation Santa Clauses. But Santa Claus himself is a mutant hybrid styled after the shamanic practice in Lapland of handing out red and white mushrooms at the winter solstice.[37] Not to mention the Renaissance Fair. Any other occasion, forget it. Depending on where you live, there is an unspoken code for what's a one-time-only deal and what's a "little black dress," as if what we wear were not dictated by both bodily and cultural flux. This is the unsavory truth of all clothes. They are not just secular frivolity but memorials, tombstones, to your being that you air to the public, whether you think every day is Halloween or not. Even people who dress in constant parody of the norm are at some level playing serious, as if it were easy to distinguish between inside and outside, as if life were not perpetually the seventh grade. Though style may appear a timeless thing—whereas fashions seem to change—both subsist in clothes as at once historical transports and trans-historical ports.

If there were an immediate link between putting on a coat and simply being cold, the first step of selecting a coat is something altogether different. To seek warmth in advance of being cold elevates a practical concern to an idealistic one. Buying a winter coat on sale in the spring is not the same as a hamster storing food in its cheeks. The selection process already demands a certain abstract "idea" of what is warm. When we are cold, we are attracted to things that "look (meaning they seem like they might in theory be) warm"; conversely, we worry about people who "look" cold. It is because of this meta-level needing—the need to ward off needs and to seem as if we have no needs—that need and want are so hard to distinguish. We have coats for all temperatures, so that we can perfectly suit ourselves to the weather, as if to have mastered unpredictability not by algorithms but by jackets. In this vein, you could easily find a reason to need several designer coats.

Marx's famous "overcoat" conveyed the symbolic power of social status, whereas, without it, he was no one.[38] Covering up for the sake of protection from the elements is, then, already making a heated philosophical claim. "A raincoat protects against rain, but also and indissociably, it points to its status as a raincoat" (Barthes 1960/2013: 38). This is because you have gotten the idea that it would be good to control your needs, and perhaps to rid yourself of needs altogether. So Prometheus stole fire, and Adam and Eve ate the fruit. The need for control rears itself most vividly in those who insist that clothes are merely protective coverings. This is, ironically, the sign that clothes are not only satisfying a basic necessity, but also providing a soapbox for making utilitarian claims.

Even rebels against fashion take fashion as the standard against which they rebel. They are breaking laws, and in doing so, their obedience is vintage. Rebelling against any law requires bowing down to that law in order to break it. If the law were truly impotent, there would be no motive to transgress (or transdress?). Fashion victims and fashion police suggest that styling yourself is a dangerous maneuver. If you do care, and you decide to follow a trend—be careful not to do it too perfectly, lest you become cookie cutter. On the other hand, if you do not follow it perfectly, you run the risk of looking like a wannabe. A badly done trend is like a badly done argument. It has an obviously re-circulated air.

Bad arguments have taken over the racks and shelves of department stores. We veer toward the casual, non-conflict, invisible. But we have an invisibility complex. Shopping for a means to "blend in" is still shopping for a variety of poetic identities: boot cut, flared, skinny, ripped, faded, acid-washed, distressed, aged. What is more, we are living in the era of Amazon and Facebook, where knockoffs are quickly becoming indistinguishable from originals, and images have overrun people. It has never been so easy to try, and never been so common to give up. If we are giving up because we imagine there is no connection between our outerwear and inner self, what of power suits and performance wear? In our secular habits we accidentally bow down to the idols of comfort and potency—two things more closely related than they may at first seem.

"Real" Clothes and Buried Selves

Night is upon us in sixteenth-century Florence. Niccolò Machiavelli is writing about his after-dinner workwear in a letter to Francesco Vettori on December 10, 1513:

> When evening has come, I return to my house and go into my study. At the door I take off my clothes of the day, covered with mud and mire, and I put on my regal (*reali*) and courtly (*curiali*) garments; and decently reclothed, I enter the ancient courts of ancient men, where, received by them lovingly, I feed on the food that alone is mine and that I was born for. There I am not ashamed to speak with them and to ask them the reason for their actions; and they in their humanity reply to me. And for the space of four hours I feel no boredom, I forget every pain, I do not fear poverty, death does not frighten me. I deliver myself entirely to them.[39]

Machiavelli finds it inappropriate to read ancient texts in dirty clothes. Earlier in the letter, we learn how Machiavelli's clothes were soiled; he was out catching thrushes, with Dante or Petrarch, Tibullus or Ovid, under his arm. There is apparently something about Italian and Latin poetry that is more suited to mire. Poetry muddies, obfuscates, and makes the truth harder to see. To read in an orderly fashion Machiavelli must re-clothe himself in "regal (*reali*) and courtly (*curiali*) garments"[40] so that his finest exterior will beget his finest thoughts.

The Italian word for "regal," *reale*, puns on another word, *reale*, which means "real," "true," or "actual." The courts of the ancients are the courts of dead men, for which it is necessary to look authentic. This ritual purification does not, for Machiavelli, entail the removal of your clothes altogether, but rather, donning the clothes of reality/royalty. In these new clothes, Machiavelli becomes more himself, and feeds on the food that alone is his and for which he was born. Time ceases to matter. He is not afraid of death, pain, or poverty. Machiavelli tells Vettori in the next paragraph that his communication with the ancients has led him to write *The Prince*, though only on the poet Dante's advice—Dante says that "to have understood without retaining does not make knowledge." The *Prince* is therefore given to Machiavelli on the advice of the ancients,[41] but it is written by Machiavelli on the advice of a poet. He begins his letter with a line from Petrarch—"Never were divine favors late." The relationship between philosophy (or truth-seeking) and poetry (or the dressing up of truth) seems implicated on every level of Machiavelli's actions. Is it Dante who suggests that Machiavelli re-clothe himself? And if so, is Machiavelli's "real" outfit still covered in the mud of poetry?

Machiavelli's most regal garments are in this way akin to a beautified image of his nudity. In these clothes, he can be real with the ancients. He is not embarrassed to ask them anything; and they answer. This is a radical transparency of thought by way of a transparency of outfit, not unlike opulent papal or royal robes, which do not signify material wealth so much as the richness of divinity or rulership. Machiavelli sees through his clothes; or rather, his clothes are a means of *seeing through*, and so his clothes are a metaphor for his words. In princely clothes, Machiavelli writes a princely work. But again, it is hard to imagine that this transparency is as pure as Machiavelli proposes. Something about the look of the real is contrived. When Machiavelli loses track of time in his study, he ceases to be subject to the whims of fortune (time; death; pain; poverty). He is not bored, but completely engaged—completely active—in his deference to higher thoughts. This echoes the state in which Machiavelli's prince hopes to find himself.

Do clothes, then, in some way signify a longing to transcend our mortality—a longing to control our fortunes? After all, how else can we explain the wish to hang onto one's youthful appearance as long as possible? It is not as if wrinkles lead directly to death; but they are the signs that there is no turning back. Even the plaster casts made of baby shoes are ambiguous: a hopeful marker of the first growth or a pessimistic reminder of the immediacy of decay? Children sometimes put their teeth under their pillows; the elderly do not. One might also think of open-casket funerals, which do not display nude corpses, but corpses made-up and wearing clothes: an everlasting image of the "real" person—at least the person we knew—boiled down to the memory of a last vestment.

In 2019, several scholars claimed that they might be able to identify the skull of Pliny the Elder. How? A skeleton was found "heavily bejeweled," as Pliny might have been (Lidz 2020). Bodies grow up and die faster than clothes and records deteriorate. Dead, we are jewels and memories of jewels. Antoine Picon suggests that something similar is true of architectural ornament: "One of its [ornament's] roles also consists in reminding the living of the passage of time and the existence of those who preceded them. Just like writing, ornament is inseparable from both present experience and memory" (2013: 82). Fashion, then, might be an alternative pathway to the immortal self; it is certainly swifter than having children. Nowhere is this more apparent than in the most extreme version of plastic surgery: mummification.

Herodotus gives an account of the ancient Egyptian practice of mummification in Book 2 of his *Histories*.[42] According to Herodotus, the ancient Egyptians took immense precautions to try to transform the body after death, and in some cases even before it. The procedure of embalmment began with special practitioners, who displayed to their customers painted, wooden replicas of the dead, as if these statues were paradigmatic representations of life. The highest-paying customers received the most exemplary imitation, which "belongs to One" whose name it is not holy for Herodotus to mention. The One is clearly Osiris.[43] This leads Seth Benardete to conclude, "The mummy is a god … The whole corpse is not a god, but the empty shell, cleansed and emptied of its vital organs, the mere surface of the body is" (1969/2009: 56; Hdt. 2.86). In order to keep the corpse corpulent, it is given a head to toe face-lift, filled with injections and ointments, and then wrapped up as if mortality would heal. How strange that the living have taken so much care to transform the dead into imitations of life, since after they are shrouded, no one can see them (something similar seems true of the selection of opulent caskets, which are interred and not visible). The covered body is then placed in a hollow, wooden form that resembles the dead person's shape, which the relatives, not the embalmers, construct. While most bodies can be embalmed immediately after the period of grieving, the wives of noteworthy men cannot be embalmed for three or four days, lest the embalmers want to have sex with them (2.85–90). Hold on—according to Herodotus, the ancient Egyptians seem to imagine life as a fixed state, as the "look" of life. For three or four days, death is more or less like life. This is not limited to the erogenous qualities of body. While the Scythians have their dead over for dinner (4.73), the tombs of Egyptian kings (e.g., Pharaoh Zoser) were filled with frozen replicas of living motion, such as stone pillars made to imitate plants and stone doorways with their curtains forever furled. This fixed flux is proto-mannequin, a human taxidermy that transforms temporary beings into timeless snapshots, into bodiless clothes (i.e., mummies)—into gods. Immortality is a wooden replica of life: a statue.

The "classic" look also bears the mummy's stamp: timeless, indistinct, statuesque. In models and mummies we idealize the freezing of time. Clothing and cosmetics stand parallel to the extremes of burial and cremation: complete concealment or complete evaporation. Like the earth used to cover up a corpse, morticians provide cover up with powder and blush in order to make the deceased look less lifeless. Living bodies sometimes need these treatments, too—a little collagen filler, a little face lift. Clothing and makeup, like coffins, cover up our vulnerabilities, the most delicate of which is our impending demise. The fig leaf obscures the signs of the life-giving genitals; but the concealment of the aging process by way of maquillage achieves the same goal. Erasing fine lines is not so much about remaining beautiful as it is about deleting the signs of decay from your visage. Under-eye brighteners and serums can make your face appear a little livelier, a little less like death.

Cremation, on the other hand, completely obliterates the body. Physicality vanishes in a puff of smoke and nothing lingers except a memory. This seems to be the flip side of burial, which cakes on the cover-up in order to conceal the wounds of time. Perhaps cremation is more fantastical in this regard; it is like trading your body in for an avatar. But both burial and cremation get rid of the material evidence of body and put up a symbol to its disappearance: an ode to an urn and a profile picture. A symbol does not have the same constraints as a body. It gives what was time-sensitive a makeover in metaphor. In ancient Egypt, the living body was itself transformed into a symbol. The same is true of timeless clothing, which makes the wearer into a symbol onto which anything can be printed. Free fashion has long allowed us to write and rewrite our own tombstones on a whim, with every hair cut or wardrobe change. The clothes we wear—our vestments—are the tablets on which we poetically design our own epitaphs.

But there are limits. The word "investment," which comes from the Latin *in* + *vestire*, literally means, "to be clothed in." Figuratively, "investment" is the sign of being "interested." Vested interest is black-tie interest. It parades itself around in a designer suit that says, "I'm interested!" To be vested is quite literally to wear clothes. That interest and clothing should be linked is not so peculiar, since apparently erotic investment and fig leaves go hand and hand. Clothes not only conceal the signs of desire but they also seem to point to some kind of shame or nobility surrounding them. To be caught with our pants down would make us blush, but we can turn it around to laud nudity as the crown jewel of freedom. *vestire* is certainly related to *vestis* ("garment") but it pays homonymic homage to the word, *vestigia*, "tracks," or "impressions." Consider Lucretius' characterization of images as leaving "certain tracks (*vestigia*) of forms" (4.87). Truth is like a wild animal, and we are sniffing out its footprints (1.403–9). The impressions left in clothes are the traces of the passing of our lives. So Hecuba laments to Hector's corpse:

> "Now beside the curved ships, away from your parents,
> the writhing worms devour you when the dogs have had enough
> of your naked body; yet there are clothes laid aside in the house,
> finely woven, beautiful, fashioned by the hands of women.
> Now I will burn them all in a blazing fire,
> for they are of no use to you, you are not wrapped in them—
> I will burn them to be an honor to you in the sight of the Trojan men and
>   Trojan women."
>
> (*Iliad* 22.507–14)[44]

There is another interesting word in Greek, *tokos*, which means not only "offspring," but also "bank interest." Investing your interest, whether inside an alluring ensemble or a secure savings account, is a way of building interest, not just concealing it. We are overly protective, since we wear not just over-wear but also under-wear. Clothing disguises the signs of our literal intercourse with the world with figurative suggestions of sex and excrement. These are the signs of our intakes and outtakes—our mortal motions— which we euphemistically entitle, the "private parts," or in Greek, *aidoia*, "the shameful (or perhaps revered) things." You might wonder if they are private because they must remain secret or because we do not understand their secrets.

Profanity and Disinvested Vestment

Is the figurative not then equally dirty? What kind of foul emission is speech? Doesn't it, too, like a corpse or a piece of shit, require cover up? Perhaps the more speech is covered up the more poetic, and so, the more immortal, it becomes? Speech can be eloquent or vulgar. In Thomas Carlyle's *Sartor*

Resartus, we learn of a fellow called Diogenes Teufelsdröckh ("God-born Devil's shit," or "Holy Shit"), a Philosopher of Clothes, and professor of "things in general," which is to say, nothing in particular. So begins Carlyle's parody of German idealism. This will be discussed in greater detail in Chapter 5, but let me briefly mention Carlyle's primary accusation: this Pontificator of Packaging, this Philosopher of Sheer Garments, is a Professor of Bullshit. In Carlyle's chapter on "Aprons," we learn that the rags which receive all the cow-shit of the Laystall are later transformed into paper onto which books are printed. We are made to identify writing and shitting, nudity and cursing.

To curse is to display an honesty apparently so emotive it must be edited out with asterisks (****). Asterisks are another apron we have for protection against shit. We use them to cover up words like "fuck" and "shit" with linguistic fig leaves, just as we cover up the signs of fucking and shitting with clothes. "Explicit" speech is apparently so forthright that it can't even be spoken. But what exactly is the naked, literal meaning of an obscenity? It seems to be used for lack of a better word. Profanity expresses our investment or our emotion without pointing us to any clear origin. For example, "fuck" may mean "Oh fuck!" "Fuck it." Or, "fuck yes!" It is malleable in its spectrum of frustration, apathy, or delight. Speech can apparently convey meaning even when it has no idea what it intends. We tend to think of profanity as wrong in its openness, but it is really speech running up against its limit, when it is forced to appeal to a meaningless word due to its inability to find a word. These are feelings of intensity that in times of leisure we might seek poetry or philosophy to explain to us. Curse words are the lingerie of our longing to express ourselves—a mantle that makes our feelings apparent with blatant opacity. They point to the impenetrability of the sacred as they blaspheme it by calling it out; they slide together the ordinary motherfucker with Oedipus. It is very interesting, too, that curse words are more usable than words with narrow definitions, because in meaning nothing and everything, they can be served up on a multitude of occasions—as interjections, nouns, adverbs, adjectives, or verbs.[45] They highlight speech not as meaning but as musical digression.

In English, the word "to swear" can be divine and profane. You can swear on your life or swear at a bad driver. In both cases swearing is a sign of investment. When we talk about "investment" we are again really talking about interest—something is at stake. Often what is at stake eludes words; we have to coat it in poetic phrases, which like curse words, simply mean to mean. If someone is disinterested, then, this would be akin to being naked or not giving a fuck. And yet, nudity is likewise a taboo "word" whose explicit appearance causes us to draw a blank. It pretends to show us everything, but only presents us with another, shocking surface that may cause us to cover our eyes in the absence of another's cover-up. Perhaps we wouldn't be abashed in a nudist colony or a love affair, but then nudity ceases to be nudity, and becomes a norm (which is to say, an outfit). Whether you willingly take your clothes off or say that clothes simply do not matter, both dismissals are ways of clothing the self in nonchalance. This is to be invested in disinvestment—to insist passionately that you don't care about what you wear. Yet, if this were really true, there would be no passionate insistence. Clothes are expletives, whether pious or defiant.

Editing, too, is a nasty business of the mouth and the mind. A good poet will hide the shitting and fucking of the editing process, in which you must be stung by frustration, ask questions, and other embarrassing emissions that suggest you actually aren't sure what you are saying. A clever poet will appear to have transcended these activities, which are reserved for the impious, ugly philosopher. To ask a question or wonder about something is to chew on it, or perhaps to vomit up what you cannot chew (Nietzsche suggested that his reader "ruminate" on his writings like a cow regurgitates its food in order to rehash it).[46] People seem to be divided over whether or not thinking's discourse should be as private as intercourse and childbirth in its streams of consciousness and verbal diarrhea. Even in secular society, we still cover up expulsions with bedroom, bathroom, and university doors.

This may be why philosophy looks so freakish. Philosophy attempts to publicly divest both convention and self, since the truth cannot be something dressed up in bias or perspective. When we think about what really is we must try to be neutral to our own opinions—to put on *reali* clothes. We cannot bristle at our own nudity as if it were profane. The seeming truths of opinions, on the other hand, are connected to adornment and distraction, hence fashion's bad reputation among the philosophically inclined. To think about truth you cannot inject the truth with your own persuasion or preference. Yet, if you are totally neutral or nude to truth, you won't be able to genuinely ask questions, since then there will be no curiosity—no investment. The trick is to generate a kind of disinvested investment—a nude suit or a leisure suit—but without the residual animosity of those who heatedly assert they are not invested.

In antiquity, the latter sort of people would be labeled "sophists." The ancient sophists admit of greater and lesser degrees of sham but for the purposes of my argument, a "sophist" will be a sort of person who is concerned in some way with having the look or reputation of knowledge. Socrates is Plato's more self-aware version of disinvestment. His most famous fashion statement was that he only had "knowledge of ignorance." Socrates may have been ugly, but he liked to play dress up. He would go around cleaning the faulty opinions out of other people's closets (particularly of pretty boys like

Alcibiades) and he would never replace them with anything new. As a sterile, unerotic midwife who could bring to bear other people's ideas (or abort them) without ever falling in love or getting pregnant himself, every piece of his wisdom was obtained second hand.[47] Aristophanes concluded that he was an airhead. The city of Athens concluded that he was a criminal. Either way, his awareness required accessory.

But if it turns out you cannot finally "divest" yourself completely, the Socratic admission of naked ignorance looks forged. Perhaps it is not that Socrates was perfectly disinvested; he simply lacked any particular investment.[48] How did he stop himself from thereby sinking to the level of a sophist or ascending to the heights of a god? Athens surely thought he was both corrupt and impious; he was tried and executed on these very charges. We might ask the question more generally: is it possible to imagine a human being without envisioning that being in clothes, and thereby suspecting a cover up? When we separate nudity from clothing we divinize ourselves. The more we think we can be without our clothes the more we think we know where alterity begins and identity ends. The ability to control our identities—now made nearly possible by the contemporary wardrobe of identifiers and the malleability of social media personalities—would also allow us to become greater identity thieves. We could don any identity for any occasion, as in the *Iliad* Aphrodite appears to Helen as a wool-weaver after she has just saved her lover Paris from being killed in battle. Aphrodite is an agile weaver of character—a good poet, like Homer.

This power of transforming identities into icons is something that philosophy shares with poetry. It has an endless, some might say incessant, power to visit the ordinary as the wondrous. A poet and a philosopher can both take a common straw man's hat, and show it off as if it were woven with Rumpelstiltskin's gold. This is more like musing or tailoring than designing. And it is a power usually attributed to people who know how to put themselves to together—to good lookers. To become aware of the way things truly are seems to necessarily mean looking at them through a looking glass. This is the sign that vanity deserves a double take. Not in high fashion or low fashion but somehow in no fashion. Genuine philosophy doesn't have a uniform; nor is it patently stitched. It seems to be perpetually good looking, sewn at just the right moment with just the right touch.

2

Phantom Selves

"And thus I clothe my naked villainy
With odd old ends stol'n out of holy writ;
And seem a saint, when most I play the devil."
—William Shakespeare, from *Richard III*

I say, beware of all enterprises that require new clothes,
and not rather a new wearer of clothes. If there is not a
new man, how can the new clothes be made to fit?
—Henry David Thoreau, from "Walden and
on the Duty of Civil Disobedience"

In the spring of 2020, the world shut down, then continued to limp forward, entering a mandatory masquerade to stop the spread of a novel coronavirus. Masks divided into two types: austere medical masks and friendly fabric masks—tragic and comic—the former reminding us of the spread of disease and our impending mortality, the latter attempting to conceal the possibility of death in various prints and styles. Masks or no masks came to signify the degree to which you love your neighbor, for the only tax on Americans for not wearing masks was to appear to lack empathy for others or to believe that the virus—perhaps even death itself—might be a hoax.

But there is an interesting relationship between the face of the friendly mask and the longing to conceal the fragility of human life: like lollipops and fake plants at the doctor's office, friendly cloth masks suggest either a resolution to die or the denial that death is transpiring at all: "a sweetish, medicinal smell, associated with wounds and disease and suspect cleanliness" (Mann 1912/1989: 52). Masks, like clothes themselves, seem a disinfectant, a germicide, a shade on the setting sun. For that disagreeable body that decays there is the more everlasting presence, the comforting vessel of inanimate cloth. On the other hand, with the invisibility of half of the face comes an anonymity that pretends to liberate our instantiation in flesh. What were once proper nouns, when masked, become common nouns: you are one of a herd and your most noble action is now your disappearance. You recede into oblivion behind the mask, where accolades are won in obscurity, since wearing a mask is a sign of virtue. But this anonymous charade is rendered duplicitous by the variegations of colors, hues, and patterns in which masks are found. In Greek the word for a "hue" is *pharmakon*, which also means both "poison" and "cure," captured in the latter senses by the ambiguous English word "drug." Socrates uses the word in the *Phaedo* to cryptically point to hemlock as either a remedy or venom for life—venom, too, in Latin *venenum*, is either a pun on Venus (her divine serum) or a toxin, for the two share the root (*wen-*, "to strive for" or "desire"), and Vergil makes the pun explicit in the *Aeneid*, where "Venus orders Cupid to deceive Dido with *venenum*" (Snyder 1980: 107).[1]

Are clothes, too, thus a drug—a phantom hallucination of our true selves that threatens to either bury or free us, or both at the same time? The phenomenon of the "makeover" does double duty as de-drugging and re-drugging—de-clothing and re-clothing—in such a way that you become a new version of you, resurrected and detoxed from an earlier you. This need not involve all the flourishes of a top-to-bottom aesthetic renovation. It could be as simple as a trim that makes you feel crisper, sharper, and more like yourself. But it's strange, isn't it? Compared to *what* version of yourself is this new self now imagined to be truer? Isn't the old self as much the self as the new self? Wasn't the old self once new? The standard of the self that we long for when we "freshen," "clean up," and "make over" ourselves seems as ephemeral as our ever-changing bodies. What then are we doing when we aspire to be more than what we are, and so to be truer to our "selves"?

Euripides' *Bacchae*: The Tragedy of Punk and Prep

In the *Bacchae* we find a portrait of clothes that ascribes to them a transformative magic. The worry that clothes can drug us, change us, or even make us lose our minds is palpable in the fear that philosophers have of being insidiously stitched up in fashion, as if this would be to drink the Dionysian wine of poetry or to lose sight of reality, tripping on adjectives and other accessories to truth. In Euripides' version, half-godly Dionysus will force his mortal cousin Pentheus out of his preppy garb into antinomian threads that will ultimately dissolve his identity. Pentheus is very scared of dressing up. Perhaps we, too, should be wary of the styles in which we coat ourselves, lest they begin to stick to our souls.

The *Bacchae* opens with Dionysus and his body double "wine" arriving in Thebes with a chorus of Crazies, plus compulsory followers who are dubbed "maenads," from the Greek verb, *mainesthai*, "to be mad or crazed." He has come to punish the women of Thebes, who slandered his mother, Semele, by saying she lied about having slept with Zeus. Dionysus' punishment is to make every female in the city go crazy in worship of him. They deck themselves out in wreaths of ivy and fawn skins; they wield thyrsus wands with which they can milk the earth. Yet despite the fact that Dionysus has only infected the women, he spurs on two wannabe male worshippers, Teiresias and Cadmus. They are already wearing Bacchant gear when the play opens. We don't know if Cadmus has convinced Teiresias or vice versa to pretend they are on Dionysus' side—since, even if Dionysus is a liar, says Cadmus, it doesn't hurt to say Zeus is part of the family. Meanwhile, sober Pentheus, son of Dionysus' aunt, Agave, does not believe Dionysus is anything but a fraud. Teiresias chides Pentheus for his painfully mad sobriety, for which "neither by means of drugs (*pharmaka*) could you get a remedy, nor without them would you be sick" (326-7). Pentheus is apparently incurably, insanely, drunkenly sober. His sickness is a drug for which there is no drug. And its origin is unexpectedly Dionysus himself, who will appear the cause of the delusion of sobriety as both drunken honesty (punk) and mad pretense (prep).

Teiresias describes Dionysus as liquid Demeter, a libation poured to the gods—

> The flowing vine, drunk to the full, provides
> Sleep and forgetfulness from daily pain,
> nor is there any other cure (*pharmakon*) for trouble.
> This god is poured as offering to the gods,
> so through this god comes human happiness.
>
> (281-5)[2]

Dionysus is the drug that can give relief by making you forget; he can also foretell the future with the frenzy he invokes (298); he has ties to Ares (302), and he does not force the women to be moderate with regard to *Cypris* (315)— this word, meaning "Aphrodite" (who was born off the coast of Cyprus), also means "sex." It is repeated at line 773, "without the gift of wine, there'd be no sex (*Cypris*)." Dionysus is Demeter, Apollo, Ares, Aphrodite, the son of Zeus, and also a libation to all the gods. He is the divinity that consecrates divinity, and, as the gift of wine that leads to sex, he makes possible human generation.[3]

But is Dionysus a god or a human? And what does his identity have to do with fashion? According to Semele's sisters, Cadmus claimed Dionysus was born from Zeus to protect his daughter's name. As a punishment for lying, Zeus blasted Semele with lightning (how else can you explain the scorched earth where she once dwelled?). Alternatively, Dionysus was either conceived by or born from Zeus' lightning. In one version of the story, Hera tricked Semele into asking Zeus to reveal himself in his true form, which immediately killed her. Dionysus was then sewn into the thigh of Zeus as a surrogate womb, which Teiresias recounts as a misunderstanding of a pun: *ho mêros* (the thigh) is a mishearing of *homêros* (hostage).[4] Human beings divide one continuous sound into two notes. This division of a liquid whole into discrete parts has something to do with the importance of the mortal shape into which liquid Dionysus has been poured, and finally, with the impossibility of seeing human character apart from the morphology of clothes.

Dionysus announces himself as follows:

> Here: I am come to Thebes: I, Dionysus,
> son of Zeus and son of Cadmus' daughter,
> Semele, midwifed by the lightning's fire.
> Shifting my shape (*morphê*) to mortal from divine,
> I am here at Dirce's spring, Ismenos' river.
>
> (1–5)

Dionysus appears as a mortal and says so. *I am a god*, though I don't appear to be. The word "shape," *morphê*, appears again in the same speech, when Dionysus reiterates, "That is the reason I took mortal shape (*morphê*) / transformed to human nature in my looks" (54–5).[5] Now, regardless of whether Dionysus is lying, if he is indeed himself he cannot appear as literally himself, since literal Dionysus is wine. He is liquid, fluid, unable to be seen without being shaped. His power likewise produces in others an inability to see themselves. Those overcome by the Dionysian drug lose their awareness of their actions. For Pentheus' mother, Dionysian madness dissolves the difference between the shapes of humans and animals. She will forget who she is and who her son is. She imagines that he is a lion she has hunted and killed. But Dionysus can make others mad only because he does not appear himself crazy. His articulated instantiation in mortal shape is akin to the sobriety of Pentheus. Even the Chorus itself, though it is made up of raging maenads, appears controlled in its reflections on insanity.

There is something critical about the female shape madness assumes in this play. It is not unrelated to the association of fashion with femininity—an association that, in turn, seems partly responsible for the perception of fashion as a lesser art, if it is even considered an art at all. To be taken seriously, it must masquerade under names such as "textiles" or "costumes." But during times when dress was more closely woven to status, outfits now considered outlandish or effeminate might have been seen as masculine and posh. In antiquity, being a foreigner like Dionysus was associated with having feminine or luxuriate looks. Theseus arrived in Athens looking like a stranger with long braided hair and a floor-length tunic. Pausanias recounts that some roof builders jeered at him, asking what a maiden was doing wandering around alone?[6] Philosophy's modern and contemporary hatred of fashion may bear some trapping of its association with Dionysian femininity, too—not connected to any reality of "women" but to that phantom femme who is perceived to be careless in mind and fanatic for frills. The Victorian obsession with "manners" renders "fashion" more "proper"; it is refashioned into something like "virtue," and so comes to fit the historically masculine aesthetic of looking righteous rather than overdone.

Dionysus' fashion is unabashedly of the more outstanding sort. Pentheus instructs his attendants to "run through town and catch the girly (*thêlumorphos*, 'female-shaped') foreigner" (352-3). He addresses Dionysus directly: "Well, stranger, I can see you are attractive (*not amorphos*), / to women anyway—that's why you came here" (451-4). At line 491, Pentheus accuses him of being in a bold frenzy and "not *agymnastos* in speeches." Emily Wilson captures the implications of "not *agymnastos*" as "not untrained," along with its connection to *gymnos*, "naked," by translating the line, "What bare-faced brashness! What a practiced sophist!" One exercises naked in the gym, and so, gym-training is quite literally training in nudity. Dionysus' skill is clearly of this sort; his cosmetic tint is a natural release. Pentheus, on the other hand, is normal to a fault. Dionysus' plan is to trick him into becoming eccentric, foreign to himself and so foreign in the city, a design he reveals to the Bacchae as follows, speaking about himself in the third person (his shape apparently requires a distance from his shapelessness)—

> [Women,] The man is heading for the net: he'll go
> to where the maenads are, where he will die.
>   Lord Bacchus, now the work is yours. You're near.
> We'll make him pay: but you first drive him mad,
> out of his mind; insert a dizzy madness.
> If he were sane, he'd never do it;[7] veering
> away from sanity, he'll strip for me.
> I want him to be laughed at by the Thebans:
> I'll lead him through the city in a dress (*gynaikomorphos*),
> after those dreadful threats he made before.
> But I will fashion Pentheus in the dress (*kosmos*)
> he'll wear to go to death (*Hades*), a trip to slaughter,
> killed at his mother's hands. He'll recognize
> the true god, Dionysus, son of Zeus,
> most dreadful and most gentle to mankind.
>
>   (848-61)

gynaiko-morphos, "woman-shaped," again emphasizes that the net in which Pentheus will be caught is female in form.[8] "Supposing truth is a woman—

what then?" (Nietzsche 1886/1989: 1). Pentheus cannot feast his gaze on the maenads clad in the dogma of the city.

Dionysus' trap becomes even more interesting with his use of the word *kosmos* for "dress." "Dress" has here, as it does in English, a generic and a particular meaning—it can mean general fashion or a particular decoration often associated with femininity. But the word can also mean "world" and "universe," and refer to the adornments therein. In Pherecydes, Zeus (Zas) gives a wedding present to Ground (*Chthoniê*)—a robe called "Earth" (*Gê*), which represents the terrestrial world. Ground then becomes Earth, referred to by her robe's name, her worldly adornment becoming identical to world. The stars and planets, too, are sometimes depicted as if they were jewelry, *kosmoi,* and the bird's eye view of the *kosmos* a bedazzled spectacle.[9] "Beautiful order" applies to both meanings of the word.

Now Pentheus must cast off the conventional for the cosmopolitan. Putting on a dress (*kosmos*) inducts Pentheus into the Bacchic *kosmos*. A simple garment will have the power to change how Pentheus sees the world and how the world sees Pentheus. Would that the world itself could appear in a dress, revealing to us in the partiality of the phenomena some truth about the whole! Would, too, that the fullness of our character and identity could appear in the partiality of our shapes. We would then have no problems of honesty or authenticity; we would simply wear our *kosmos* on our sleeves (also, *kosmos*).

Pentheus is terrified that donning the feminine raiment will transform his identity—"What? Will my status change, from man to woman?" ... "But I could never put on a woman's clothes" (822; 830). Dionysus hopes Pentheus will become "the mirror image" of his aunt and mother—an important detail when later his mother holds his mutilated head in her hands. Pentheus does not disappoint. He emerges looking in shape (*morphê*), "Just like a Theban princess" (916–17). Shape in these latter passages is directly associated with placing clothes on the body. Pentheus seems to be the only male in the play who is noticeably affected by the process. As soon as Pentheus puts on the dress, he begins to see Dionysus as a bull. Whether this is a real or placebo hallucination, Pentheus attributes a magic to clothes that he explicitly denies to Dionysus. This does not reveal a stable, singular Pentheus, but a shapeless Pentheus—one whose fear for his identity only makes sense if his identity is not fixed. Dionysus, then, is the shapeless god who reveals the shapelessness of human identity by way of the "clothes" of madness. Normal people like Pentheus are apparently the most insane.

But can there really be clothes of madness: true clothes, free clothes, honest clothes? If these will aspire to the level of Machiavelli's "real" robes, then they would have to appear to invoke reality. To Pentheus the naturalness of the Dionysian shape appears outside of law. It looks anarchic, crazed, illegal. The chorus sings, "Every woman in the land has left her shuttle, left her loom, infected by the sting of gadfly Dionysus" (116–19). Although leaving the loom is supposed to be a punishment, Agave reinterprets it as liberation—"I left the loom and shuttle, and I rose / to greater things: I hunt with my bare hands" (1235–6). Meanwhile, Pentheus threatens to capture the women and send them back to the enslavement at the loom, but Cadmus advises Pentheus—"Stay home with us, don't live outside our ways (*nomoi*)" (514; 331). *nomos* can mean a variety of things—"way," "law," "custom," "tune"; it might even be translated as "fashion." Here, the Dionysian anti-*nomos* appears to be the *nomos* within which Pentheus must live. In a similar twist, liberation from the shuttle may appear to free Agave from the weave of civilization, but it is also an elaborate trick contrived by Dionysus to wreak havoc on Thebes. The antinomian is thereby shown to be within convention in a double way. The divine illusion that one can be in harmony with nature is the punishment of the gods for the city's blasphemy. Divinity itself may be the attempt of mortals to approximate a transcendence of their own deathliness.

Newly untethered from the shuttle, the maenad dress is not woven but taken whole from the animals they kill.[10] When they wear their skins, the line between human and animal is blurred.[11] As they deliver themselves from joyful romping to rabid mania, the ivy wreaths in their hair become snakes that lick the blood from their cheeks; the deer they suckle as surrogate babies become their prey; and they themselves are also compared to leaping fawns, which makes it difficult to know if they are hunting or being hunted.[12] The shepherds and cowherds report to Pentheus that as the maenads swooped down on a herd of cattle, "The flesh that clothed their bodies got torn off / quicker than you could blink your royal eyes" (746–7).[13] Flesh that is torn off is repurposed as clothes, but the maenads also eat raw flesh.[14] There is no telling whether they are eating or being eaten.

As clothes become flesh and bare hands become weapons, the metaphorical becomes the literal. The maenads lose distinction between images and reality. They have returned to a Hobbesian state of blissful horror. In this state, their oneness with nature renders them unaware of humanity. What is more, they cannot be seen as seer-less without destroying what sees them, whether it is the outward gaze of an onlooker or their own internal gaze on themselves. The former comes first in the plot of the play. Dionysus lodges Pentheus high in a tree—*cryphêi su crypsin hên se cryphthênai chreôn.* Literally translated, this means, "you will hide (or 'be hidden') in the hiding place in which you need to be hidden" (955). But the very words already expose Pentheus' hiddenness. His concealment is manifest, and the maenads end up seeing him. Then, his own mother and aunts, as if a single body, ruthlessly tear him apart, behaving like priestesses in a sacrifice. You want to know the secrets of nature? You cannot see them without destroying your own vision. As Pentheus' hiddenness reveals him, so the maenads become more arcane the more visible they are.

When Agave returns home with the dismembered body of her son, Cadmus refers to Pentheus as "the offshoot from your bodily cavity [womb]" (1306).[15] Agave, who is holding Pentheus' head in her hands, looks upward, then back down to see the image of herself (for femininely decked Pentheus had looked like his mother). Agave's apparently naked vision was in reality woven on a Dionysian loom. The outcome for Cadmus is similarly intriguing: as punishment, he is turned into a snake (*dracôn*, 1330). Echion, Pentheus' father, was one of the Spartoi, or "Sown men," who came to be from the teeth of the dragon (also, *dracôn*, 539) that Cadmus had slain in the founding of Thebes. To be sent into snake-form is to become the pre-Theban ground of mythical autochthony. Agave's uncivilized liberation is the counterpart to returning Cadmus to the city's roots, and the suggestion in both cases is that nature is a political invention. Cadmus, after all, was a Phoenician.

The gods haunt us in many outfits: Zeus appears to Europa as a bull and Leda as a swan. It doesn't go well for Semele when Zeus tries to show up as himself. The polymorphism of the gods, as well as their variety, appears to be a shaping and a fracturing—a clothing—of their shapeless potentiality.[16] But Dionysus is the god who pretends to give mortals a way to see gods—to tap the secrets of shapeless nature with liquid divinity. The same thing seems to be true of our clothes. They are the symbol of our partial vision of the world and ourselves. And like gods, they reveal secrets not as truths but as enigmas. In clothes hides not reality but exposed hiddenness. We never appear as we are. The gods wear the opacity of our reflections.

Meanwhile, the fashion industry parades, even celebrates, the tragic partiality of its shapes as if they could carry within them the gravity of an entire *kosmos*. The *kosmos* is a dress and in a dress. Versatility pretends to give us human morphology writ into fabric, as do shapeless clothes, baggy clothes, obscure-the-body-free-the-soul clothes. This would bring us closer to the mystery of ourselves than would *this* or *that* shape or outfit. But the *Bacchae* is about the impossibility of revealing the shapelessness of human character except in a shape. Even the drunkest, most unleashed version of the human will still have a look. And the clothing of immediacy which pretends to be no clothing is in fact designed by Bacchus; these are the "maenad fakes" (1060).

From the chorus of crazed Bacchae, we learn that "crazed *doxa* ('opinion')" can make *nomos* seem—after a long time—natural (887). Those with crazed *doxa* disregard *nomoi* and get hunted by the gods. True drunkenness in this play is the illusion of the natural to which convention aspires, and which Dionysus' faux liberation mocks as a punishment. There is no escape from shape, no outside of *nomos*, and so no outside of fashion—which is to say, there is no way to see the "insides" of mortals through the secrets of either gods or clothes. To be drugged on reality is the most contrived of all hallucinations: the thought that you have exited the cave. The tragedy of gods, which among them can only be comic, is a metaphor for the tragedy of mortality: to be doomed to only see one's shapelessness in a shape, to see time on a line, and the *kosmos* in a dress. The different fashions and shapes of this dress may affirm and deny one another but cannot affirm or deny dress itself.

Bacchic Leisurewear

Perhaps less visibly pharmaceutical is the Bacchic mask of sweatpants. Sweatpants are a version of sportswear, which originates in the mid-twentieth century, prefigured by the use of pliable fabrics for everyday clothes, the shortening of dress hemlines, and the increasing acceptability of females in pants. Eventually this morphed into the trend of athleisure, which I will come to in due course. However, what is so amazing about sweatpants as a species of leisurewear is that unlike the bodycon look, sweatpants are frumpy and shapeless by default. Where sweatpants count as legit street wear, private life seems to bleed into the public realm. It segues into Reality TV, true-life stories, and a fascination with the psychology of British Royalty or even the troubled pre-history of superheroes like Batman. The public at large arises as political analyst, crime investigator, and moral judge. Sweatpants are the voyeur's choice, a way to knock everyone down to size, the garment in which one tweets.

Sweatpants are "a sign of defeat," declaimed the late Karl Lagerfeld, despite the fact that there is such a thing as Chanel sweatpants (2013: 56). At Paris fashion week (Fall 2014), Lagerfeld showcased a neon-pink moth-eaten sweat set on a Chanel supermarket runway. The sweats were later donned in real life by Kim Kardashian, herself now a passé trend. True, Chanel's sweatpants are more of a knit overstatement than a fleece understatement (fleece is for some reason obviously less high-end than knit). But they provide an interesting angle on the contemporary invisibility complex. Glamorized invisibility used to be the terrain of daytime soap operas, only to be replaced by the One Direction clones of American Idol—a reimagining of ideal beauty in a more reachable, common denominator. On the one hand, it seems good to push back on elitist standards. But standards make possible individuality as well as prejudice, since without them we have no way of liberating ourselves from them. The body positive, now countered by body normative,[17] and free-the-nipple movements are welcomed only to be damned by the cave-poets of virtue bullying, who police how free and how positive the shadows are allowed to be. The impetus to turn scrutiny away from bodies and outfits counterintuitively subjects them to a more rigorous microscope. But body is an event: the arrival of personhood in flesh, a constantly moving target wherein one can never finally locate the self. Billie Eilish channeled the spirit of the times by disembodying herself in shapeless clothes to try to prevent body-typing. Yet this, too, created an anti-body-typing type, and Eilish caused an upset when she posed in form-fitting lingerie on the cover of British *Vogue*. Can we un-drug, un-type, un-shape ourselves? Or do we need to be—do we even enjoy being—mired in shapes and clothed in "social constructs," so that we can criticize these very constructs from our sweatpants, watching with fascination as the world goes down in flames. The poetry of our biases makes for a novel tragedy, in which we imagine we have escaped convention only to discover that such escapism is sophistry. Is the road to the light tricked out in shabby chic and scotch-taped ties?

In America, sweatpants signify the elevation of the lookless look, a meek humility unconcerned with petty frivolities. Somehow this breakdown between fantasy and reality, served to us by Reality TV and sweatpants, paved the way for Donald Trump.

> Reality television is a mechanism for making "stars" out of everyman/everywoman figures—Snooki from *Jersey Shore* or Omarosa from the *Apprentice*. Donald Trump was and is a reality television star generated by a culture industry whose precise mechanism in this instance involved deleting the difference between larger-than-life Hollywood stardom and reality, letting the star mantle fall on a common man caricature.
>
> (Bernstein 2021: 207)

In Aristophanes' *Knights*, the character Demosthenes flatters a Sausage-seller as having all the traits of a demagogue—"always make over the people by sweetening them up with cooked-up phrases, and besides, the rest of what befits a demagogue is present in you too—you have become a shrill, perverse voice, and you are of the market-place: you have united everything necessary for a government" (215–19). The government in this case has become a "typical erotic contest" for the affections of old man Demos (a "gullible old man") in which "the people," also *dêmos*, have become eroticized (Arruzza 2019: 153). The commonality of mere existence is a site for endless possibility, and this exposes that transitional point through which democracy's openness to citizen rule falls prey to the fantasy of the *dêmos* incarnate. Noncelebrity celebrity is catching: an Everyman ruling from the oval office, the rise of YouTube nobodies seen by the late-night glow of a smartphone screen. They are *just like you*. Sweatpants seem to be stranded between a "time out" from life and the profession of laziness that is the amateur cultural critic. They are a curious platform that allows you to hide from the world while at the same time enabling you to spout theories from the guise of anonymity. If you cannot be judged in sweatpants—for you are not yet clothed—you are as of yet unconquered. Sweatpants render you invisible, then pave the way for your feeling indomitable.

In the *Republic*, Socrates, compelled by the longing of Glaucon and Adeimantus, paints invisibility as a sticking point to a perfectly just city: the rogue, rebel thoughts of the unchained mind are hidden and prone to deviate without brainwashing, eugenics, and dress codes restricting poetry and legislating nudity.[18] But Plato, a poet himself, knew the human mind could never be turned into a sheep. The sheepish secretary in *Zootopia* reveals the terror of having the wool pulled over your eyes. The most frightening specimens of psychopathy seem to be puerile beings. Power is somehow more striking when it comes from a seemingly benign source. Enter sweatpants. With the bar of beauty as a loose fit, we enter a more human era, but one that grows together with the more complicated suggestion that a catch-all is sufficient to grasp our insides. So special are we that none of us are. How strange that this relativistic pretense toward equality comes at the same time as advances in plastic surgery and Photoshop. You don't have to be an expert photo editor to "filter" your selfies to such a degree that you are reduced to a pair of come-hither eyes and lips. On Instagram, noses for a time didn't even exist. It is all a blur. *Forget reality*. Good looks are a vanishing act. That invisibility has become a coveted beauty mark ("no filter") is perhaps the most palpable sign of our revised standards. Truth is we always valued intelligence. The trouble is we judge it, even in academia, on the basis of looks.

The canceling of style in sweatpants may even be in some way a reflection of the modern longing to cleanse the stains of previously bad style, i.e., the patriarchy, misogyny, and racism. In the *Republic*, Socrates is already musing on a similar tack: how to purify his perfect city of any and every injustice, which involves the cancellation not only of poets, especially Homer, but of any style that is not strictly narrative. Of the guardians' education, Socrates wonders, "Then shall we so easily let the children hear tales they happen upon fashioned by just anyone they happen to meet …?" The sentence is uttered just after he had compared the activity of educating his hypothetical citizenry to "telling tales in a tale" (376e; 377b). Dreaming up cities seems to be just the sort of tale that could never exist in this dreamed-up city. It can have no awareness of its own impure origins, and "the guardians will scarcely know that their city has a history, let alone what that history was" (Pappas 2020: 128, 144).[19]

Clothing in its entirety will have to go for the very same reason, because writing and weaving go together. Pregnancies, too, are carefully screened and monitored by a philosopher-ruler, since they are hidden inside women's bodies as thoughts in the mind, and so are not transparent. When the tyrant is subsequently unveiled at the end of Book 8, he appears as an image of the public itself, and a shadow of the "Big Brother" philosopher-monarch—"the tyrant's overthrow of democracy is simply the individual appropriation of the ideal of sovereignty enshrined in democratic liberty" (Arruzza 2019: 131). We thus meet a danger of fashion's fashioning, namely, imagining that there was a time when it was not present, when we were virginal blank slates just waiting to be dressed in social garlands, or when we knew not how besotted with cultural costume we already were. But fashion's constant deviation is a foil for time's movement. In *The Human Condition*, Hannah Arendt writes the following words in her section on "The Public and Private Realm": "Only goodness must go into absolute hiding and flee all appearance if it is not to be destroyed" (1958/1998: 87).

Our comfort surrounding the things we are comfortable seeing or being associated with signifies a kind of abstraction from our contact with ourselves, a longing for disembodiment, which is what fashion pretends to give us, and why its talons can be so compelling when they take hold. "Even the Silicon Valley style [an ancestor of normcore] of casual wear has become a kind of dress code: if a sweatshirt and flip-flops demonstrate a single-minded focus on innovation, a suit and tie betray an outmoded concern with appearances and status" (Ford 2021: 5). You aren't supposed to trust a CEO in a suit; we call them "suits," as if they were made of clothes. Clothes are signs that you wear on your person that tell a story about who you are and where you have come from, just as the look of age preordains what "chapter" of your life you are in. Is this view dictated to you by the outside world or is it masterminded by individual artistry? It seems those two might be unhappily aligned. And anyway, it doesn't seem possible to think of life as a story without having already lived to the end of it. The body underneath clothes is merely a pretense to another pretense. You would need to go under the skin, deeper than even the bones and sinews, past the particle-wave duality, in some unknown direction of the unseen self. By this I do not mean the Freudian unconscious, which is clearly just another closet. Clothes suddenly stand not for packaging but disembodiment—a longing to access a changeless individuality, or in more contemporary language, a liberation of identity. Yet, absurdly, the way this shows up is a transcendence of flesh, which the real-life necessity of appearing continues to mock. Avatars and social media have challenged that necessity but they also set a trap for suicide—"a bottomless rabbit hole of melancholia" and "Hamlet-like inner-spiralling self-doubt"

(Critchley 2020: 19). Death, or at least an attack on the self, seems to follow almost too logically from our growing attraction to disembodied voyeurism. So, the rise of sweatpants in America mirrors the intellectual and political climates that emerge from a breakdown of private home life and the public sphere. But I write all this, of course, in sweatpants.

Euripides' *Helen*: Greek Expectations and Trojan Clotheshorses

Memory is the cruelest month. We pay Charon for a ride with a faceless shade, a one-trick pony phantom that lives on but at what cost? Helen must be imagined. She was supposedly the most beautiful woman in the world, but as a figment of Homer's poetry, she was not and is not exactly visible as herself. Just as an imagined Socrates can be uglier than a fleshy, bodily Socrates, so too Helen can be even more beautiful when we don't see her. Her impression is fleeting, constituted by some loose-fitting notion of beauty rather than any particular silhouette. Yet how can we imagine her without imagining a specific *her*? In an early riff on Helen's story, Euripides imagines that Hera sent a phantom (*eidôlon*) to Troy, and hid the real Helen in Egypt. The root of the word *eidôlon* is *weid-*, "see," and it is related to the perfect tense Greek verb, *oida*, meaning "I have seen," and so, "I know." *eidôlon* is also one of the words used to refer to the "shadows" on the cave wall in Plato's *Republic*: a shadow is twice removed from reality and yet related in look and etymology to the *eidos* ("form") in which it shadily participates. *eidôlon* as "idol" gets its sense as both copy and icon, or imitation and stamp of authenticity; so Helen is ambiguously called the *eidôlon hieron*, "sacred idol" of Hera (1136). *eidôlon* can also mean the "shade" of a dead person in Hades. The shade is the afterlife of what was visible of the person, but without substance—their looks detached from their content. Shades are mere clothes, since clothes without body underneath them can only be thought an analogue of the immaterial. "It is curious … to think that appearance, the most despised of realities, owing to its ephemeral and insubstantial character, has the capacity to persist longer than the human beings who originate it" (Carnevali 2020: 43).

It is the specter of Helen, the detached concept of Helen, the clothes of Helen, that went to Troy. How exactly did Hera pass off a phantom for an actual woman? Well, Paris was dumb. He didn't seem to notice that his prize was made of air. Or perhaps he saw what he wanted to see: a trophy wife. The *Helen* play proves to be about this phenomenon of recognition, which gleans its shape from our expectations of what we think is behind what we see.

At the start of the play, Helen gives two versions of her origin. Like Dionysus, her divine parentage is open to dispute. Either she is the child of the mortal Tyndareus (along with her "twin," Clytemnestra, who is definitely not launching any ships) or she is the child of Zeus who raped Leda as a swan, from which Leda also bore the twins, Castor and Pollux. Here is Helen's opening declaration:

> I come from Sparta; Tyndareus was my father.
> There is another story—if it's true,
> that Zeus became a swan and flew disguised,
> chased by an eagle, into my mother's bed,
> and tricking Leda, he achieved his end.
> I am named Helen. I would like to tell
> the things I've suffered. Once, for the sake of beauty,
> three goddesses met Paris in the cave
> on Ida, so that he could judge their looks (*morphê*):
> Hera, Aphrodite (*Cypris*), and Athena (*diogenês parthenos*).
> My beauty was what Aphrodite (*Cypris*) offered—
> if curses count as beauty—and she won,
> by promising him me. So Paris left
> his cowsheds and arrived in Sparta, seeking
> my bed. But Hera, hating having lost,
> turned my affair with Paris into wind.
> She gave king Priam's son an empty image (*eidôlon*),
> not me but something like me, made of air
> but breathing. So he thought he had me,
> but it was just an empty false appearance (*dokêsis*).
>
> (17–36)[20]

There is something striking about this opening. Helen has just revealed that Hera sent her image, not her, to Troy. But why on earth should we believe her? What if a fake Helen has come to us to announce that it is not a fake? Hera is certainly capable of more than one trick. Even if this Helen is *the* Helen, she has already claimed that she is double: either she is Helen of Zeus or Helen of Tyndareus. Menelaus later suggests that even Zeus may have a mortal double: "The woman said she was the child of Zeus. / Is there some man who has the name of Zeus / beside the Nile? There's only one in heaven" (489–91).

Helen continues on—"So 'I'—not I, my name—was made the prize" (43). Helen's name is the clothing used to identify her.[21] In addition to being a phantom image, she also calls herself a false "appearance," a *dokêsis*, literally, a "seeming," and so a "reputation," "expectation," or "suspicion." The latter appears to be a hunch, the former a ghost. Helen refers to herself (as wallowers do) in the third person—"A woman who was neither Greek (*Hellênis*) nor foreign (*barbaros*), / Leda, produced an egg, with Zeus as father, / or so they say: a pouch of chicks, all white" (256–9).[22] Helen is neither *Hellênis* nor not *Hellênis*; she is neither Helen nor not Helen; she is neither human nor divine. Helen is rumor. Helen is reputation. Helen is unknown. The name for the Greeks, the "Hellenes," comes from another story and another Hellen, but the pun cannot be an accident, for the tragedy of the Trojan War that led to the tragic fate of so many Greeks (including Helen's mother, brothers, and daughter, 280ff.) is the result of one Helen or another.

But was it really Helen's fault? Helen was promised to Paris by Aphrodite, who convinced Paris to pick her in a contest of beauty with Hera and Athena. But Aphrodite was only capable of such a trick because Zeus selected Paris to judge the contest (he turns out not to be a very good judge of appearances). Then again, Eris was responsible for the contest itself: he was angry at not being invited to the wedding of Thetis and Peleus, so he showed up with a divisive wedding gift—a golden apple bearing the message, "to the fairest." In Euripides' play, Hera one-ups Aphrodite: she divides Helen into an image and a reality, so that Aphrodite's victory is now an illusion. Despite the fact that the contest seems to be more about who is cleverest, the nesting of action within it makes it difficult to know who and what is *not* a phantom. What Paris did was caused by Aphrodite, what Aphrodite did was caused by Zeus, what Zeus did was caused by Eris, and all of this is caused by Euripides (and perhaps, as is said of Shakespeare and Homer, Euripides wasn't really Euripides). Everything that happens looks as if it is the shade of some alternate reality. Is reality, then, only another level of Hades?

The gods seem to be using mortals to pull each other's strings, as if human life were an elaborate game of foosball. When we first meet Teucer, Ajax's brother, we learn that Athena is responsible for his suicide. She makes Ajax go insane and murder a bunch of sheep imagining they are warriors. Mad Ajax is thus the *eidôlon* of rational Athena. The gods vent their grudges in mortal outfits. In a similar move, during the one-on-one combat between Menelaus and Paris, Aphrodite simply removes Paris from the fight because she knows he is too weak to win even against a mediocre fighter like Menelaus. But Euripides' Helen stages a trick to compete with her divine rivals: imprisoned in Proteus'[23] house with his son, Theoclymenos (who is hoping that Helen will eventually forget Menelaus and marry him), Helen turns the real Menelaus into a phantom in order to engineer her own escape.[24] Unlike Hera's trick, however, Helen's is orchestrated on the basis of word of mouth and clothing. Menelaus will become what he seems to be in his dirty clothes: not Menelaus.

But how did Menelaus get to Egypt? He appears unexpectedly and rather conveniently shipwrecked at the house of his about-to-be-revealed-as-missing wife. It doesn't seem at first as if this can be altogether bad, but then there is Menelaus' family inheritance—

> O Pelops! In that famous chariot race
> in Pisa when you raced with Oenomaus,
> <after you served as food to feast the gods,>[25]
> if only you had died that very day,
> before you fathered Atreus, my father,
> who had two famous sons by Aerope:
> Menelaus—me!—and Agamemnon.
>
> (385–92)

In these lines, Menelaus refers back to his ancestor Pelops, the son of Tantalus. Tantalus wanted to test the gods, and so, he cut up his son Pelops[26] and served him to the gods in a soup. Demeter was sad that day, because her daughter Persephone had been kidnapped by Hades, so she unwittingly ate a piece of Pelops' shoulder (Clotho later had to refurbish it[27]). Tantalus was then punished with eternal thirst. Because of this, the house of Atreus was cursed from the start. Menelaus is born into a chain reaction of doom. All of his actions must be the phantom images of the deeds of his ancestors—a fact which could be said not just of ill-fated parentage, but all parentage. If your parents are not the reason you are the way you are, then perhaps it is culture or circumstance—perhaps your identity is even traceable all the way back to the big bang or Gaia's generation from Chaos, so that you yourself are, in fact, a phantom, responsible for nothing. Even to explain that you are "so-and-so" is to create a phantom image of yourself that is not subject to the progress of time (as, of course, you, the apparent non-phantom, are). The real "you," the spectator of the specter "you," remains in Egypt, watching the whole identity crisis.

Take another phantom Greek: Odysseus. When he turns up in Ithaca dressed as a beggar, you may not believe that he is who he claims to be, because you can "sense" that he is not who he says. But what makes possible that sense? Is it the way his clothes fit, the way they are worn, the bouquet of their threads that smells of deceit? Odysseus already seems to be the person who is never who he is, as he arrogantly demonstrates in his encounter with the Cyclops by announcing himself as *outis* ("No One"). He is later outed by a grammatical pun on *mêtis*, which also means "No one" and is a homonym for "mind" (9.366 and 9.410). Plus, his cleverness so enthralls him that he cannot help but reveal himself as "Odysseus!" as he is making his escape. In Book 8, it is Odysseus' tears at hearing Demodocus' song about the capture of Troy that leads Alcinous to ask him about his identity. As he weeps he pulls a purple cloak over his head, presumably to hide the exposure.[28] But his grief defies the false clothes in which he hides himself. He is ultimately recognized by another visible mark—a scar he bore from a boar that Eurycleia, his childhood nurse, notices when she is washing him.[29] Like Odysseus' tears, it is not the mark but the moment at which the mark is recognized that transforms recognition into knowledge.[30] Clothes are in this way akin to song. They are a vessel through which one sees the inside glimmer but not the inside itself.

It is likewise the distortion of Helen's identity that makes possible the insight into her real self. We see this first in her expectations about others. Because Helen is in Egypt, she is not expecting to see Menelaus; therefore, when she sees Menelaus, she does not see Menelaus. Teucer tells Helen that Menelaus might have died (128), from which Helen concludes that he has died (279). She expects the worst, and so, fulfills it in her mind. Theoclymenos, on the other hand, hears that Menelaus is dead from a man who he does not expect could be Menelaus because he has just been told Menelaus is dead. In each case, it is the phantom that proves integral in defining the "who" of the encounter. On the one hand, this makes human recognition seem quite shallow. We appear to be forced to use visual cues to distinguish phantoms from realities. But how do we stop ourselves from deceiving ourselves? Helen is not even sure that she can distinguish herself from Helen.

Teucer, who is fleeing Salamis on his way to found a new Salamis (a phantom Salamis),[31] does a doubletake when he sees her. He is angry at first, but because they are not in Troy or Greece and because she is not with Menelaus, he concludes she must just be an uncanny counterfeit (back home, she could not be so lucky). When Helen learns that Teucer went to Troy, she asks whether Menelaus retrieved her doppelgänger:

> HELEN: Did you see (*eides*) that poor girl, or is it a rumor?
> TEUCER: I saw her face to face,[32] as I see you.
> HELEN: Was it an apparition (*dokêsis*) from the gods?
> TEUCER: Let's change the subject—no more talk of her!
> HELEN: But can you trust (*dokein*) this sighting (*dokêsis*)? Was it her?
> TEUCER: I saw (*eidomên*) her with my own eyes, and my mind.
> (117–22)

Teucer makes explicit the connection implicit in the words *eides* and *eidomên* (related to *eidôlon*) between sight and knowledge. Helen questions Teucer's sight with a suspicion that it is dosed with *dokêsis*, but he assures her that what he saw "with eyes" he also saw with his mind. The visual shell of Helen was thus, as Helen suspects, thought to be the real Helen. Although her looks throw Teucer for a loop, he concludes, "Your body is like Helen's, but your heart / is very different, not at all alike. / May she die, and never reach the banks / of the Eurotas. But to you, good luck!" (160–3). So this Helen is not Helen but the body of Helen. In being the "real," "bodily" Helen, she cannot be the true Helen for whom so many Greeks died, for then they would have died not for an idea but for a mere individual.[33] Helen herself appears to be already dead, since her soul and her body are severed between two lands. The lines following this exchange demonstrate the fracture: Helen joins the chorus. Her reflection on herself is not the same as how she is perceived by others. People think she is one way; they see her *eidôlon*. But Helen experiences herself another way. The real Helen is trapped inside the *eidôlon* and cannot get out. She is her own captive, *helein*.[34] Yet without the "clothes" of her detached image, Helen has no identity—for if she is not Helen of Troy, she has no husband, no lover, no city, no family. And yet if she *is* Helen of Troy, she loses all of these things by the same turn—

> The worst of all is this: if I went home
> to Sparta, they would bolt the gates against me,
> thinking that I was Helen back from Troy
> without my Menelaus. If he'd lived
> we would have known each other by the signs
> that no one else knows. That won't happen now.
>
> (286–91)

"By the signs that no one else knows" literally reads, "by the signs (*symbola*) that are visible (*phanera*) to us alone." What are these *symbola*? They are manifest only to those who can recognize them, a kiss between phantom images, wherein you imagine that someone has seen something about you that identifies you as *you*, and so, perhaps, in seeing the reflection of your own sight in their eyes, you recognize an intimacy that cannot be cloned.[35] But again, suppose this conviction is an illusion? Suppose Helen is the bad seed we all imagine we are in love with, and who makes us believe she loves us, too. We envision in her eyes the expectation of our private wishes being fulfilled. Maybe it is the illusion of a real woman that is the true phantom? Maybe the real Helen is the fake.

The recognition between Menelaus and Helen occurs as follows. Menelaus arrives shipwrecked in "shabby clothes" of which he is ashamed (415–17). He comes to Proteus' palace, and straightway judges the man who lives in the palace by the way the palace looks—its splendid gates, its fine walls, and friezes. But he learns from an old woman at the gate that the man who lives in this splendid house is dead, and this is his tomb.[36] He also learns from this woman that "Helen" is inside. But the name Helen could mean any Helen, and Menelaus does not believe *this* Helen could be *his* Helen, even when they meet face to face and express to each other how like each is to the other Helen and the other Menelaus. Helen is the first to see through Menelaus' dirty looks:

> HELEN: Gods! It's a god to recognize *familiars*!
> MENELAUS: Are you a Hellene? Or a native here?
> HELEN: I am Hellenic. And what about you?
> MENELAUS: I never saw a woman so like Helen!
> HELEN: And you're like Menelaus! I can't speak.
>
> (560–4)[37]

"It's a god to recognize familiars" or "friends" is like saying it's strange to recognize what one knows. It is strange too that we come to know those we do not by re-cognizing some sign in them that feels familiar, as if to get to know them was to have already known them. The ambiguity between phantom and ideal is identity's secret. Theoclymenos' prescient sister, Theonoë, will say that she has a "temple" in her nature (1003–4). "Believe in yourself," goes the contemporary idiom, as if to be yourself required a piety to the fact that you were really there. Divine favor turns imitation to intimacy.

What is it in Menelaus' behavior that allows Helen to see him? Is it that she thinks that he's him and he thinks that she's her? She seems to have no trouble allowing his look to identify him, while he requires further proof, despite her cries that "I'm not a nightmare vision. You can see me!" (570). This is Helen's conundrum: her aim is to gain her independence from the other Helen, but she lives her life entirely on the basis of her Helenic look. Menelaus finally believes her identity when a servant announces, "Your wife is gone, into the folds of sky. / She's taken. She's invisible. She's hidden" (605–6). Yet this seems equally dubious, as if now that one Helen is gone, it is okay for a clone Helen to take her place. However faked their recognition of one another is—one wonders if these two are in love with anything but their images of themselves?[38]—they now band together to escape from Proteus' house.

Helen asks Menelaus, "Do you want to die in word (*logos*), but not in fact?" (1050). The plan is to trick Theoclymenos into believing that Menelaus has died at sea. Helen says she will put on mourning clothes, cut her hair, and scratch her face. The last claim comes as a surprise. Could such a beauty scratch up her spotless visage? Helen subsequently appears in black with shortened locks, but no scratches on her face are mentioned.[39] Meanwhile, Menelaus arrives again in his "disgusting clothes" to bring the news of his own death (1204). The two of them then convince Theoclymenos to give the phantom Menelaus a burial. When Theoclymenos asks if one can bury an absent shadow, Helen appeals to the Greek *nomos*—to bury those who die at sea in "empty woven folds of cloth" (1243).[40] Theoclymenos thinks this is a sign of sophistication: in Egypt, you need a body, but the Greeks are more abstract.

Helen and Menelaus will eventually sail away in the very boat with which Theoclymenos has provided them. In this coup, Menelaus appears successful and heroic; he rouses the Greeks together to destroy Theoclymenos' men, as if he were his brother Agamemnon. In the end, Helen and Menelaus are transformed into divinities by Castor and Pollux, who imply that if Zeus had made them gods before, they could have saved Helen and avoided the Trojan War (1658-61). Is it Pollux and Castor, then, who finally have control of reality? Yet the success of Helen's escape hinges on Theonoë, who is first called Eidô, until she matures into a teen and acquires a more particular name.[41] Helen must coerce her into concealing the truth that she would otherwise reveal because she is the *noê* (thought) of a *theos* (god), knowing the potential of the phantoms of the future. Theonoë is only convinced to keep Helen's secret because of a debt to her father Proteus and to Hermes for bringing Helen to Egypt. Theoclymenos assumes that his sister is directly responsible. He is ready to murder her for mutiny, but the chorus[42] won't let go of his "clothing" (1628). He was never promised Helen, so he is not really owed anything. Everyone seems to be attached to everyone only by a thread. But threads are critical here, for they seem to inspire us to seek realities.

Is Greece—Hellas—the real loser? It went to war for a phantom. But again, war does not really make sense unless it is for the sake of some "idea" beyond just killing people. Armor is the necessary abstraction that allows you to tell friend from enemy, and so, to imagine that those you are killing are not *real* people but phantom limbs of cities. Still, if this is the case, then the war which defined who the Greeks were—Teucer tells Helen that there is barely even a trace of the walls left of Troy (108)—was all based on a false expectation, the armor of Helen, that led the Greeks to don their armor. In this, even Helen finds herself enslaved to her own image (275). Is there something in Helen's identity, then, that is a metaphor for the identity-seeking of the Hellenes, and, despite their success in the Trojan War, the impending failure of their unity?

Although looks seem a phantom emptiness, you only need to imagine the Trojan Horse to see how they can kill. Emptiness exaggerates the power of appearances, making them seem invulnerable and transmutable. Fabric, which might be now construed as material metaphor, can be taken from one body and placed upon another, as that symbolic cloth called a flag, for which so many have died, imagining they are interchangeable with it. Burial, too, is a "sophisticated" operation of "empty folds of cloth"; for what we bury is the shadow of what once was but is no longer. We bury a memory and a tomb becomes a memorial.[43] Is the concern of being identified with one's clothing the fear of becoming a mere memory? Helen appears consumed by this fear while also being completely enamored of its powers. She treats the tomb of Proteus as if it is the house of a living man, camping out in squalor beside it (though, strangely, she never appears dirty).

In a converse fashion, Achilles, too, was drunk on the power of his image when he sent Patroclus into battle wearing his armor, as if the mere look of "Achilles" would do the killing for him. "Night, your singer's cloak. / Night, on your eyes, like a shutter. / Would a seeing man not have joined Achilles to Helen?" (Tsvetaeva 1989).[44] Achilles-like, Helen believes in the power of her outer shape, whether it is her own fate to be indistinguishable from her bad reputation or Menelaus' deceit by means of a phantom *logos*. The servant who brings news of the other Helen's disappearance can tell as much: "As for prophecy, / it's useless, full of lies! I see that now. / There's nothing solid in the flash of fire / or in the cries of birds ... Calchas said nothing, made no sign at all, / when he could see us dying for a cloud" (744–7). But the chorus of captive Greek women brings this foreboding message, "What mortal can think it all through and explain what is god, what is not god, and what's in between?" (1140). And if to recognize friends or familiars is itself a god, "Our inability to recognize friends would therefore call into question our ability to be just. This, in turn, calls into question the justice of the Trojan War, a war that begins with a violation of the laws of *xenia*— guest-friendship" (Davis 2011: 117).[45]

But why does the chorus rebuke Helen by comparing her to Persephone?[46]

You burnt offerings down in the chambers of the earth
that were wrong and unholy,
and, daughter, because you dishonored
the rites of the mighty Mother,
her wrath is upon you.

(1353–7)

There are textual problems with these lines, but the accusation—that Helen made unfit sacrifices to Demeter—is echoed in the rest of the antistrophe. Helen prided herself on her "beauty (*morpha*) alone" (1368). She believed she could launch a thousand ships, or at least that she could escape home in one, even though it was in both cases the consequence of a phantom image. Still, Helen is *taken* by Paris (courtesy of either Aphrodite, Hera, Zeus, Hermes, Eris, or some combination of all of them), and Persephone is *taken* by Hades. What did either of them do to deserve rebuke? Helen's mistake can only be that in her disavowal of her own phantom she believed in the power of phantoms, which meant dishonoring the very phantom ("mother") that produced her. This is complicated by the second strophe, where Zeus sends the Muses to soften Demeter; Aphrodite is apparently there, too, dancing and blowing a pipe. This reminds us that Helen is the gift of Aphrodite to Paris, and Aphrodite, too, prided herself on her shapeliness.

At the end of this chorus, the wrath of Demeter shows itself in Dionysian revelry. In contrast to Helen's belief in her clothes or the outsides, Demeter and Bacchus stand for the insides. Without their fertility and sowing there would be no sprouting or harvesting, and so, no *appearance* of life. Helen's piety to the outside is an impiety toward what was *underground*—for graves and wombs are connected as coming to be and passing away—and this is what constitutes her unholy sacrifice. Helen is thus doomed to use the very power that caused her disappearance to escape. This power—the power of how things appear—is the fruition of her longing to be a god, a longing to be fully real or authenticated by manifesting her inner self as the reality behind her outward shadow. Yet, the "inside" once made visible seems to be equivalent to an outside with no inside. Is the wish to become a god the wish to become a shade of oneself? Is the only way to be fully real to be half-real? That Helen becomes a god in the end means she has failed to materialize herself; she becomes more like a phantom the closer she comes to escaping her phantom-hood.

For fashion, the analogue is this: in the clotheshorse of phantoms born from the patterns set by poet-designers, which models, fashion influencers, and trendsetters follow, the spirits of past costumes seem to cycle in and out of fashion regularly, as if phantoms circulating independent of the agency of originals. The time has come for spandex biker shorts (once a huge no-no) and high-waisted pants. While no one would say "jeggings" anymore (there is a brand of jeggings called "Faded Glory"), the slim-pants-no-pants craze is nothing to sneeze at, some fifteen years after their advent (despite the quarrel between millennials and Gen Z[47] over the width of one's pant openings). There is a strange nostalgia for the '90s that Gen Z groundlessly channels with less Prozac and more environmental politics. Daisy Dukes are everywhere, hearkening back to Duice, even if they don't go by that name anymore. Delia*s has returned along with diaries (complete with lock-and-necklace key), Dickies, and Doc Martens. The internet has changed things, to be sure, but even cyberspace has taken on the look of its late '90s debut with "lo-fi" forums like Reddit, a digital grunge that hearkens back to dial-up modems and chatrooms.[48] It is so-called fashion influencers (the latest rhapsodes, literally, "stitchers of verses"[49]) who dictate what ends up selling, and they do this not just by wearing clothes but by promoting a certain way of wearing them. That is to say, it is the *fashion* in which fashion is fashioned that leads to its reproductive traction. But readers of the *Helen* play want to know: are we who follow trends doomed to be mere copies of the copies of the originals, as phantoms of history or mortals to divine poets of fate?

Following a trend does not involve—in fact even denies the possibility of—a perfect collapse between you and your fashion icon, whether it be a Helen or an early incarnation of Madonna (back in her days of religious iconography). Kant seems misled that "[i]n fashion there is still a compulsion to let ourselves be led slavishly by the mere example that many in society give us" (7:246). As slave to fashion's rhythm, you want to both aspire to the "beyond" of your inspirations but also to be capable of launching an equal amount of ships. By imitating your inspiration, you at once engage in pious flattery and a wish to be the original. To supersede what you are and become what you are not is a wish to become more yourself, not just a phantom of the original, but a replacement for the original. Selfies ("little selves," diminutive selves), too, are a longing through the lens of seeing yourself in a phantom copy to become the you of the inside: a longing to transcend your mortal coil by way of an imitation. Again that idiom rears its specterly head, "believe in yourself": aspire to be the thing you already are as if it were at once preordained and inscrutable.

To be able to control the gap between how you perceive yourself and how others perceive you would be to control the power of appearances—the prophesy of what you were, are, and will be. While at first this seems to be what prevents things from being recognized as real, by the same turn it also seems to be what makes possible our experience of the real. In Helen's case, her longing to banish her ghost, and so to experience her own reality apart from her "clothes," is the same as the wish to die and become a god. But the revelation of clothes as deceptive phantom images discredits the sanctity of clothing only to replace it with a faithful conviction in the power of its deceit. This latter point is true in spades of that age-old position that looks don't matter.

Normcore's Mean: Democracy and Tyranny

Normcore: the grandest of all delusions of grandeur, the worst of all Renaissance Fairs. An article in *The New York Times* referred to normcore as an undertaking "in which scruffy young urbanites swear off the tired street-style clichés of the last decade … in favor of a less-ironic (but still pretty ironic) embrace of bland, suburban anti-fashion attire" (Williams 2014).

As a fashion, normcore is nearly corecore: ordinary to the max or hardcore normal. It takes its bearings by an ironic adoption of the image of the so-called masses—what "normies" wear—the I-blend-in brand of sweatpants. This is the stylized living dead, a sober satire of common zombie garb. The more you camouflage with the norm, the hipper you are. Normcore made normal into an exclusive club. In this, it seemed to owe its look not only to religious prototypes but also to the professional "philosopher" of Plato's Academy, clad in anonymous gym clothes.[50] Academic ascetics reified this styleless idol in a separation of plain facts from the ornamentation of value or the use of sesquipedalian diction that only a few can decode. Proof that one is a generic scholarly spider is ironically gained by brand-name degrees and looking too smart to be wrinkled by questions.[51]

> Popular is he, this poor peripatetic professor of posing, with those whose joy it is to paint the posthumous portrait of the last philanthropist who in his lifetime had neglected to be photographed,—yet he is the sign of the decadence, the symbol of decay.
> (Oscar Wilde, "The Relation of Dress to Art," 1885)

How quickly we lose the magic of inquiry clad in ostentatious bibliographies and button-down prose! Academics will not like to hear that fashion "signifies union with those in the same class, the uniformity of a circle characterized by it, and, *uno actu*, the exclusion of all other groups" (Simmel 1904/1957: 544). The way out of the cave is surely the fastest way back in. It matters not whether normcore has outlived the publication of these words; it has been in style among academics for centuries.

If the common academic is an obligatory fashionista, following the latest trends[52] while behaving as if thinking required initiation into the Mysteries, what do sweatpants, or more broadly "leisurewear," and philosophy have in common? Philosophical nonidentity requires some form of negating the presence of the self, so as to broadcast arguments from the ivory tower of No One or "one." Philosophy cannot engage directly because that would mean to get involved, which would involve potential bias. If to acknowledge your bias is another outfit—the negation of the negation of playing dead—suppose, then, that we begin negative, that we begin already in clothes, and so, longing for clothes that would strip us.

If nudity, philosophical or otherwise, involves the impossible feat of subtracting your clothes (or conventional biases) from your self, maybe the solution is to subtract your self from your clothes—to disinvest your in-vestment, and so to dress down. Dressing down entails diluting your personality with your outfit (read: metaphorical sweatpants). Hanson attributes dressing down to the disgust philosophers seem to have for a business that operates entirely on "changing desire," and which draws attention to human transience (1990: 109). "[P]hilosophers seem to reserve a special disapprobation for fashionable dress ... even while they enjoy a meal of veal and baby vegetables, kiwi soufflé, and cognac to follow" (108). Steele similarly comments, "Clothes, then, are a taboo subject, a forbidden realm of pleasure. Many of the very same professors who censoriously dismiss the pleasures of dress may well lavish time and money on couture cuisine, stereos, Volvos, computer gadgetry, skis, travel, and wine. But not clothes" (1991).

"I must tell you that I am not at all interested in clothes," said Simone de Beauvoir, with an air of elegance. She sat impeccably clad in a tweed dress, garnet earrings, black heels, and vibrant lipstick (Judah 2019). Unwittingly, philosophers dress up their notions of dressing down, sometimes in word, sometimes in deed. The climax might be to dress oneself out of dress altogether: to put on the invisibility dress. Harry Potter had a cloak that made him invisible, so did Arthur (its name was "Gwen"), and so did fashion photographer Bill Cunningham. Cunningham prowled New York City "unseen" on his bicycle, always clad in a simple blue utility smock. While this look was intended to help him blend in, it ultimately became his signature. Of his work, Cunningham said, "It's important to be almost invisible, to catch people when they're oblivious to the camera—to get the intensity of their speech, the gestures of their hand" (Horwell 2016). As with Bill Cunningham's iconic yet commonplace blue jacket, Socrates' lively practice of dying became a trend in its own right. Starting out with the impulse to disappear in order to capture dress in its natural habit and habitat, both set standards that became legendary. Cunningham became a decorated presence in the fashion scene; Socrates became a notorious gadfly. You might ask: how does the attempt to disappear move so quickly into the limelight? And how does the limelight morph so quickly into a death sentence, as it did for Socrates? Idolizing blurs the line between emulation and envy. Was Socrates executed because being good at looking was perceived by Athens as a *bad* look. Did *bad* mean *too good*?[53]

In Plato's *Protagoras*, the acclaimed sophist Protagoras announces himself as one who does not need a "cloak" for his sophistry. But this claim to be uncloaked seems a new cloak, and Protagoras, for this reason, a sophisticated sophist. According to Thucydides the Athenians had initially worn golden cicadas in their hair (1.6)—a patriotic allusion to their being autochthonously generated from the soil of Attica.[54] Later on, the Athenian adoption of a more modest Spartan dress, as well as the Spartan fashion of exercising naked, ironically expressed their claim to democracy—for clothes seem tethered to convention, like laws or opinions, so that removing them poses the result of either anarchic freedom or refined equality. The wish to blend in order not to be seen incorrectly is very close to the desire to be seen in the act of not being seen, to be seen as no one in particular, which is to say to be seen as equivalent to everyone.

It was first in ironic mountain-man hipsters that artisanal nudity permeated contemporary fashion like a hand-tossed ceramic. But the golden mean of normcore dressing took this up a notch with a super-*sprezzatura*: a hyper-attention paid to your outfit that miraculously disappears in the final product—a disappearance that cannot and must be signaled by the casually inserted flaw. On the one hand, dressing down the assertion of the self seems to go together with a democratic wish for the equality of the self with its self and with others. But the intentional imperfection of a perfectly adopted normalcy bears a strange air of tyranny. It generally does seem to matter that people think that you thought it didn't matter what *they* would think; you might notice that it is often the people who don't dress up who get the most defensive about not caring about clothes. To strip and to clothe are woven together, and their unproblematic togetherness is granted only by the illusion of effortlessness.

Effortlessness, like comfort, placates everyone. It is the oxymoron of a natural shade of lipstick that must be artificially realistic or the pricelessly amorphous silhouette of luxury sweats.[55] You are investing in a drapery of nothingness: thrown on, without reference to any particular pattern. *You* are a ghost. *You* are a phantom. But, as with artificial intelligence—a worry contained in imitation branding—effortless reproduction can only be justified by those inward signs that were so hard to recognize in Helen. The need for the inside to show on the outside has emerged as fashion's attempt to become politically, socially, and environmentally conscious, as if it were itself an individual with distinctive views; the clothing brand Reformation has made "genes" for jeans with a fabric dye that traces the "story" of your pants. This makes it possible to verify that these jeans have good intentions sewn into them. Yet the point of effortless authenticity is that there is no detectable will or intent, since that is what it means not to show effort.

So, too, *you* are most conspicuously *you* when you are not perceived (and so, clothed) by anyone at all, *including* your own self-perception. That is to say, you are most you when you are not contrived. Self-awareness and self-forgetting, like egoism and conformism, seem to go hand in hand. Yet the self that does not doubt itself is indistinguishable from a patchwork of allusions to others, drifting hither and thither on borrowed wisdom. What better way to refuse credit for your own inventions than to say the ill-fitting shape is the fault of a Banana Republic investment? Wasn't it Descartes' evil demon who threatened to put the philosopher's brain in a cravat?[56] The self is like a coin whose value we are constantly deferring to some other figure, like Marx's phantom coat.[57] The deferral of value is paradigmatic of clothing, which is, loosely speaking, always symbolic of some identity. Symbols are sticky, but also pliable—where the symbol becomes divested of content and all clothes are treated alike, a devaluation of content occurs. The ironic result is normcore: the wish to blend in so well that individuality ceases to be perceived as a noteworthy event. But again, its image vacillates on a precipice of democratic and tyrannical evanescence. Bari's characterization of Magritte's surrealist paintings of suited men applies equally well: "They are the visual definition of the nondescript, spookily vacant, like the void of the zombie dead. They could be anybody, and so nobody, all at once, banal and terrible in the same brushstroke" (2019: 106).

There are stranger things though: you are *really* you when you are, in fact, not you. Feeling "seen" involves feeling yourself coming at yourself from the outside, as when a person who knows you so well sees a garment in a store window, and says, "that's so *you*." This standard *you* evaporates and resurrects your individuality, as in Helen's phrase, "it's a god to recognize friends." One thinks of other catchphrases such as "you do you," "on brand," and "suit yourself," as if you could wear the self that suits. You want to be seen as yourself which means in a way not to be seen. But the act of "wearing" demands that you elect to give yourself up to someone else's design, even if it is your own, for once a garment is placed on your surface, the perception of your identity is not entirely under your control (a problem that also inheres in names). In Plato's *Republic*, democracy's comparison to a *poikilon* ("embroidered") cloak, embroidered with every habit, seems the problematic parka par excellence (557c5).[58] This cloak reflects the variety of the citizen body (which is also described as *poikilon*, 561e4), and also contains all of the looks of the other regimes. Democracy is a cloak that contains so many cloaks that no cloak in it can really be a cloak. We are left to wonder who will wear it or if it will simply double as the *kosmos*.

The impetus behind "normcore" fashion is, then, the apex of all fashion: to perfectly outfit the self as the generic self, and so, to display its true nature. In the Garden, the insecurity of looks is lodged in dress broadly categorized as shame; in contemporary society (and, oddly, in ancient Rome) it seems to be the fear of betrayal. We are suspicious of what is being concealed or of what others might think we are concealing, whether it is clothes themselves that hide deleterious opinions or others' opinions about our clothes. The "authentic" used to arrive on the scene in a crisp toga draped in the appropriate folds, but this is now replaced by "sweatpants" which are designed to neutralize judgment altogether, or to simply bypass it. Social media sweatpants allow you to recede into the virtual reality of self-avoidance. But philosophy, too, dreams ironically of sweatpants. It nourishes fantasies of jettisoning mirrors, either out of a full-blown narcissism or a complete rejection of appearances and flux. Surprisingly, the two—one arrogantly drunk on its own image, the other humbly refusing to look at its own reflection—are siblings, for they are motivated by a similar quest for the insularity of the real, occupying an impossible nexus of a democratic claim to express the self as other and the tyrannical obliteration of the otherness of the self.

Is authenticity a farce as impossible as nudity? Do we seek a confirmation of our image in an out-fit in order to make sure we do the right thing (and so, fit in) or to make ourselves conspicuous? "Fashion is about going ahead, not about memory"—another gem from unexpected poet Karl Lagerfeld, and a riff on this line from Coco Chanel, "In order to be irreplaceable one must always be different." One must, then, disappear again and again. If you never repeat yourself, this guarantees that you can never be pinned down and that you will remain irrevocably unique, impossible to copy, a trend that evades trendiness. Although sweatpants at first appear to be rejecting this aristocratic stance, they are the vulgar version of conspicuous disappearing—an attempt to erase history, to recede from memory, to be so far on the cutting edge as to already be preemptively out of style. Sweatpants are high society incognito. The proof is athleisure, which passes its judgment from the high church of nonidentity.

Seeing without Being Seen: Gyges, Sweatpants, and World Domination

I end this chapter with some disappearing acts. First, a pair from Herodotus and Plato. Both concern a man named Gyges who attempted to wear invisibility. In Herodotus, Gyges becomes a criminal through the act of becoming invisible (a scary prospect for clothes, and one that is clearly evident in charged reactions to them). Herodotus tells the story of how the Lydian king Candaules ordered his advisor Gyges to contrive to see his wife in her true form—that is, naked. In the king's words, "'Gyges, I don't seem to persuade you when I tell you about the *eidos* ("form") of my wife (for the ears of human beings happen to be less trustworthy than the eyes). Contrive (*poiein*, "make"), then, that you observe her naked'" (1.8.2). Candaules seems to have confused form with body. That Gyges must contrive to view the queen without himself being seen is a second-order nudity that requires making his own influence *barely* perceptible. Nudity and invisibility go together. Seeing the truth for Gyges means escaping notice.

But what about Gyges' perception of his own act? He is at first uncomfortable with the idea of seeing another man's wife in the buff. This is because he can see himself seeing the queen—an envisioning that is tantamount to the queen seeing him. To be as you are—to act natural—you cannot see yourself being seen; you cannot be self-conscious. This is likewise a problem for the queen. The queen will not be unveiling her true beauty if watchful eyes clothe her, whether the onlooker's or her own. Social media feeds into this Gyges-like predicament—that is, the possibility of a voyeur that goes undetected, a spy on reality (a god?), as if self-consciousness were only a philosophical advance and not the roommate of paranoia and insecurity.

Berkeley's claim that "to be is to be perceived" threatened to relegate anyone alone in a room to nonexistence, at least in the absence of divine oversight.[59] Fashion could be accused of having the same motto. In Herodotus' account, the secular kernel of consciousness looks over your shoulder, whether you are reprimanding yourself to button up or repeating the words of a text in your head as you read them. Gyges' failure is crucial for this. He remains reluctant, despite the king assuring him there is nothing to fear. Unfortunately, the queen sees him. She immediately realizes what her husband has done. In order to get revenge, she orders Gyges to murder the king and marry her (1.11). The moral of the story, as in the case of Pentheus and the maenads, seems to be that to see without being seen is unable to be conceived. This has implications both for the neutrality of the philosopher and for the invisible voyeurism made possible by sweatpants and social media. If we cannot see without being seen, privacy may be as fictional as invisibility. In clothes and because of clothes you will always be wondering—am I being watched?

In Plato, Gyges makes his cameo in Book 2 of the *Republic* in the puzzle of whether the just man is better than and indistinguishable from the unjust. If you are going to be perfectly vicious, the best way to be so seems to be to wear the clothes of virtue. This is how you get away with murder. The innocents are the breeding ground for devils. As in Herodotus' version of the story, there are two levels of intrigue. On the one hand, being just means seeming to be what you are (being naked). On the other hand, it involves perceiving what seems to be as it is (rather than being duped by yourself or others). In Glaucon's version of the story, Gyges is either a shepherd or the ancestor of a shepherd who finds a ring on a larger-than-life dead body—the confusion is important since, if we take the reference to "the ring of Gyges" at 612b3 seriously, the dead man might be Gyges himself. Like Herodotus' Gyges, Plato's Gyges is from Lydia, where there is apparently a trend of wanting to go unnoticed.[60] That the ring is found on a corpse is not a good sign, but Gyges snatches it anyway and soon realizes it has the power to make him invisible when he turns the band inward.[61] When he turns it outward, he reappears. Gyges' newfound power makes him *isotheon*, "equal to a god" (360c3), and he uses it to seduce the queen and kill the king, but only after first contriving to become one of the king's messengers.

But it's perplexing—does Gyges convey messages while invisible? Wouldn't this be suspicious? Also, how does he plan to sleep with the queen? If he only uses his invisibility to sneak into her room, wouldn't she be shocked when he suddenly appears? Or does he have disembodied sex with her? Is this like Zeus sleeping with Leda in the form of a swan or the Annunciation, action at a distance? The Herodotean Gyges' wish not to be seen seems to be entangled with the Platonic Gyges' wish to pass unseen: a longing for invisibility that segues into a longing to stalk the world as an influential ghost—to have your effect on reality appear to come from an undiscoverable (perhaps divine?) agency. The gods, meanwhile, are naturally effortless. They wear shapeless clothing that can permeate any and every shape, which means that they themselves are akin to nothing. To be nothing is apparently most divine, and the longing for nondescript, shapeless, or shape-shifting clothes seems to be equivalent to the wish to pass among mortals as a god.

The Gyges parable in the *Republic* prefigures another image of non-appearance worth mentioning. Following Socrates' proposal to found a city in speech in order to magnify the image of justice in the soul, he takes a detour to reveal three waves that will be required for the city's perfectly just constitution. In Greek, the word for "wave" (*kuma*) also means "pregnancy," literally, a "swell." The first "wave" is that everyone must be naked, both men and women: "Then there must be stripping for the women guardians, since they'll dress themselves in virtue instead of cloaks" (457a7–9). This next-level nudity is something like "soul nudity" (Pappas 2016: 191; 222). The citizens will instead be *clothed in virtue*. The trouble, however, is overcoming the laughter at the naked bodies, especially when they are wrinkled and old; erotic attractions between sexes will clearly also be a problem, and the second wave addresses this: women and children must be communal. No one can know who their parents are. How Socrates will get around the nine-month gestation period or the suspicious resemblances among citizens is left unexplained; incest is as forgotten as the parricides of regime change will be. It is not until the third wave that there is any indication of how babies will even be "made," or really, "manufactured." The third wave, about which Socrates is most hesitant, is that a philosopher-king (or queen[62]) must rule the city. The ruler plays matchmaker to the citizens. Even while the citizens believe they are operating of their own free will, in reality the philosopher-psychic acts as Cupid, so that no one is mismatched and the citizens come to be the best they can be. The greatest threat to justice in the city must stem from unplanned pregnancies—not just literal childbearing, but also thinking. Pregnancy (*kuma*) is *the* problem. Both babies and thoughts have to be controlled, since anything eccentric to the city, whether in the mind or the body, is potentially hostile, because unpredictable—"the eugenic oversight will ensure that no one appears out of nowhere, as tyrants do" (2020: 126). "Pregnancy" is the sign of such potential insurrection, in which beings seem to appear *ex nihilo*, or at least from some hidden source. There is no guarantee from the city's perspective that babies won't grow into rebels, unless virtue is somehow made genetic and visible, if only symbolically.

That Socrates' own thoughts are referred to as "pregnancies" suggests that hostility to the city may be implicit in the activity of dreaming cities up. It was anticipated when Socrates had declared that the origins of the city must be concealed in a "noble lie (*gennaion pseudos*)"—a bold gloss on this might render it a "genetic lie." The citizens must believe that they were predestined in the roles they play and the fashions they wear. You can now see why such a city must be a nudist colony, since in it there could be no gap between nature and convention—no difference between the mother and fatherland and individual parents. What is meant by nudity is not necessarily the absence of clothes so much as the absence of contrivance. Yet, Socrates' own pregnant thoughts indicate that contrivance is at some level inescapable (natural?). The hiddenness of nature must be covered up with a noble lie if perfect convention will reign. But, to go back to Heraclitus' dictum, why is nature "fond of hiding"? We often suspect it of being pregnant with design. It would be the clothes of virtue that could perfectly hit that human mean between social pariah and haughty elitist, beast and god. But it is as if, the more layers we remove, the more layers are revealed. It seems to be clothing all the way down.

Modern people may worry that Gyges' insecurity was misunderstood. We meet a self-effacing Gyges in Virginia Woolf's short story, "The New Dress," the tale of forty-year-old Mabel Waring, who commissions a dress to wear to Mrs. Dalloway's party. Mabel selects the pattern from one of her mother's books of Paris fashions, thinking that vintage fashions are much more attractive than new fashions. But when she tries on the finished product and gazes at her own image in the mirror, she is horrified by what she sees. "But she dared not look in the glass. She could not face the whole horror—the pale yellow, idiotically old-fashioned silk dress with its long skirt and its high sleeves and its waist and all the things that looked so charming in the fashion book, but not on her, not among all these ordinary people" (1927/1989: 171). Mabel is reluctant to go to the party but finally decides to go anyway. As she is pretending to gaze at a picture in the main room in an attempt to conceal her awkwardness, a mean-spirited guest comments on her new dress and tells her she looks "rather ruffled." In Mabel's mind, she is like a "meagre, insignificant, toiling" fly trying to crawl out of a saucer. She toils to fit in with ordinary looks, but always ends up mortified by insecurity. In her embarrassment, she decides to make an early getaway from the party. She concludes to herself that,

> She would go to the London Library tomorrow. She would find some wonderful, helpful, astonishing book, quite by chance, a book by a clergyman, by an American no one had ever heard of; or she would walk down the strand and drop, accidentally, into a hall where a miner was telling about the life in the pit, and suddenly she would become a new Person. She would be absolutely transformed. She would wear a uniform; she would be called Sister Somebody; she would never give a thought to clothes again.
>
> (176)

Mabel wishes to become a "new Person" by means of wearing a uniform—to reinvent herself by purifying her consciousness of "clothes." Clothes here mean that the fly is trying futilely to crawl out of the saucer. Some flies, like her friend Rose, are better at crawling among ordinary people. They do not slip back into the teacup and drown. But Mabel cannot help but retreat into self-consciousness; she always feels herself as inferior to others, and is unable to shut off the overbearing voice of anxiety. The one exception is when she is not looking directly in the mirror, but at her reflection in the kind eyes of Miss Milan, the tailor. The mirror is much less forgiving. Mabel longs to exorcise herself of self-reflection. To become Sister Somebody is like becoming nobody, bar none.

Then, is the point where a dress is right and not wrong that covetable nexus where the dress disappears altogether? The quandary of longing to be *right* in the individual sense—either by staking out our sameness with ourselves against otherness or by engulfing otherness into ourselves—waffles between the democratic and the tyrannical. To reconcile the two in our experience of ourselves in the world seems to be the liberation promised by malleable, floppy sweatpants. Anything is possible with the roomy freedom to expand. The elastic waistband allows you to forget your body's boundaries, to render shapeless and indistinct the limits of your own physical space. You recede into the world until you are indistinguishable from it: invisibility by means of assimilation.

For the city of ancient Athens, the more it expanded its dominion, the less it could experience the freedom made possible by its expansion. This was a story that had an earlier reflection in the Persian Wars. Herodotus quotes the Persian king Xerxes saying that he will reveal "the Persian land as cohabiting the ether of Zeus" (7.8.1). Persia would then disappear as Zeus' realm becomes a world of Persian design. As Xerxes crosses the Hellespont, someone mistakes him for Zeus, exclaiming, "O Zeus, why do you wish, looking like a Persian man and putting forth the name Xerxes in place of Zeus, to make (*poiein*) Hellas rise out of its place, bringing along all human beings?" (7.56.2). The word *poiein*, earlier translated as "contrive," is cognate to the English word "poetry." It means "to do" but also "to make" in the sense of "create" or "poetize."

In Aeschylus' *Persians*, Xerxes' rule is depicted as equivalent to his robes. At the beginning of the play, his mother, Queen Atossa, reports a dream in which two sisterly apparitions appear in Doric and Persian dress, respectively. They divvy up their father's land between them into Greece and Asia.[63] This creates strife between the two that Xerxes seeks to check. In the dream, Xerxes falls to the ground, and, at the sight of his father pitying him, he tears his robes. The rending of clothing then becomes a reigning metaphor for the rift of kindred lands, symbolized as a univocal Xerxes destroying his own threads. The sentiment of the dream seems to be that the foreign and the Greek are of common origin, and so, Xerxes is not personally responsible for the failure of his conquest.

The Queen subsequently summons the ghost of Darius, Xerxes' father, who instructs her to "Gather up rich and brilliant cloths, and go / To meet your son; for he, in grief, has rent / His embroidered robes to shreds" (834–6).[64] This thought disturbs the Queen more than anything else: the "dishonor of the clothes around my son's body."[65] She resolves to gather up *kosmos*, either "adornment" or the "world," to bring it to Xerxes. The word appears again at line 920 to mean "the ranks (*kosmos*) of men whom a god has slain." The diremption of Xerxes' *kosmos*, doubly an internal and external ordering, is both the outcome and the image of the war with Greece: "My garments (*peplos*) I rent at my woe," 1030; "I am stripped (*gymnos*, 'naked') of escorters," 1036; "Break the fold-swelling garment (*peplos*) with vigor (*akmê*) of hands," 1060.[66] Adornment is here a royal raiment like a crown; Xerxes takes out the failure on his own image, as if it signified the failure to compose a unity under the Persian image—in other words, as if he were identical not just to Persia but to Greek and non-Greek. If Atossa's dream is correct, and the two sets of clothes—Greek and Persian—have the same parents, then the othering that is signified by clothing is a natural strife. Its repair under the auspices of nature appears imperialistic, and only replicates the divide.

That the order of a dress mimics the order of a city is an old idea that permeates new fashions. "Self-rule" is a form of mastery, even where it pretends to thoughts of "dressing only for yourself," or self-care and improvement. As we poetically tailor our horizons to feel more comfortable and more flexible—to give ourselves more space—the distinction between self and other recedes. To preserve our boundaries, we forsake them—an unwitting tyranny made possible by the democratic collapse of public and private, in social media as in sweatpants. The wish to rule the world is not so far removed from the remote control of the couch.

3

The Dead

FASHION: *If we were to run together for the prize, I don't know which of the two of us would win the trial, because if you are running, I'm traveling better than at a gallop; and if you faint from standing in one place, I melt. So let's start running again, and while running, as you say, we'll speak of our cases.*

DEATH: *May it happen soon. And since you are born from the body of my mother, it would suit you to profit me by doing my business in some fashion.*

FASHION: *I have already done it, in the past more than you think. Firstly, I, who annul and twist all other customs continually, have never in any place let the practice of death end, and for this reason you see that she endures universally from the beginning of the world until today.*

DEATH: *A great miracle, that you haven't done what you could never!*

FASHION: *Why can't I? You show that you don't know the power of Fashion.*

—Giacomo Leopardi, "Dialogo della Moda e della Morte"
("Dialogue between Fashion and Death")

In Leopardi's dialogue, Fashion takes responsibility for *not* annulling or twisting the fashion of dying. Death's universal endurance is the result of Fashion's own device. Death, portrayed as Fashion's sister, chides her: you do not have the power to change me even if you wanted to. Fashion quips back that Death does not know her power. Indeed, Fashion is akin to Death in being able to quicken the demise of human beings by contorting their bodies (e.g., in foot-binding and corsets[1]), forcing them to wear inappropriate fabrics in adverse weather, or exposing them to toxic chemicals (e.g., vibrant arsenic green dye or the mercury fumes that made hatters go mad[2]). But this is nothing in comparison to fashion's power to enfeeble human action, and to make existence more "dead than alive." Anyone who has an intellectual capacity, says Fashion, now longs for Death and looks to her for hope. Thanks to Fashion, immortality has gone out of fashion, too. The reasons behind the fashionableness of wishing for death are murky. But let me pose this question as a start: is it possible to see hope in the finality of death without longing for something akin to eternal life?

Leopardi's dialogue was written in 1824. Today, in the twenty-first century, beauty products and fashion ads evoke an eternally youthful space, where every attempt is made to reverse or conceal the aging process. Anti-aging elixirs claim to help you appear as if you are not subject to time. This does not stop you from aging, of course, only from appearing to live, which is to say, it presents the hope of time stopping as if it would abate rather than reproduce the image of death's finality. Herein one finds an analogue to Greek tragedy: what we understand as a longing to live forever from another perspective appears a hope for a premature death.

The reader will soon meet Antigone, an anti-aging icon, or, let's call her, an early goth. Meanwhile, the 27 club beckons. More glibly, we have the saying, "I can die now," as if death is proper when you've reached a certain peak, because if you were to die at this *prime* time, you would have achieved some pinnacle of selfhood that makes your life somehow fulfilled as a life. Into this prime we harvest the self with facial peels and firming masques, not in an Ouroboros-renewal, but as if strive toward a point where becoming most approximates being, an ageless median between wannabe and has-been. "How *becoming*," we say, as if coming to be had suddenly presented itself as a fixed state. To the young, the beauty industry offers a bit of maturity, to the old a bit of immaturity. Yet in the alluring concoction of the "prime" of life, you somehow emerge as your best you, a combination of Solon's two famous maxims: "Count no man happy till he's died" and "I grow old ever learning many things."

Is being in your prime the same as looking in your prime? To think of life as if it had a beginning, a middle, and an end seems to mean to imagine it as a story. In the plot of such a story, the prime is that honeymoon period before the midlife crisis—the perspective from which you supposedly come to understand that the young you is not equivalent to *you*.[3] The self goes toward its prime as if it were coming to know itself denuded in its most fitting outfit. The prime drums up ideas of potential specialness and other myths that are promised to the young and reminisced about by the old. This is the state of unexpected promise, where the reader doesn't know the ending but the storyline is just starting to get good. The clock ticks, but patiently, so that time seems neither fleeing nor finite. But when is this goldilocks state of being neither too young nor too old?[4]

In the *Rhetoric*, Aristotle clocks the prime age for the body at between thirty and thirty-five, while for the soul it is fifty minus one. Fifty minus one is forty-nine, just prior to fifty, and well over the halfway point of the usual life span (probably about seventy), when you are declining over the hill and are ready for the advent of being past your prime. Forty-nine is not a prime number—a number that has arrived at a point only divisible by unity and self-unity—but seven times seven, and seven was an important number for the ancient Greeks, especially the Pythagoreans, for whom it carried divine significance.[5] There were seven wonders and seven sages. But apart from numerical mysticism, Aristotle's specificity for prime body versus prime soul suggests that the physical achievement of being in your prime does not correspond to the psychical experience of being in your prime. Such a variance would make it possible to look in your prime without being so, and to be in your prime without looking so. Enter fashion and sophistry. If we age, why can we not un-age? If time moves forward, why can it not retrace its steps? Baldwin's words ring true:

> It is perfectly possible—indeed, it is far from uncommon—to go to bed one night, or wake up one morning, or simply walk through a door one has known all one's life, and discover, between inhaling and exhaling, that the self one has sewn together with such effort is all dirty rags, is unusable, is gone: and out of what raw material will one build a self again? The lives of men—and therefore, of nations—to an extent literally unimaginable, depend on how vividly this question lives in the mind.
>
> (1964/2008: 51)

Fashion and Philosophy in Their Prime

In the *Rhetoric*, Aristotle divides human character into three stages: youth (*neotês*), prime of life (*akmê*, related to "acme"), and old age (*gêras*).[6] In the initial list, being middle-aged is placed in between old and young, as it seems to be chronologically. In what follows, however, Aristotle begins with the young, then moves on to the old, and leaves the middle-aged for the end. He concludes by saying, "Let such things be said of youth, old age, and prime of life, and of what sort of character each is." The temporal sequence of growth—first we are young, then we reach our peak, and then we get old—is altered in the sequence of understanding. In order to come to understand the middle, it looks as if we must first be—or imagine ourselves to be—both young and old. We would then come to the middle age after already having "lived through" old age. But this would mean it would be impossible to be in your prime and know it, unless you could travel to the underworld and back like Odysseus or Er. Or, unless you could jump out of your life, like Aristotle, to attempt to understand the ages of life from the perspective of having died. We come to know the ages in an altogether different way than we experience them, for as we think of ourselves as young we grow older, and as we imagine we have aged, we can only imagine it from an impossible point of view.

> Present experience has, I am afraid, always found us "absent-minded": we cannot give our hearts to it—not even our ears! Rather, as one preoccupied and immersed in himself into whose ear the bell has just boomed with all its strength the twelve beats of noon suddenly starts up and asks himself: "what really was that which just struck?," so we sometimes rub our ears *afterward* and ask, utterly surprised and disconcerted, "what really was that which we have just experienced," and moreover: "who are we really?"
>
> (Nietzsche 1887/1967: Preface, ¶ 1)⁷

Incest and parricide look as if they might also be viable possibilities for attempting to flash-freeze the self in an imitation of being self-caused. In the same way, the tragic poets of beauty and fashion sell us the story of our lives, and anti-aging regimens as a vaccine against fate (*Forever 21*). That way, we stay locked in the cave and continue to buy the shadows.

The young, says Aristotle, are imbued with passion. The world is their oyster, but at the same time they are powerless before their desires, especially in regard to sex. Their wants are extreme, but also prone to change on a dime—"For their wishes are acute and not great, just as the thirst and hunger of the weak" (1389a4–5). Aristotle describes the young as both *thumikoi* ("spirited") and *oxythumoi* ("sharply-spirited" or "quick-to-anger"). They follow after their impulse and are weaker than *thumos*. *thumos* means something like "spirit" or "the will to live"—so much so that you would be willing to give up your life. With both *thumos* and desire, then, the young flit about uncontrollably, flying after their wants, climbing on soap boxes and becoming easily agitated at being belittled or wronged. They are hot-headed, as if naturally drunk, and above all, they want to be superior or victorious, more than to have money or honor. They are very trusting, too, because they haven't experienced much failure or deceit. This makes them foolishly hopeful, and so, both confident and prone to embarrassment (*aischuntêloi*), "for they don't yet assume other things are beautiful, but have been educated solely by the *nomos*" (1389a10–11). *nomos* as "law" or "custom" seems to indicate that the young are conventional. However, in its other meaning as "musical strain,"⁸ there is the suggestion, too, that the young are swept up by the melody of their lives. So immersed are they in the plot that they do not yet know that their view of the world is not their own (they "live in character more than in calculation"). As *megalopsychoi*, "great-souled," they imagine themselves worthy of great things and are afraid of looking ugly. They pursue the beautiful and do not care for the useful. Their mistakes, consequently, are made from hubris. And they are fond of laughter, since wit, says Aristotle, is "educated hubris."

Those who are "older and those past their prime," on the other hand, are "mostly" opposite to the young. The "and" makes one wonder if the old are the same as those who are past their prime, or if Aristotle means that you can be old and in your prime? The relative degree of "older" along with the word—"mostly"—seems crucial, since the old were, after all, once young, and their moderation appears to be the result of their formerly youthful confidence. Unlike the young, the old are shameless and focused on necessities. They are certain of nothing. While the young do everything in excess (they don't listen to Chilon's maxim), the old are excessively under-excessive, more so than they ought to be. Looked at in this way, the old are young in their oldness. They add qualifications to everything, thinking all the time but never knowing anything. They are *micropsychoi*, "small-souled." The young are hot and impulsive; the old are chilled by fear. Their passion is directed toward what is absent, which, since they live in memory more than hope, seems to be the presence of their youth. Their *thumoi* are acute (*oxeis*) but weak. In this, they reverse but remain as charged as the young, to whom the compound form, *oxythumoi*, was attributed. The old, then, are as powerless as the young, but oppositely; their desires lead them now toward profit and away from the beautiful. The young donate; the old save, but both are marked by an excess of passivity toward the self. At the end of the section on old age, Aristotle concludes the following: "since all accept the ones who are similar and who speak speeches in their own character, it is not unclear how in using speeches they will appear such, both they themselves and their speeches" (1390a17–21). Age again seems to be associated with an appearance of character, and one that a rhetorician could imitate in order to appeal to certain age groups.

At last, Aristotle comes to those who are in their prime (*akmazontes*). He uses an active participle, as if being middle-aged were an activity you could do. The middle-aged are in the in-between (*metaxu*[9]) of young and old. But isn't every age in between coming to be and passing away? Having learned of the foolish hope of the young and the calculated memory of the old, one wonders if those at the acme of life have knowledge of ignorance. Their state is at the "mean" by a removal of the excesses of both young and old. They are neither overly bold nor overly fearful but they hold beautifully with regard to both. They don't trust or distrust everyone but they judge instead according to truth. They don't live by the beautiful or useful (good) alone but by both. They seem to occupy that delicate position of being *kalos kagathos*, "beautiful and good." In as many things as the others are excessive or lacking, those in their prime are the measure and the attunement of these. That is to say, the middle-aged have excess and lack but in the proper measures. In the young and the old, one finds moderation and courage separately; in the middle-aged, moderation does not lack courage and courage does not lack moderation. This holds for *thumos* and desire, too. But again, if what is found in youth and old age separately is found together in the prime of life, how does this state emerge without the prior awareness of both? The middle age seems to have aged like a fine wine, and Aristotle's own account of it needs both the boldness of youth to jump out of life and the voyeurism of old age to observe it. The assessment of the relative status of the ages can only come to sight for someone who isn't occupying any of them. Is middle age, then, after old age in thinking but before old age in experience? Is being in your prime a nostalgia that you only discover in retrospect or from imagining yourself dead? Is age itself in some way a state of mind?

Supposedly, Baudelaire's Monsieur C.G. and Rousseau both began writing around age forty-two.[10] Monsieur G., says Baudelaire, retained enough youthfulness to add an "unexpected seasoning" to his artwork (1863/1995: 6). Age forty is pivotal for Mabel Waring, as it is for Nietzsche's Zarathustra, who at forty descends from his mountain haunt. Forty seems to be a mysterious point of midlife ripeness, perhaps in some way the descent of resurrection. The metamorphoses of Zarathustra also confuse the order and meaning of age: the passive camel (Zarathustra's Avestan namesake) seems to be akin to youth, but the jaded lion has already aged too quickly, and the final shape of the child seems only now to invoke a prime state of possibility. But this all needs to be paired with another detail concerning age in Greek antiquity: the beard.

At the beginning of Plato's *Protagoras*, a comrade asks Socrates if he is coming from the hunt for "the bloom (*hôra*) of youth" of Alcibiades, whose beard is apparently just filling in. It is Alcibiades season, because Alcibiades is in season, which is to say in a prime state, about to be in full flower.[11] He is budding, coming into his adulthood, and while the comrade seems to be insinuating that he is a bit too old to be hunted by Socrates, Socrates responds, "aren't you, however, a praiser of Homer, who said the bloom of youth (*hêbê*) was most graceful for the one just getting a beard (*hupênêtês*), which Alcibiades now has?" (309a–b).

Socrates more or less "quotes" here a passage that occurs twice in Homer, at *Iliad* 24.348 and *Odyssey* 10.279.[12] The word used for "bloom of youth" is not Aristotle's *akmê*, but *hêbê*, who is also a goddess. Both lines are references to the god Hermes, who in each case arrives having likened himself to a young man just getting a beard. In the *Iliad* he is sent by Zeus to help guide Priam safely to Achilles' tent. In the *Odyssey* Hermes comes to show Odysseus the moly root (itself an image of Hermes' in-between looks) that will make him immune to Circe's potions. Hermes is the go-between god and his looks identify him as in a state of conspicuous transition. But as a divinity, this is not Hermes as a physical Hermes, but only a representation of his role as middleman.[13] In Plato's portrayal of Socrates citing Homer, Homer himself is in a transitional state. Socrates rejuvenates the old Homer with a slight misquotation that, like writing, makes him seem ageless. Or is it the sign he has aged well? As with Lucretius' remark on the same state, in which the fuzz on the face is referred to as a garment, time too stops in the prime to give us a look.

Alcibiades' bloom is likewise the sign of a loss of youth, as if a blush, suspended between knowledge and ignorance.[14] The young Hippocrates will blush when Socrates gets him to admit he wants to go to Protagoras to become a sophist—embarrassing because it means admitting he is concerned not about wisdom, but about its reputation. Blushing is an uncontrollable physical manifestation of the psychical perception of yourself as uncontrolled; it is even possible to blush at a blush in a flush of embarrassment at having revealed that you are embarrassed. While the season of blushing and blooming seems more appropriate to youth, the strangeness of applying rouge to the face depicts the attractiveness of this just-jaded innocence at all ages. Rosiness signals a time when you can dream and be disappointed in equal measures. But the measure of eternal bloom that cosmetic blush seeks to replicate is again the sign of impending decay, for it is verbal in nature—a rise just before a fall, which is recognizable in Alcibiades especially. He wants to be taken seriously, as a grown-up—and he *will* be taken seriously, when eighteen years later he convinces the Athenians to go on a disastrous expedition to Sicily, in no uncertain terms a midlife crisis.

The *Protagoras* has a dramatic date of around 433 BC; Socrates is at this time about thirty-four. Hippocrates arrives at Socrates' house before dawn to wake him up to beg him to take him to Callias' house to see Protagoras, whom Socrates later compares to Orpheus.[15] This and what follows depict Socrates descending into a sophistic underworld, where he will meet disembodied ideas, a.k.a. shades. Callias is rich, and this may be a reference to Pluto (better known as Hades), whose name means "wealth." The people whom Socrates encounters divide into the same number and grouping as those that Odysseus meets in Hades. If Socrates is young enough to be somewhat unknown, could it be that by the time Socrates emerges from this Hades, he has the glow of a Socrates in his prime? Encountering sophists may be a form of cryogenics for philosophers, just as the old are parasitic on the young. In Book 1 of the *Republic*, Cephalus suggests that he needs some enthusiastic youths to inject his house with life—though he also admits there are benefits to no longer feeling fraught with sexual desire.[16] Are philosophers, too, turned on by spurious wisdom (read: fashion)?

There is another stereotype that haunts the *Protagoras*. Protagoras, whose age is a bit of a mystery (he could be anywhere from early forties to early fifties[17]), draws attention to his maturity, saying, "I am indeed already many years in the art <of sophistry>; for my years, too, are altogether many—and there is not one of you whose father I could not be" (317c1–4).[18] Protagoras cites age as a natural hierarchy, perhaps to elicit a compulsory conviction from his audience. This appeal to something irrefutable that sets him above the rest allows him to adopt an anti-democratic standpoint without countering Athenian convention. Time itself looks anti-democratic, since, even if our selves might be somehow equal, they age at different moments. The idea that we could "be" at a certain age turns the fleetingness of being in time, and so appearance, into the illusion that appearances could be controlled. The perfect age, like a perfect outfit, would be a state in which you are least foreign to yourself and most at home. Protagoras' own maxim is a cryptic indication of this—if man is the measure of all things—does he also set his age? Protagorean relativism attempts to give human beings control over appearances, and so, time. This is mirrored in fashion (both contemporary and ancient), not only by way of anti-aging products but also by way of leisurewear.

Protagoras wants to create the impression that he is a fully matured parental figure pontificating to a room full of children—he is grooming himself for his audience (Socrates later describes Protagoras as "beautifying himself for us," 333d1). But the association of knowledge with age is as finicky as the association of ignorance with youth. It requires the assumption that knowledge is stuff you naturally get more of the longer you live. While this might be true, it is by no means necessarily true (as Aristotle suggests, old age can make you either crochety or Gloria Swanson). So the chorus of Aristophanes' *Knights* turns to face the audience,

> Moreover, he [Aristophanes] knows that you [the audience] are seasonal
>   by nature
> and betray the earlier poets in their old age:
> Magnes knew and underwent this when his gray hairs came down,
> he had won very many trophies over rival troupes:
> he had let go all keys, plucking strings and fluttering wings,
> turning into a Lydian and a gnat, dipping himself in frog-colors
> —but it was not enough. Coming to an end in old age, since he was not
>   in bloom,
> he was cast out as an antique and abandoned because of mocking.
>
> (518–25)[19]

Unlike Protagoras, who is foreign (from Abdera), removed, and older—as perhaps we think wisdom would look—Socrates is familiar, available, and seems to know less the older he gets. Hippocrates marches right into his bedroom without knocking, and seems not to regard him as either famous or wise enough to teach him; Socrates is merely his ticket into the sophist salon. Socrates' boutique midwifery is like an ancient episode of What Not to Wear, guided by a *daimonion*, who helps him determine which fashions are bad and should be trashed, and which are good enough to nurse to fruition. But people cling to their bad fashion, like Linus clings to his trusty blanket. They then want to bite Socrates, and this seems to be where he gets his reputation for childish antics. In the *Gorgias*, Callicles tells Socrates, "I've been taking note of how, if anyone gives in to you on any point, even as a joke, you hang on to it with glee the way teenagers would" (499b6–7).[20] In the *Euthydemus*, Crito worries about Socrates' suggestion that the two of them ought to go back to school. Socrates is only concerned that Euthydemus and Dionysodorus will be called, like his music teacher, Connus, a *gerontodidaskalos*, an "old-geezer teacher.[21]" But in the *Protagoras*, the sign of Socrates' teen spirit paradoxically lies in that fuzz on Alcibiades' face. While Alcibiades is a pretty boy, Socrates is particularly attracted to his scruffy countenance.[22] Is Alcibiades' look of "bloom" the physical manifestation of knowledge of ignorance?—on the one hand, being too young to know, on the other hand, being old enough to acknowledge your own youth?

The contemporary beauty industry conflates this look with its psychical equivalent, as if the face of Alcibiades would signal promise by default (Thucydides advises otherwise). As an acme of beauty, Alcibiades is more of a common stereotype for feminine looks, which are glamorized as high when they are high, then suffering a sharp plummet, accelerated by childbirth and wrinkles. There are all sorts of creams and tonics that are supposed to assist you in looking as if you froze at some pre-maternal peak, when dew glows freshly on your cheeks and a gleam of curiosity sparkles in your eye, before you are deflowered by sex and knowledge. Meanwhile, masculine looks plod along with much less negative attention drawn toward their aging; the look of being older, and so, supposedly wiser, is as prized as the look of the eccentric young genius. Still, the anti-aging elixir is not so much about being young as about time being staved off, curated, creamed, oiled, etc., fixing the story at its juiciest, most lively point. The attraction to the bloom of youth is spiked with the spellbinding intellectual connotations of blooming. The charm of the two together has made its way into the singular image of Petite Meller, a philosophy student and popstar whose signature look is very strong pink blush. Or maybe ex-philosopher and Contrapoints fashion-philosophy idol,

Natalie Wynn. Perhaps there is something of Protagoras' foreignness in the exotic come-hither look of intelligence where it is least expected, from frills we do not assume could be sagacious, whether verbose poetics or overdone fashion. But the conflation made by an association of age with intellect (in whatever direction) suggests an interest in the appearance of knowledge: the fashion in which it is brought to bloom. Hippocrates is not so smooth as to question Protagoras' claims to age; but Socrates is certainly recording the whole thing in his mind, for he immediately retells the conversation to an unnamed comrade.

In other places, too, we meet a budding Socrates, even in his later life. In the *Symposium* Socrates claims to know "erotics" (177d8), while in the *Theaetetus* we learn that Socrates has no intellectual children. His practice of dying and being dead is a neutralization of the self's progeny (a procedure bottled and sold by Euthydemus and Dionysodorus). Perhaps practicing dying and being dead, then, would be philosophy in its prime, having gone down and come back, returning to the insight that the bloom of death is the prime of life. Coming to know is like growing up—but repeatedly—with the result that philosophy appears to be prime-arily for perpetual adolescents and dead people. Words themselves stay stranded in the adolescent stage of communication, the hermeneutics of which Hermes is again the emblem. Aging is, like fashion, nonlinear, and in every argument the ideology of adulthood, anti-fashioning, threatens. Fixating on either permanence or impermanence will lead one to fly the cave too quickly.

In a myth at the end of Plato's *Gorgias*, Zeus is said to have stopped the trials of souls in clothing. The age of Cronos was in this regard unfair, since "wicked souls" could appear "clothed in beautiful, well-born, and rich bodies"; and even the judges themselves had their souls veiled by clothes. Removing the clothes of judges and judged meant removing cloudy judgment, a state akin to a thorough death:

> Then, they must be judged naked of altogether all those things—for it is necessary to judge them dead. And it is necessary, too, for the judge to be naked—being dead—observing with the soul itself the soul itself immediately after each has died, deserted from all kin and leaving behind on earth that *kosmos* (adornment) entire, so that the judgment may be just.
>
> (523e1–6)

If being naked is death, the arrangement of the *kosmos* itself looks as if it could be beguiling. To judge well requires leaving not just the body in which the soul is clothed but also the world of which the soul was a part.

Death is like exile, its force to denude the order you had previously taken for granted.

Antigone's solution is given to her accidentally: she is the vertical product and the horizontal sibling of her father and brother Oedipus. She is also in love with death, and her name literally means, anti-aging, anti-generation, or anti-birth; the *anti-* prefix might also mean "in place of." As a paradigmatic adolescent, she is at the nexus of being both caused and cause; for Heidegger, being thrown (*geworfen*) and projecting (*entwerfen*). Incest threatens to combine these conjunctively, where in growth we meet them disjunctively. So, Antigone is a living character who claims to be dead, and the only "nonvisibly monstrous and wholly human being" ever called a "monster" in Greek tragedy (Benardete 1999: 50; cp. Pl. *Euthyd.* 296e2). Despite their varying appearances, goth and prime-of-life are strangely inspired by a similar wish. Death becomes them.

Contemporary goth is a form of suburban punk, part deconstructionism, part rockabilly: shredded garments, lace-up-bondage, a touch of pin-up, black eyeliner, tattoo sleeves, and unexpectedly, cute cuddly animals. Goth has an intriguingly wide range from campy to belle époque: Marilyn Manson posing with a kitten, creepy undead Claudia in *Interview with the Vampire*, Eugène Delacroix's *The Young Martyr*, Elvira with a furry puppy backpack, beach goth.[23] Bloodstained lips and pasty white faces somehow easily mutate into a caricature of everlasting innocence. The Thanatos Archive, a database of Victorian photographs of dead people, also for some reason has a lot of photos of cats in human clothes. The personified kitten and the evil child are more dramatic versions of household familiars who shock us by revealing nefarious lives we never imagined. If the prime is the best part of our life story, goth is the riveting plot twist, a caricature of death's bloom. We don't suspect the goody two-shoes of poisoning the teacher. Children, particularly babies, recover eerily quickly from both wounds and tantrums, almost as if they are made of immortal plasma, at once fragile and impenetrable—half monster, half ingénue—*in-fans*, an unspeakable thing which itself does not speak. Especially on the streets of Tokyo, gothic fashion is a dreamy Nabokov nightmare, taking its cues from Madame Alexander and Chucky.[24] Eternal death meets eternal youth. Undead hippies are somewhere in there, too, aiming at the eternal summer.

Fashion at large engages in other morbid behaviors that are more difficult to crack—capturing moments in the coffins of photographs—photo-"bombing" and "shooting" people are strange expressions for making images; recording every "first" of every baby; setting up tombstones to a million meaningless details on the graveyard of Twitter. Tattoos have become increasingly mainstream as a way to affix a memorial to one's body.

Light-hearted morbidity flits about with similar ease. Alexander McQueen's skull scarves are now a common pattern; you can even buy yoga pants with human skulls printed all over them. During the season of Halloween in America, children dressed as murder victims roam the streets eating candy bones and wearing wax vampire teeth. It is a seasonal mockery of death, which in quips seems to be in fashion all year long. The casually delivered—"I want to die," "I'm dead," "I'm dying"—are a near ritualistic trivialization of fatality, as if death were an option. Even lampooning un-PC speech seems to favor a look of preserved innocence over the complicated decay of the history of words. We want the impossible: to be like shades in Hades, transparent in speech and action, so that we can be not only the perfect manifestation of what we are, but of what we were and what we wish to be. The only way is to live as if you already know your tragic flaws, and so, can now safely avoid them. Subcultures and fetishes are the next targets of this errorless sieve, to be safely replaced by virginal icons, such as babies, prudes, and dead people—all of which had a marked presence in the Victorian Era. One wonders if the regressive trend in twenty-first-century fashion toward high-necks and puffy sleeves is telling us something about ourselves.

Time is the trouble, as it always (so often?) is. The wish to freeze is not random; we stop rather at Aristotle's mean—that moment when to blush is still possible but also forgivable, or when you are not so aware of your exterior as to commit a terrible injustice to your interior. To put blush on your face is to paint on the look of intentional "knowledge of ignorance." But this changes its Socratic hue. If you could have a cloak of justice, a bit of blush, why wouldn't you behave like a criminal? Meek fashion and eternal youth go together in this way. Both are wrapped up in looking innocent on the outside and blooming with cleverness on the inside. The world did not expect Pinky (Blushy?) and the Brain; the wolf should prefer to masquerade as the sheep; and the anti-aging elixir? If we drink this, does it make us not only purer and younger but also invincible?

This standard of appearing as your most arrived self seems not only fleeting but also unpredictable and liable to change at different stages of life. "Who wore it better—the former self or the future self?" Without even a hint of argument, fashion posits a transcendental ego. This look can kill with a sudden Q.E.D., even while the plasticity of the self continually denies its own certainty. Fashion creates the false hope that somewhere in the netherworld of our closet lies the self-expression we covet. It must likewise leap to the conclusion of an original self as a blank slate: a self that was once unclothed or at least unfashioned. But each self that we try on we are compelled to judge in relation to what came before and what could come after, as if we knew where we started or where we were going. And just as fashion drugs us with notions that the right dress today will be wrong tomorrow, so beauty "rituals" defer to a meta-self to whom one sacrifices a series of alter egos: "Believe in the possibility of transforming yourself into a fixed self," fashion seems to say. Philosophy is suspicious of this apparent "revelation." Fashion is not really about controlling our aging bodies. No, fashion invokes the crazier notion of transcending the body altogether. This takes us back to a youth so young it lies before notions of time itself. It is the illusion of a prime self that magically transforms itself in each particular person, as each person's self in each particular moment, and as that basic self that existed before stylized selves. Fashion runs—for it will melt if it stops—and in running it manifests itself as a continual rejection of its own appearances in favor of the specter of its peak, in which it senses but cannot know the flavor of its permanent impermanence.

    We thus meet another accidental shade of philosophy. Socrates uttered that infamous line that philosophy is the "practice of dying and being dead" in the context of comforting his friends who were worried that there would be no philosophy after Socrates. Philosophical suicide is his solution to the problem of his execution: only die-hard intellects are willing to cast aside flux in order to secure a unity with unchanging being. It is, and Socrates knew it, clearly a nihilistic wish that only makes sense to the living, since to achieve a moment of such singularity would result in the annihilation of your self-awareness. To want to die is to wish to be and not be simultaneously. Fashion presents this irrational view as if it were self-evident. Fully realized, particular selves grace the pages of fashion magazines, where their potential is actualized. For this, fashion earns and maybe even deserves philosophy's ire. But it is not so much its faulty logic that incriminates it. It is rather its uncanny mockery of that conviction with which we search not for the perfect self but for the perfect truth. Somehow the desire to fashion the self just right and to annihilate it are heading toward the same thought. It is the thought of fashion and philosophy in their prime. A conviction in the fully realized self is the alias of a conviction in the neutralizing effect of self-knowledge. Fashion shares with philosophy that damning adornment of self-elevation through self-negation. Just as philosophy begins as a reflection (and therefore not at the beginning) that steps out of the continuous flow of experience to assess it, and yet in its very act is still part of the flow, so too fashion's bloom may be like beauty's, an unexpected burst of selfhood that is then revealed to be just another moment in the experience of the self. We come to know clothes through the second thought of fashion—the popped collar that presumes a time when collars couldn't pop—and through these second thoughts we come to the thought of a self beyond clothes. Fashion's changeability at once seems to stand for time and our longing to transcend it.

Sophocles' *Antigone*: Anti-aging Goth

So we meet Antigone, frozen in a state of adolescent angst. Her name and its anti-genetic connotations make one think of plowing mother earth to dig graves rather than to sow seeds. As the daughter of Oedipus, who married his own mother, Antigone really should've never been born. But she has a story, and by her own lights it's rather predictable. She says that she "knew that she was going to die," since "her soul died long ago in order to serve the dead below" (460; 559). From the start of the play, then, she is a zombie. Antigone's anti-aging elixir is burial, concealer, cover-up. She is special as a tragic character because she claims to *know* her own fate as if posthumously. Perhaps the singular point of suspense is her actual death: she hangs herself. But even in this elevation, Antigone seems to wish to identify the depths of Hades with the heights of Olympus. She has transformed death into an object of worship—"I am in doubt," utters the Chorus Leader, "what is this surprising monster?" (376).[25]

Antigone is not alone. Her living sister, Ismene, is the addressee of her opening lines:

> Oh common selfsame sibling head of Ismene,
> do you know any evil from Oedipus which
> Zeus has yet to accomplish for the pair of us still living?
>
> (1–3)

Antigone's strange emphasis on the commonality and sameness of her sister anticipates disagreement. This is further indicated by her reference to her and Ismene as a "pair." The word "pair" translates the dual number in Greek. The dual is used to refer to a "two" that is somehow a "one," an inseparable unit, neither singular nor plural. For Antigone, Antigone and Ismene are one entity with two heads. For Ismene, on the other hand, it is only dead brothers who can be paired in this way:

> No word, Antigone, of friends,
> either pleasant or painful, has come to me since
> we (plural) two were robbed of our two (dual) brothers
> on a single day, as a pair dying by a double hand.
>
> (11–14)[26]

Ismene refers to herself and Antigone with the plural, while their brothers are dual. Antigone makes no distinction between dead and living. A brother is a brother, just as a sister is a common head. The plight of their two brothers, Polyneices and Eteocles, is the catalyst for the plot of the play. The two of them had originally agreed to alternate the rule of Thebes, but Eteocles became greedy and refused to give up his turn. So Polyneices took seven against Thebes to invade his own city. Polyneices' misfortune of appearing on the outside leads Antigone's uncle Creon (now in charge of Thebes) to consider him a traitor. So his corpse is left "unwept, unburied, a sweet treasure-house for birds on the lookout for a free meal" (29–30).[27] Eteocles, meanwhile, gets a full burial. He is completely covered. Antigone seeks to rectify this injustice. She decides that she *must* bury Polyneices. All brothers deserve to be treated alike, no matter what crimes they commit. It is not the city, but the dead below, who say what must be done with the dead.

The Chorus Leader flatters Creon with the opposite sentiment:

It's your pleasure, child of Menoeceus, to make (*poiein*)
thus those who are ill and well-disposed to the city,
and to use any and every law, this is in your power,
over the dead and as many of us as are living.

(211–14)

Creon's tyrannical authority is at odds with Antigone's perception of underground justice. But you might wonder: why is it better to be buried rather than exposed? What does it matter to the dead, if they are no longer in their bodies? Creon's suspicions about Polyneices seem to emanate from the *poly-* ("many") in his name. Anything double or multiple has to be left out in the open, if the city is going to be kept safe. It is "impossible (*amêchanon*)," says Creon, "to figure out the soul and thought and judgment of any man until he is brought to light, tested by rules and laws" (175–7). Whatever lies buried inside of someone is of no consequence; the only means to distinguish souls is by their exposure in political acts. Burial presents onlookers with a false unity on a complex thing; it is mere cosmetics. For Eteocles this process is justified because his allegiance looks simple. But Polyneices is *for* the city and *against* the city at the same time, and Creon cannot reckon this double stance. The solution is to expose Polyneices as a criminal, since hiding him somehow replicates his crime. Anyone trying to bury Polyneices' corpse is to be punished by death. Burying a body no longer means paying your last respects. It is an act of criminal concealment tantamount to murder.

A guard soon appears with some news. He had drawn the unfortunate lot of informing Creon that someone has dusted the corpse of Polyneices. He was reluctant to come, and so, he says he didn't arrive quickly by taking up a "light foot" (*kouphos pous*). "Foot," *pous*, is hard to ignore, not only because it is part of Oedipus' name, which means "swollen foot," but also because it is the word for a metrical foot in poetry. The guard says he spent so long debating the pros and cons of going (or not going) that he ended up in a mental traffic jam, which he calls *anastrophê*. Anastrophe is what happens when you dance all around yourself, and try to go in one way and another, strophe and antistrophe, at the same time. This circular confusion takes its cues from the language of a tragic chorus, and it frustrates Creon. He wonders why the guard insists on, quite literally, putting his pain "to rhythm," *rhythmizein*? Of course, the guard is hesitant because he doesn't want to tell Creon the bad news. Perhaps he should just turn (*strephein*) and go? When the guard does disclose his news, Creon begs him to be silent. *Anti*strophe is as stressful to Creon as *Anti*gone will be. Creon had instructed the chorus not to repeat anything that he did not order (215; 219). Later, when he has second thoughts about sentencing Antigone to death, it is already too late to turn back, and the act of doubly thinking seems to him all the more criminal (1096, cp. 389). There is a suggestion being made here, and it will become more apparent later, that poetry—with its double entendre and invisible notions—is hostile to Creon's ears. Poetry buries intentions in metaphor, and even takes pleasure in this concealment.

Creon refers to the "perpetrator (*autocheir*)" of the burial with the same word he had used to refer to the double murder of Eteocles and Polyneices (306; 172). Antigone's is the poet's crime: piety toward the unseen. The pluralization of the criminals goes together with this. While the guard had said, "there was no sign (*asêmos*) of any doer" (252), Creon replies, "the ones who've carried out these things did them for pay" (293-4). Perhaps Creon is referring to the other guards, but at line 490, he similarly slides Ismene together with Antigone—"She, and her sister too, won't (as a pair) avoid the worst fate; yes, I blame *her* equally for plotting this burial." All sisters are perpetrators, because they are in some sense related to the crime. Of course, Creon is *also* related to Antigone. But he is not the child of Oedipus, and anyway, in the city, citizens are "relatives" not by literal but figurative blood.[28] Antigone, too, is inclined to interpret her familial relations as "simile" rather than difference. We see this inclination in her words to Ismene: "Such are the declarations they say the good Creon holds over you and me—and really I mean *me*" (31-2). For Antigone, the unity of siblings is in their intentions or not at all. Ismene cannot be considered her sister, when she won't go along with her plan. Either Ismene shares in Antigone's thoughts, and so, can be a blood relation or she has different ideas and is cast out of the family ("you'll incur my hatred, and the hatred of the dead man too, justly so," 93-4). It is easier to posit similarity when your siblings are dead. Antigone forms her familial relations through ideas not genetics.[29] She imagines that she is betrothed to Acheron.

The Plot to Bury/Kill

"What's the matter?" inquires Ismene, "Clearly, you are darkening over some word" (20). Antigone's thoughts about burying her brother are visibly underground. Ismene begs her to be reasonable, and at the very least, "Ok then, don't reveal this deed to anyone, but cover <it/him> up in secret, and I'll do the same" (84–5). That is, if you have to bury him, bury your burial, too. The word "secret (*cryphêi*)" is cognate to a word Antigone had used to say that Eteocles was "hidden" (*cryptein*) in the ground. Apparently, covering up a corpse only sprouts a new one. Death is not the kind of dirt you can simply dust off your hands. You must conceal your concealment. While it has been proclaimed publicly—the word is *ekkêruxai*—that no one is allowed to conceal Polyneices, Antigone tells Ismene that she will not hide her cover up but proclaim it—again, *kêruxai* (27; 87). Antigone will reveal the burial not in the name of political rebellion, but as a divine spokeswoman for the dead.[30] Antigone's allegiance to the dead seems to make no distinction between the gods above and the dead below. She is only sure she is extraterrestrial. Both like and unlike her father, she boasts of tragic awareness and her acceptance of it as a boon. "You have a hot heart for chilly things," says Ismene—"you love impossibilities (*amêchana*)" (89–90). What Creon deems "impossible"—to reveal a man's soul except by visible deeds—Antigone challenges by way of burial. Burial hides from view mortal decay. Its concealment seems to be metaphorical for a darkness in thinking.

This is all but a re-killing: burial covers up the evidence of death, as if its exposure would remind you that you are complicit in the crime of mortality. While a dead bird might make us wince and turn away, a dead human body prompts a need for action. We don't lay out our dead or even our living bodies in plain sight. We take care to keep them hidden in crucial ways or to get rid of them entirely, as if death put our deepest vulnerability in the nude. Perhaps we cover up out of a recognition of our kinship to others of our same species, too, but in this recognition lies a concern that waking life, the civilized world, is no place for death. Death is the sight of the unknown, and we do not want to see that we cannot see it. The city helps this along with its patriotic assimilation of a "citizen body" to the soul of its state. The fabric of the flag glosses death as a symbolic act of immortal camaraderie.

In this cloth is your passport to the underworld. And although fashion seems more malleable than a grave, since we can re-invent our memorials to ourselves on a whim via clothes, what remains constant is the sense that something *must* be done with our bodies. No, we seem to say, we are not naked animals. Our nudity is a choice, like a leopard print coat. No, we do not decay. We can choose to stay young, to keep the body trained or "fit"—in good "shape." But this is another version of that wish for immortalization that also takes the form of the written word. Would that our bodies could be writ in indelible ink, tattooed with indelible fashion. But then they would cease to be bodily. We are anything but fixed selves or bodies in time's death march, yet still the illusion of your "self" is compulsory, even if it can only arrive the second before it disappears.

We find Antigone, then, stranded between two conflicting sentiments: "And if I die before my time, I call it a gain; for how would one who lives, like me, beset by evils, not gain by dying?" (462–66). But later on, Antigone will lament her fate: as her brother is "unwept" and "unburied," Antigone is "unwept, unloved, unmarried" (876). She seems to need to bury her brother to conceal her own mortality from herself, and then, to comfort herself by proclaiming it loudly as if she does not care. This seems a conflict for contemporary mortals, too, where death is frequently seen in the compelling fictions of the silver screen and the chilling events of real life, which mostly arrive second-hand on the news. We grow accustomed to death's simulation even as we fear its actuality. Does Antigone really want to die? Suicidal thoughts seem to be the expression of a wish to live on without conflict, since only alive can you lament the cruel fate of living.

The old motto, *memento mori*, "remember to die," meaning perhaps, "remember that you have to die" or "that you currently are dying," once referred to the macabre trend in which gothic curiosities such as skulls were laid out to remind you of your impermanence. In its literal translation, death isn't a far-off future fate, but rather an ongoing, present tense reality that you cannot escape. The imperative, however, casts it comfortably into future time; it is frequently translated, "remember you *will* die," which delays death to a later date. Perhaps this makes it sound a bit more tolerable? Death has been transformed into something you could long for rather than something you are already unwillingly undergoing. So too, Antigone's gothic claim that she knows she will die and that she is already dead takes possession of her fate in a way that plays at the idea of her being beyond death—or at least *so over it*. Her fascination with the impossible is picked up in the most famous chorus of the play, which begins in this way,

> Many are the wonders, the terrors, and none
> is more wonderful, more terrible than man.
> He makes his way, this prodigy, over
> the dim gray sea (*oidmata*),[31] riding the blast
> of the south wind, the swells

> of the deep cleaving before him;
> he wears away the Earth, mightiest
> of gods, imperishable, unwearied—
> his plows turn her over and over, year
> after year his mules plod on and on.
>
> (332–41)[32]

Among the wonders and the terrors—two words that translate the single word, *deina*—none is more terrible (more *deinon*) than a human being.[33] *deinon* means both "clever" and "awesome," or "canny" and "uncanny." The togetherness of its opposing traits would be something like a prime human: clever in such a way as to be a force to be reckoned with.

Human beings stand before the awesome sea in horrific fascination. Then, they build boats. The untamed earth threatens to subdue them. Then, they invent farming and agriculture.[34] In the first antistrophe, we learn that human beings go hunting in wild lairs and yoke "the shaggy-maned horse and wearless mountain bull." In the second strophe, humans are said to teach themselves language and "windy thought," and "how to live by laws." But, in spite of their over-cleverness, there is one thing they cannot escape: "Hades." No matter how many resources, cures, or nets human beings contrive, human beings cannot escape their own mortality. Antigone seems to be peculiar for having thought she could find a way out by embracing it. But the word "Hades" is already complicit in the cover up, since the dust of euphemism buries it. This is the unlisted survival mechanism of the chorus itself: poetry. Human beings make the earth bow down to their feet not only with the turns of plows but also with strophes of their poems. Both are signified in the cryptic word *nomoi*, as songs and laws (369). Poetry puts reality underfoot not by wiping it clean or making it dirty, but by metaphor's imitation of love and death. There are echoes of this in a later chorus, where Eros is described as—

> roaming over the gray sea
> and into the lairs of the wild—
> you even the immortal
> gods cannot escape, nor anyone
> among men who live but a day: he
> who catches you is driven mad.
>
> (784–90)

Eros makes even immortals swoon with madness; he haunts the sea and the expanse of the wilderness, but love is not something either human beings or gods are canny enough to master. Eros' present absence is the counterpart to death's absent presence.

Antigone attempts again to cast it off by joining a choral ode that yokes her doom metrically; she adopts the function of the chorus as revealing the fate of the characters—in this case, her own. But the power of fate is *deinon* (951). Antigone compares herself to Niobe (a goddess who lost her *children* not her brothers). The Chorus Leader corrects her: "But really, she was a god and a god-born / while we are mortal and born to die" (834–5). In line 869, we get another glimpse of Antigone's horizontal vision: "Oh! Brother, you hit upon a wedding of misfortune!"—a double entendre that refers both to Polyneices and to Oedipus (Antigone's other unfortunate brother). "If my husband died, another could take his place, and a child from another man, if I lost *this one here*, but with my pair of parents, mother and father, both hidden in Hades, no brother could ever come to light" (909–12). "Child" seems to be on the verge of brother, and brother again seems to mean father, too; the claim recalls Pericles' suggestion that if you lose your child in battle, you can simply give birth to another.[35] The city (the parent), on the other hand, and by extension here the citizens (brothers), are irreplaceable. Both Antigone and the polis seem to have Oedipally confused siblings and progenitors. Antigone's incestuous patriotism is a metaphor for the city's conflation of vertical genetics with relations of same and other.

Consider these lines: "And yet, from where could I get a more glorious glory than putting my selfsame sibling[36] in a grave? All these men (*indicating the chorus*) would gladly agree with this, if fear hadn't shut up their tongue" (502–5). The idea of death as a salvation of the self is a vindication of suicide made possible by the celebration of the city as if it were a self. It says, "Go to war and die for the glory of your country, as if for a parent or brother." Antigone declares, "It is a beautiful (or noble) thing for me to die doing (*poiein*) this." The use of the word *poiein* suggests that this view on death is a poetic one. The enjoyment of her own plight is something of which Creon accuses her—"Take her away as soon as possible and enshroud her in a vaulted tomb, as I've specified, / Leave her there, solitary, if she wants to die or, living under such a roof, to go on performing burials!" (885–8). Can it be that to stage a funeral is to erect a flag to your family? Antigone makes death come alive in her love for the impossible. In the city, as among goths, death is romanticized. Antigone loves Hades, whose name, *Haidês*, is a pun on "invisible (*a-ïdes*)"; she ignores her boyfriend and cousin, Haimon (Creon's son), whose name means "Blood." Her attraction to what is underneath is displayed as an erotic longing to clothe her brother's body, and this seems to be signified by the dusting that follows.

In the account of the second burial, the guards brush the dust off the corpse, then sit and watch. The corpse is said to be "damp" (410), the dust is twice called "thirsty" (245; 429). Their watch is broken by a huge dust storm that fills the plain (*pedion*). It is so bad the guards have to shut their eyes (419–20). After the dust settles, Antigone lets out "the sharp cry of a bitter bird, when she sees the bed of her empty nest orphaned of nestlings" (423–5). The nestlings seem to be the dust particles that the guards brushed off the corpse. Antigone has been robbed of her concealment, and she shrieks at the absence of tiny particles that seem themselves the presence of an absence. "Dust," *konis*, can mean either literal or metaphorical dirt; in Homer it is described a "countless multitude."[37] Dust seems to gain its substance in generality more than particularity. Its particles are so miniscule that to acknowledge them is already to abstract from them and wipe them away.[38] Antigone cries out for her dust baby, the burial that is her brainchild, the absent presence of a present absence. Dust, like ash, while bringing humans closer to invisible things like fire, gains its value through what isn't present. In this way, it is like poetry—obfuscating reality while at the same time clarifying it. But if the corpse was damp and the dust thirsty, after a dust storm that was so great the guards couldn't see anything, how can Antigone tell the difference between *her* dust and the wind's?

Clothes as Poetic Dust

As the generative timeline is replaced with symbolic generation, physical roads become mental roads. The one who can see best is the blind Teiresias. Dying in this play is likewise a simulacrum. As is true to tragedy more generally, we don't ever see death happen on the stage. But Sophocles goes out of his way to exaggerate this in the *Antigone* play. The ravaging of Polyneices appears an empty threat. Teiresias says he heard the cry of birds plundering the corpse. But Antigone's cry at 427 was also like that of a bird. The boy who is Teiresias' guide tells him something unusual is going on with the sacrifices, as if the meat were the corpse—but still, this is symbolic. When Haimon dies, he does so with a verb that is cognate to his name (*haimassein*, 1175). His suicide, too, seems a poetic act. Antigone's own death of being buried alive in a cave seems no death until she kills herself by an ascending descent. By the end, only Creon and his strophes (the messengers and the chorus) are left. He assumes he killed everyone; the chorus suggests it might have been an accident. Creon is thus the reflection of Antigone. He longs to be responsible for his own actions. But the signs of Sophocles are everywhere, for burial is the act of "clothing" that is implicit in all poetry.

In the guard's first account of the dusting of Polyneices, he reports that the doer left no sign of wagon wheels nor stroke of a mattock. The word "wheels (*trochoi*)" is related to "trochees (*trochaioi*)," one of the variations of metrical feet. The wagon wheels reappear again as cycles, when Teiresias warns Creon: "Indeed, know well that you won't yet / finish many racing circuits (*trochoi*) of the sun / before you yourself will give up one from your loins / a corpse in exchange for corpses, / since you've thrown below one from above / and have made a soul dwell dishonorably in a grave" (1064–9). When Creon first enters, the chorus announces him as the leader of the *chôra*, a word that means "land," but which is also a homonym for "chorus." The verb used for his "coming" is another homonym, *chôrein*. After Antigone is discovered, she is referred to four times as a *korê*, yet another homonym, which means "girl," or the "pupil" of an eye.[39] Eyes, of course, are also of extreme importance in the Oedipus trilogy, second only to feet. Haimon will advise Creon not to "strain the foot" (*teinein poda*)[40] of his ship too tightly, lest he be "turned," *strephein*, "on his back" (715–6).[41] *strephein* is again cognate to strophe, and this line is a perfect double entendre for metrical extension; it is a meta-metaphor for the city as a ship and a ship as a poem. Perhaps Haimon thinks his father's foot will become swell or his poetry too strophic? When Eurydice, Creon's wife, gets a report of both Antigone and Haimon's suicides from a messenger who was at the scene, the messenger says that Antigone followed Eurydice's "husband," *posis*, who was followed by a "foot attendant," *podagos*, to the end of the "plain," *pedion* (1196–7).[42] *posis, podagos,* and *pedion* are all instances of footed doubletalk that impede the listener.

Poetic images are here not symbols of realities but rather, blood, birth, and death are symbols of poetry. The very sprinkling of dust is a symbol of burial, which is a symbol of death—and this is implicit in every act of symbolizing. Antigone's familial patriotism makes physical blood a matter of symbolic allegiance, while Creon's political patriotism makes physical allegiance a matter of symbolic blood. This allows Antigone and Creon to easily generate enemy blood in Ismene and Haimon. Antigone's erotic imaginings bring on a thumotic rise. *thumos* is also the object of Teiresias' annoyance at Creon: "Such are the steadfast arrows I've aimed at you like an archer, at the *thumos* of your heart—for you vex me!" (1084–5). In an earlier exchange, Haimon tells his father: "Let go of your *thumos*, then, and allow yourself changes" (718). But Creon is confused: "To yield is terrible (*deinon*), but the opposite, to strike *thumos* with terrible (*deinon*) ruin <is terrible> too" (1095–7). Creon defers to the chorus, who tell him to go bury Polyneices and resurrect Antigone. But Creon's consistent belief that burial should be buried seems to be equivalent to Antigone's longing to bury her brother and herself. Are these twin perspectives on poetry? Antigone believes that metaphor is essential to revealing reality, Creon that metaphor covers reality up with dust. Yet poetry uses metaphor to bury reality in order to reveal it.

Antigone's burial revives the thought with which we bury the body, the thought of our own death. If, however, human cleverness imagines a way out of death, Antigone is the idealization of that mortal sentiment. She is a perfect martyr for the sake of death itself, annihilated by her fate the moment she is conceived. We see her living and moving but she is really just a perfect poetic illusion, a figment of Sophocles' imagination. She stands for the bringing into reality of, the giving birth to, what is anti-generative, what is born not from the possible but from the impossible. She is the realization of the poetic, for in Hades, thumotic shades stripped of eros are the only reality. This is the city's darkest aspiration for itself, since only there could familial attachments and other irrational attractions cease to have sway. Only there could the city's clothes be equivalent to reality.

Buried alive in a cave, fashion's shadows reek of substance. Dusting is akin to dressing. It can be used to make things invisible—to bury a body, to sweeten a corpse, or to symbolize the abstract idea of siblinghood, whether through conspiratorial blood or a flag. The city interprets the former as murder and cover up, though it itself uses dust—for example, in myths of autochthony—to avoid looking impure. Antigone, as an attempt to encapsulate the living dead—as Sophocles' doll come to life—eradicates the distinction between dead and alive. She seeks to be the author of her own fate and a character within that fate simultaneously. Is it possible to be the creator of your own image and the inhabitant of that image without risking losing yourself in the process? Clothing yourself involves attempting to understand the design of your character. It is a prototype for knowledge of oneself as an agent, and to achieve it seems only possible by going goth. In putting on clothes, we learn to die.

Blood and Armor

Clothes are not our guts. They do not feel. To be sure, they are vulnerable, but like gods, only in a half-assed way. Their seams can rip, their fabric will sometimes relax, their fibers can even deteriorate, or their colors bleed in mock vitality. But all of this happens painlessly. Their insensitive bodies hang like ghosts in our closets, daring us to believe in their power to make or break us, daring us to appropriate them as if they were human skins. Alas, poor Yorick, fashion turns death into an artwork. It is not a species but the genus of *memento mori*.[43] Decapitation necklaces and skull paperweights precede the melancholic allure of The Munsters, but all wear vulnerability like aged denim. McQueen—who once posed resting his hands on a skull, while a cigarette languidly dangled from his mouth—said of his own work, "I like to think of myself as a plastic surgeon with a knife. ... But ultimately ... to transform mentalities more than the body ... It's almost like putting armor on a woman" (Bolton 2011: 44). But what does fashion armor you against? The danger remains unspecified: public scrutiny? The horror of being human? There is a nagging suspicion it cannot be solely the elements—that would be the province of those atomic clothes whose original whereabouts can only be traced as far as the fibers of parchment.

McQueen's countless fantastical designs incorporated such things as ethereal gowns made out of fresh flowers and politically charged collections like "Highland Rape" (a mix of Scottish tartan and war-torn English lace). Among McQueen's armored muses was avid fashion lover and heiress to the Guinness Brewery, Daphne Guinness. A year after McQueen's death, Guinness unveiled her collaboration with jewelry designer Shaun Leane: a chainmail glove. The glove was not your ordinary piece of armor; it was magnificently crafted out of 18-carat gold with a diamond-encrusted exterior. The design also included birds to symbolize freedom from the material world (you know, from gold and diamonds). Guinness said she wanted to look like she had been in a "very chic road wreck" (Steele 2011: 83). She meant, partly, that she wanted to look composed, even though she'd just been hit by a car. But she also meant that she wanted to actually look like she'd been hit by a car: mortally wounded, yet serenely untouched. Road wreck chic, fatal femme *fatale*. It sounds as if an armored glove would make her Christ. There are others, too, who use fashion statements to bear witness to some mystical purpose, like the holy spirit of "Ye" (formerly "Kanye West") or the gospels of academic journals. But if we stay strictly in the realm of fashion for a moment, we notice that body no longer means body. Instead, body is the wafer you eat when you take communion. Body means memorial to body—body bag, Body Glove. Christ, the wafer in the flesh, is a fusion of the low and the high, a transfiguration of Rag & Bone's "distressed" denim. "Distressed" fabric is already an absurd notion. What can it mean for clothes to be stressed out? You can buy denim pre-stressed, too, for a high premium, so you don't have to suffer through living with it. Distressed denim sounds like a battered sail, never mind that there is a tank top that goes by the name "wife beater." This did not originate in Marlon Brando's look in *A Streetcar Named Desire* (1951), but likely from James Hartford, Jr., who beat his wife to death and whose mugshot in a bloodstained tank appeared in newspapers with the caption, "The Wife Beater" (1947).

The vintage scene reduces the anxiety of the "now" by occupying itself with a variety of decades.[44] Instead of being of their time, vintage fashionistas are from another time. In investing yourself in a piece of experienced clothing, you can take on the look of being aged and experienced without having aged or experienced. You can then find yourself out of the court of this era's fashion judgments, though it is tricky, since the past's looks sometimes recall bad sentiments. "A 'deformed thief,' Shakespeare calls it: fashion takes from the past not to redress a lack, not to dress its naked body, but needlessly, excessively, and as a result emerges misshapen, a monstrous fabrication" (Nagel and Wood 2010: 89).

Mortal denim is one of many death-bound trends that reveal the self in its outstanding reality. The cross pendant is the predecessor to the Louis Vuitton purse (LV; IHS). This is a new agelessness by way of the faux signs of aging. The Tiktok teen who started the trend of drawing bags under the eyes posted the video to a remix of the song "Greek Tragedy" by the Wombats. Because when you look sleep deprived, you get that romantic Antigone look: tormented, insomniac, dissociated. Bee-stung lips and mental illnesses are also cool on Tiktok.[45] And something called "Dark Academia Fashion," an autumnal boarding-school vibe with a touch of goth and an antiquarian book under the arm. College sweatshirts are no longer enough. One article suggests pairing this "intellectual look" with handwritten notes and a rolled-up map: Harry Potter meets *Cruel Intentions*. I don't think Gen Z has made enough of a tiger's leap. They should do more research.[46]

During the Terror of the French Revolution, relatives of guillotine victims wore red ribbons around their necks—pointing to where the blade struck—to protest the executions. The high-fashion "chokers" became associated with so-called *bals des victimes*, dances for the afflicted families. "Choker" is an interesting moniker for a necklace. It slowly chokes you; you are a breathless fashion victim, mortally, shabbily, heartbreakingly chic. The guillotine ribbons demonstrate something fashion is rather good at—making pointed statements with no words. Causes are color-coded to draw attention to them: pink for breast cancer or rainbow for gay pride. Fashion is here armor not against nature in general, but human nature in specific. For goths in mourning clothes when no one has died, or even the little black dress, there is a bristling irony that all fashion, even when it guards (diplomatically) against frostbite, cannot help but be a public endeavor. For not only do our clothes channel personalities that alter the impressions we make on others, they also change our impressions of ourselves. If you imagine that you look good, you emit a confidence that can make you actually look good. Diogenes' raggedy cloak was in his mind a lion skin. It was all about *how* he wore it. This is the *fashion* that supersedes all fashions, where psychology bleeds into the body language of clothes. Clothing throws in our face a cacophony of stereotypes, bold-faced and cruel, alluring and deceitful, suggestive and sometimes very accurate. In this, it also reveals something about the irrational way in which we are both ruled by and suspicious of our mortal armor.

Half-mortal Achilles was destined to die like a human; he was outfitted with supernatural abilities, complete with a high heel. At the beginning of the *Iliad*, Achilles has a rift with Agamemnon, the leader of the Greek army, over a girl, Briseis, whom Achilles took as plunder from the Trojans. Agamemnon wants to take this "prize" away because he had to give his own girl back in order to avoid a plague (he had taken the daughter of a priest). Achilles—believing that he is more deserving of reward than Agamemnon—refuses to give up Briseis. At one point he even lunges at Agamemnon, and the goddess Athena has to (invisibly) pull his long hair back to stop him. Agamemnon ends up taking the girl away anyway. Achilles throws a tantrum, and refuses to fight. This is terrible for the Greeks, because they will lose to the Trojans without Achilles' model fighting. To make matters worse, Achilles' mother Thetis tells him that if he stays to fight, he will die young and win glory, whereas if he goes home, he will live a long life without notoriety. This doesn't seem to be a fair choice, since both options end in death. Achilles comes up with a solution that seems to solve both his personal and political problems: he decides to send his beloved Patroclus into battle wearing his armor. This allows him to fight without fighting. Achilles imagines that the mere image of his armor will have the same effect as himself, so that anyone who sees even a fake Achilles will be scared stiff, as if the body inside the armor were irrelevant.

If looks could kill: dressed as Achilles, Patroclus (who is referred to as "gentle") kills more Trojans than anyone else on the Greek side, including the actual Achilles. Patroclus describes Achilles as *amêchanos* ("impossible," 16.29); wearing his armor, he is "equal to a divinity" (16.705). But Patroclus is killed by Hector, and thereafter, Achilles goes on a murderous and guilt-ridden rampage. In his final face-off with Hector, he confronts an odd image. Hector is wearing the armor that he stripped from Patroclus, which is, of course, Achilles' own. Achilles ends up battling his avatar; his true enemy is himself. This is Homer's way of depicting anger as driven by guilt. Even after Thetis' ultimatum (*pace* Zeus), Achilles is still looking for a way to save face. To armor an image with the power of the self is not possible without gutting it. If only our images could have lives of their own and fight for us, while we bow out of the battlefield without anyone being the wiser. This seems to be the perspective from which the Olympians observe mortal actions. While gods may seem far removed from contemporary problems, they are really a more magnificent version of our attempt to write our public fate and face (book). Zeus' power is shown by his nodding with his "dusky eyebrows" and shaking Olympus with a toss of his "ambrosial hair," a cosmetic and cosmic motion. Gods are the ultimate beauty icons. Perhaps this is why we refer to egregiously beautiful people as "divas" (related to the word "divine"). Gods are human armor against chance; but our fabric armor, whether a designer glove or intentionally ripped, "mortal" jeans, reveals divine incompleteness—theirs and ours.

Homer does not leave us hanging in this regard. He also gives us a divine mortal who is nothing but armor—Paris. Paris stole Helen away from her husband Menelaus, and this started the whole war. Before Paris fights Menelaus, Homer gives this description of his outfit:

> But shining Alexandros [Paris] put his fine armor upon his broad shoulders,
> he, the husband of Helen of the lovely hair,
> First he strapped the splendid greaves around his shins,
> fitted with silver bindings around his ankles;
> next he girt about his chest a breastplate,
> his brother Lykaon's, but it fitted him;
> across his shoulders he slung his bronze sword
> studded with silver; and then his great strong shield.
> Over his powerful head he placed his well-forged helmet
> with flowing horsehair, and terribly the crest nodded over it.
> He took his strong spear, fitted to his hand.
>
> (3.328–39)

Not Paris' usual leopard skin dress. Homer finishes the description by saying, "And in this way too did warlike Menelaos also arm." So Paris' outfit gets described in incredible detail, while Menelaus gets one measly line. Though elsewhere Menelaus' armor gets more attention, it is ignored here just as Paris will seem to ignore Menelaus.

The battle itself turns out like this: Menelaus hits Paris' shield but doesn't hurt Paris. Menelaus then almost strangles Paris with his "elaborately embellished" chinstrap (nice detail), but Aphrodite swoops in, and causes the fabric to rip. Then, just to be safe, she also decides to make Paris disappear, much to the confusion of Menelaus. Disguised as a wool-weaver (and having pulled the wool over Menelaus' eyes), Aphrodite whisks Paris away to Helen's bedroom, where Helen is also weaving.[47] When Aphrodite arrives, she says, "Come here; Alexandros summons you home; / he is there, in his bedroom, on his bed that is inlaid with rings, / shining in beauty and raiment—you would not think / that he came from fighting a man, but rather that he was going / to a dance, or had just left the dance and was reclining" (3.390–5). Helen goes in and tells Paris that he must challenge Menelaus again, to which Paris replies that he has never desired more to make love to her. Meanwhile, the Greeks interpret Paris' disappearance as Menelaus' victory.

From one perspective, Paris' outfit is so perfectly sewn that who he is becomes naturally invisible. What he's wearing is quite literally *divine*. On the other hand, he clearly would've died if Aphrodite hadn't taken him out of the fight. Paris may be divinely knit but he's also a knitwit. He is *all* armor and no content. By wearing protection he admits he is vulnerable to attack; yet because it is so ornate and beautiful, he seems not to take fighting very seriously. War is just a dance that you do before you make love. This is either because you are very powerful or because you are very foolish.

In a later passage, Hector reaches out toward his son, Astyanax, while still clad in his armor. Astyanax moves away in fright, "crying at the sight of his dear father, disturbed and confused at the helmet and its crest of horse-hair, thinking it nodding terribly (*deinon*) from the uppermost helm" (6.466–70). Hector's son does not recognize his father inside his armor, and this makes him cry out as if he were beholding a strange being. Or rather, is the disappearance of human vulnerability itself a bewildering (*deinon*) image that makes us cry out? Casual looks are modern armor designed to defend us from passersby. So, too, will the Dandy's look of being perfectly "put together" or "composed" both repel and challenge others to a duel. But self-consciousness is a terrible roadblock; either you must murder your voyeuristic self or you must use a cloak and dagger.

What Is Not: Hair

As clothing ebbs and flows with changes of body, hair and its style and texture seem somewhat more constant. When you are naked, hairstyles remain the crown of your silhouette. Hair grows all over the body, too, and its growth—much faster than wrinkles—signifies what you have been as if it were what you are (one thinks of Aristotle's definition of essence as "what it was to be," *Metaphysics* 1029b). This makes baldness an interesting phenomenon, and Critchley's ode to the bald head—literal and literary, "hairless and blunt"—bares mentioning: "The baldness that I want to emphasize here consists in not waiting for your mother to buy you a hat but sticking your head out of the window nonetheless ... As an academic, one gets used to speaking with a lot of protective headgear, which one can arrange into an elaborate scholastic toupee" (Critchley 2021: 8). Maybe this explains that strange passage at *Republic* 454c, where Socrates suggests that bald and haired (*komētas*) are inconsequential to the nature of the shoemaker—in Greek, *koman*, "to hair" or "to plume," can metaphorically mean, "to put on airs."[48]

Unlike clothing, hair suggests that it needs to be dealt with. According to hair impresario Anthony Barrow, "Hairdressing is the oldest profession, second only to prostitution."[49] "Dressing" hair reverses the natural order of events: hair first presents itself, and only then becomes subject to combs.

Even people who have no stylistic vision are aware that a hair change will at some point be required of them: a trim, a shave, the thought—however controversial—of coloring your grays. More minimal possibilities easily entangle an unsuspecting victim. Tying back, braiding, and wrapping all awaken the opportunity to resist or tame natural growth. And while hair color, too, is of interest, especially when it is dyed, the mere *fact* of hair, as well as the fact that clothing is itself made of hairs, deserves treatment. Hair is the shadow of clothing's shadow. It is textile, the original "skin" out of which the second skin of fabric is woven (from fur, pelts, wool, cashmere, silk, or the bushy fibers of plants, such as burlap, hemp—or fig leaves), just as a text is woven out of the fibers of words.[50] More than clothing, hair exposes our deaths, since it is a secretion of deadness coiling about our persons, the sign of time's having already passed. To cut it is to stave off the impression of how long we've actually lived. How strange that we nurse it with vitamins as if it were alive and wince about split ends, since hair is, like nails, bloodless.[51]

We can shave our hair wherever it grows, but unless we laser it all off, it *will* grow back. The "negative" impression of our experience returns again and again. In some cases, the more we take to the scissors, the more fully it revisits us. Hair also seems connected, at least by way of image, to animality. The hairier the person, the more some natural coat appears, hearkening back to the remnants of our pre-Promethean existence, or whatever. This is easily romanticized by fashion theorists; but fur was long ago already the sign of an otherness as well as a kinship with animals. That we now cull animal skins into bags and hats or produce faux versions of their fur only reproduces the closeness of our distance from them. The story of our animal emergence—the history of our coming to not just be in but to put on skin—is a history only thinkable obliquely, which is to say always through time and so never in real time.[52] Hair, then, strikes out on two counts: it brings to the fore our creaturely features and showcases our aging. Even premature balding freaks us out as if some piece of the self suddenly had eroded, never to return.

The hairlessness of childhood appears as if it might be the remedy. But it is all so matted: how are we to make sense of the fact that some people will not hesitate to wax or pluck their bodies into a hairless preteen state, but are terrified of cutting the hair on their heads or breaking a nail? Is genital hair more offensive since its absence goes together with the absence of the generative powers that come with age? Hair is a shape atop your shape, an outfit that, unless tamed, seems to have a mind of its own. In Plato's *Parmenides* a young Socrates reluctantly concludes that, in addition to perfect ideas of beautiful things, such as the good and the just, there must also be perfect ideas of worthless and ugly things, such as "hair, mud, and dirt" (130c-d). Hair is mortal mud, bodily dirt. It seems to signal feelings of being unkempt or uncivilized. In Adrian Piper's ongoing exhibition, *What Will Become of Me?*, she collects her hair and nails in jars (and has been doing so since 1985). This will continue until her death when her ashes will also be displayed in a jar. These clippings of the self now become idealized dirt, a strange *alter* piece to the decomposition of her/our form. Dirty hair or slept-in hair has also acquired its own idealization. Hair shares in common with dirt (and mud, which is just wet dirt) a graininess that is more construable in a large sum than bit by bit. It can be muddy or grimy, depending on what kind of hair day it is or if you use certain hair products. Hair is partly individualized according to person, and partly impossible to understand individualistically. Without the face or body, and without more than a few strands, it would be too decontextualized to suggest its identity as "hair." It seems to be a particular brand of generality—a natural coat that slimes all over everything as if insatiate or that is so dry and needy as to prevent any traction at all. In both Greek and Latin, the word for "hair" is "hairs" plural, as in English the collective whole and the individual pieces are treated as a single herd. Such cosmetic communism is interesting because of the connection between hair and character: the finely curated mob versus the mad scientist with too many hairs out of place. There is a phrase, *ad unguem* in Latin or *ep' onychos* in Greek, which means, "to a nail," or "to a hair," and so, "exactly," "perfectly."

Hair's kinship to *vestis*, "vestment," may be its most striking feature. Hair grows out of us as if *naturally* trying to detach; and we treat it as a garment we "wear." Hair's similarity to clothing is easier to see if it is extended, and certainly more impressive this way, just as a floor-length fur coat is a more striking pinion than a wool sweater vest. Hair also suggests race, ethnicity, and personality. Shorter hair may carry connotations of bravery: you are willing to sacrifice your face to the public gaze. Long hair, on the other hand, goes with safety. But why did Artemis tie her hair up while hunting, instead of cutting to the chase and chopping it off, which would have been simpler? The Spartan lawgiver Lycurgus claimed that long hair would make the handsome more beautiful, and the ugly more frightful.[53] But Medusa's hair, which is composed of live snakes, is a handsome fright. Beauty can be hair-raising.[54] In Herodotus' *Histories*, the Spartans are seen exercising and combing their hair before the battle of Thermopylae. "This is their *nomos*: that when they are going to risk their soul, they order (*kosmein*) their heads" (7.209). Perhaps it is simply thinking ahead—what if you are beheaded? In ancient Rome, the heads of enemies were installed on platforms in the forum. Bodies may look alike; but heads are particular. Hair makes everything more dramatic with its ups and downs, and parts and waves. It lures you in, while keeping you at a distance, since it itself is only a numb link to the person to which it is attached. In Plato's *Timaeus*, hair is said to protect the *en-cephalon*, literally, what is "in the head" (76d1). But what exactly is in the head? Hair shelters the innards as if a thatch roof. It can therefore also encrypt. In Herodotus, Histiaeus gives word to Aristagoras to revolt by tattooing the head of his most loyal slave and letting his hair grow over it; the shaving of his head will then reveal the secret message (5.35.3). But long hair is risky—Periander advised Thrasybulus to cut down the tallest of his "crops" (5.92).[55] That the height of your leaves should be a metaphor for your status was especially true in eighteenth-century France, where hair height was synced with societal function. High hair seems better than a high crown because its girth is yielded by a natural phenomenon. "No crown is simpler than the simple hair" (Wallace Stevens, "To the One of Fictive Music").

The Bible is full of barbed hair tales. In the New Testament, you find that

> a man ought not to cover his head, since he is the image (*eikôn*) and glory (*doxa*) of God, but woman is the glory (*doxa*) of man ... Does not even nature itself teach you that, if a man should have long hair, it is dishonorable for him? But if a woman should have long hair, it is a glory (*doxa*) to her: for her hair is given her for a covering.
>
> (Cor. 11:14)

"Nature" is apparently responsible for a hairline distinction between the sexes. But, doesn't hair *naturally* grow at about the same rate on both men and women? The word *doxa* is translated as "glory," but in earlier Greek it means "opinion."[56] We get the word "dogma" from it, and its root *dok-* means "to seem" (related to the English word "decorous").[57] As seeming or opinion, *doxa* masks what is, like a veil. Hair is the most natural coat we own, the dogma of the self that grows out of us and into the world, the self's particular outlook, her habit, hirsute.

To be shaved is to go one step further than to be stripped. It is to have not just one's conventional coat but one's nature taken away.[58] In a letter to Magnus, St. Jerome compares matrimony to David beheading Goliath, and to the transformation of wisdom into a handmaiden by "shaving off and cutting away all in her that is dead whether this be idolatry, pleasure, error, or lust" (70). Letting nails and hair grow speeds up death and obscures truth. The longer they are, the more dirt they attract. Shaving and exfoliating are a mechanism of cleansing and reducing.

In Deuteronomy, we learn that when, "a captive woman has her head shaved, her eyebrows and all her hair cut off, and her nails pared, she might then be taken as wife" (21:10–13). Wives are captive rather than captivating; prim and trim, declawed of their natural weave, the textile that grows on their body, its dread locks. The Sheitel is a wig or half-wig worn by Hasidic Jewish women to cover their hair after they are married; meanwhile, in Leviticus 19:27, one finds the prohibition concerning men's side curls (*payot*). The reason for not cutting these curls is either not revealed, or carries implications of not appearing as an idol worshipper (indicated by shaving the hair between the forehead and the ears). In Ezekiel 44, there is a Goldilocks principle: men should neither shave their heads nor grow their hair too long. Esau's name might mean "Hairy" in Hebrew, at any rate he was. And in Judges, Samson's long hair is said to be the secret to his strength. Delilah first tries to braid it in order to control him, but it is only when she shaves it off that he weakens. When his hair grows back, he regains his force, and ends up crushing all of the Philistines and himself underneath a house.

The 1979 Iranian Revolution led to a series of dress codes for women, including that they must wear a veil. To hide the face seems a means to control the sight of the signature features of identification—the signs of human presence as a subject rather than an object. We do not so much distinguish by bodies as by heads (*prosôpon* in Greek means "face" or "countenance," literally, "what faces or is looked toward").

In Plato's *Phaedo*, Socrates runs his fingers through Phaedo's long hair, saying that "Tomorrow, Phaedo, you will cut off this beautiful hair" (89b4–5). Though Phaedo is a man, he stands for a woman. Socrates' death scene contains a cast of characters that mirrors those present during Theseus' voyage to slay the Minotaur. Phaedo is Plato's characterization of Ariadne, the longhaired lady who helped untangle the Minotaur's labyrinth by leading Theseus through with a ball of thread, only to later run away with Dionysus. Phaedo will cut his hair, but only after he leads Socrates through a maze of arguments, and then abandons him in his death. That Phaedo and his long hair are as unreliable as Ariadne is clear from Plato's very words. Plato goes out of his way to have Phaedo announce that "Plato" may have been absent at Socrates' death (he was perhaps "sick," 59b10). That is to say that it is Phaedo (the namesake of the dialogue) and his wooly opinion that are responsible for fleecing Socrates. What is preserved is not Plato's version of events, but Phaedo's dogmatic alteration. Elsewhere in the *Cratylus*, *logos* ("speech") itself is said to be either the brother or son of Hermes, in the form of double-natured Pan, who is "smooth from above, while shaggy from below and goat-like (*tragoeidês*)" (408d1–2).

When the ancient Egyptians mourn their dead, they "let the hair on their head and beard go," though at all other times they are shaved and wear only linen, newly washed (Hdt. 2.36–7). The women have one garment; the men two. Priests shave their bodies every day, and clothes need to be washed as hair would be shaved. It is only the fact of death that causes the Egyptians to leave their own dead hairs untreated. Among the academic set, shorter hair seems to imply that you are less high maintenance and closer to Ockham's razor. The Anna Wintour shortcut, on the other hand, is seriously slick, like Uma Thurman in *Pulp Fiction* or Natalie Portman in *The Professional.* Medium-length hair remains as safely neutral as blue jeans, unless it is chopped against a vista of overdone crops and lengthy layers. Hairstyles and their significations, however much they put on airs, are deeply relative. "With punk, a brand-new axis opened up: professionally cut ↔ hacked about by a brainless cretin … 'Hacked about by a brainless cretin' became not the death of hair-styling but the furthest outpost of a new continuum of possible choices about how hair could look" (Eno 2020: 312–13).

Lady Godiva grew her hair very long to cover her nudity, much to the detriment of a Peeping Tom. In Aristotle's *Nicomachean Ethics*, nail biting and pulling out your own hair are listed along with cannibalism among the "unnatural pleasures" (1149aff). To pick away at the self is to self-destruct, to pervert nature, to behave like a monster. Alexander the Great figured out that long hair was a detriment in battle, since persons can be easily captured, if the enemy grabs their hair or beard. During the Vietnam War, there were protests against long hair by anti-hippies (with slogans such as "long hair is communism"), while buzz cuts were polarizing, because they signified the draft. The "Depression Era bob," made popular by Irene Castle in 1915, originated when Irene cut her hair to avoid it being fussed about when she got an appendectomy. Short hair was up until the Castle Bob considered inelegant and coarse. In 1920, F. Scott Fitzgerald published a short story, "Bernice Bobs Her Hair," in which the main character wrestles with bluffing about "bobbing your hair" versus the effect of actually doing so, which is a kind of societal castration. Short hair was associated with being a liberated woman; for Bernice, it means freeing herself from being manipulated by convention. It was Louise Brooks who transformed the bob into a party look.

In the 2019 film, *I'm No Longer Here*, the main character Ulises (a new Odysseus) sports a distinctive hair style, recognizable in the Monterrey subculture of *cumbia* (itself borrowed from Kolombia, spelled with a K), but foreign in Queens where it defines him as an outsider. In 2021, eyebrow cuts revisited us from their '90s heyday (courtesy of Big Daddy Kane), and middle parts became the sign of youth. The factitiously titled "divisive hair part," parting your hair on the side rather than in the middle, was dubbed passé and too millennial by Gen Z.[59] That millennials think the side-part is cute identifies them as partisans of the wrong party: move to the middle, taunts Gen Z, in between the left and the right.

I want to talk about blonds, too, but god knows what people will think. There is a book, *On Blondes*, by Joanna Pitman that follows the history of blond hair from antiquity onward through its various stages, where it has been used to suggest everything from vapidity to prostitution to racial superiority. The term "blond" has been saddled with connotations of the word "White" and Nietzsche's nebulous "blond beast"; it carries the baggage of both purity and impurity, timidity and boldness. But you don't even need Disney to find the wicked queen and the innocent ingénue portrayed as the difference between dark and light hair. Dip-dyed hair color has gone in and out of style, but color needs "much more detail than dark ↔ light. It needs an axis of redness, an axis of greyness, an axis of colour homogeneity, an axis of shine" (Eno 2020: 313). There lurks here an idea about pigments, and one that seems to vacillate with time and hair dye. The ancient Greek poet Menander wrote, "no moderate woman should make her hairs yellow" (Fragment 610). Menander's view came from the association of blonde hair with hookers (though blonde was then more akin to strawberry blonde). The Virgin Mary was, at least for a time, safely brunette.

In the thirteenth and fourteenth centuries, Eve is consistently portrayed as a blonde for Menander's same reasons, while in ancient Rome, blonde hair was so desirable that women dyed their hair with pigeon dung; in Venice, they used horse urine. Our current blond stereotypes are rather freely associated: from Barbie and California surfers to Nikki Minaj and Elle Woods. For less than ten bucks, you can give yourself hair that is buoyant and light or dark and mysterious. The raven-haired beauty versus the blonde bombshell? Blonds apparently have more fun, and as Edith Piaf's "Le Brun et le Blond" suggests, brunettes are apparently more serious. Is it always society that makes us want to dye our hair or is it the hope that our internal gravity might be depicted, that our personalities might morph, if we frame our features in just the right light?

A foamy afro, dreadlocks, silvery swathes, pigtails, visible roots. Hair is a text we cannot escape reading or writing. It comes right out of the head, like Athena from Zeus. It sprouts up already with a tone and a rhythm, taking its curly cues from the poetry of the self, regardless of whether you have recently had a close shave or never been cut. Even wigs and toupees are intended to simulate a growth, whether with natural neon or sorrow-tinted black. Blondie made blonde hair with dark roots cool, Cruella de Vil style. Cherishing your roots is somehow the sign that you have a *past*—that you are not the perfect royalty of fairytales. Mulan needed to cut her hair so she could sneak into the army. *Tangled*'s Rapunzel—with auburn hair—is the only one who figured out that untangling the knot was a lot harder than just cutting it off. Her hair tethered her to an ivory tower; when she nixed it (at least in the cartoon), she was emancipated. Snow White's hair is short and dark, but it is more of a 1950s coif than a real bob—a fashion that apparently held sway for women at that time (Pitman 2003: 129).

In a cartoon, of course, whatever length or color the hair, it obeys laws because it is fiction. It does not seem possible to animate—or even to paint—ugly hair. For computer animators, the trouble is specific. Hair plays with light in a way that has no formula or order. It moves simultaneously as one crowd and as individual fibers, partly like the reflection of inanimate metal and partly like the irregular flicker of fire. Hair is stranded between unmoving objects and highly motive facial contortions: dead as a still life and lively as a secret. Nails part ways with hair here, though they are made of the same substance, keratin (from the Greek *keras*, "horn"). It is much easier, and less costly, to get a set of false nails than a set of false hairs, and no one bothers to worry that the nails are not real. Real hair extensions, on the other hand, are arguably better than fake. They can easily cost thousands of dollars, especially when the hair comes from India, where people shave their heads for money, a sign that hair is at once valuable and worthless.

The hair on the head seems to be a conduit to the holy, even a sacrifice made in the hope of changing your fate. In Hinduism, Shiva's depiction with locked hair carries religious significance. Sikhs, on the other hand, wear turbans to protect their long hair, out of deference to divine creation. While the turban wasn't originally gendered, it has come to have male connotations, and stereotypes concerning femininity likewise abound. How hair is treated seems to have to do with subduing the natural: to let things grow untouched, the way they were "intended," or to assert there are certain procedures which, if followed, will lead to good fortune.

Stream-of-consciousness grooming (or lack thereof) is the custom among some parts of Islam and among the Amish, except with respect to facial hair. Hair covers you up to such an extent that you become locked away, a captive of God's thoughts rather than your own whims. Hare Krishnas, on the other hand—puns on their name notwithstanding—shave all of their hair off except a single knotted lock, which functions as a handle connecting them to God. God pulls you upward by means of your hair. Achilles' lovely locks, too, behave as a divine wire for Athena's touch (*Iliad* 1.199–200). The communication is indirect but formless, not requiring her to adopt a shape. Hair as both alive and dead negatively images the immortally mortal. The bloodless blood that Aphrodite bleeds when she is wounded in battle can only be like the pain of a bad haircut (5.339).

Horace's *Carmina* 1.6 contains these cryptic lines:

We sing banquets, we <sing> battles
Of sharp virgins with cut nails on young men,
We, idle, in whatever way we burn
Not beyond custom, or light.

"We" means "we lyric poets"; we who are in this poem are said not to write epic or tragedy—that is, in the style of the Greeks. Instead, we lyric poets sing of light subjects, like banquets and love affairs. This is Horace as Danielle Steele. But we know he cannot be telling the whole truth, since he writes his Latin poetry in Greek meter, and announces that fact in another poem (3.30). Also, the above stanza is peppered with oxymoronic language: maidens are "fierce" or "sharp" with their "cut nails"; we burn "idle" or "empty." Is Horace describing the acute power of poetry?

Poetry is both feeble and incendiary. It appears as if it were innocuous and unarmed, an act that does not seem to act but rather merely to simulate. It is like a maiden with cut nails. But in this seeming innocence its figure is sharpened. It conflagrates a new trend (we lyric poets do something different) and normalizes it as standard (not beyond custom). Cutting hair or nails is here a metaphorical experience of weakening, which has the effect in poetry of renewed strength. We meet in hair the fear of time negating us as a natural extension, before it is woven into that negation of the negation that is our clothes. But clever as we are in meeting the uncanny, we cut, alter, and sew ourselves back together. We, idle, in whatever way we burn, not beyond custom, or light.

4

The Dandy

Human beings give more attention to that song,
whichever comes round to the listeners as newest.[1]

—Homer, Odyssey 1.351–2

You're so vain, you probably think this song is about you.

—Carly Simon, "You're So Vain"

It would be a mistake to separate fashion from movement—its pull on the body is like the rhythm or pattern of a song that lures you into moving to the beat, even when you don't want to and even when you don't know or like the song. Fashion is linked to rhythm in both style and flair, neither of which admit of being imitated perfectly without the jazz of improv. "Fashion is like music," chirped Karl Lagerfeld, "there are so many notes ... You need to play around with them"—or, more dramatically, fashion demands that you strike a pose, an attitude, compulsory free play (2013: 35). If the Academy snubs its nose at fashion, in doing so it derides rhythm as if it meant reverence to rhetoric, attempting to seduce with cadence and air rather than to prove by cheerless argument. Fashion is in this way *heard* more than it is *seen*. It comes to be as thinking comes to be—by stirring up études of wonder—and tone deafness in this regard proves fatal.

> The virtue of the wondrous lies in experiencing it, in seeing the sunset or hearing the fugue or being moved by the beat. And the virtue of the artist lies in creating an experience that either participates in the wonder of its subject—a painting of a sunset, say—or that inspires reverence in its own right—the fugue, the dance. The virtue of the philosopher, by contrast, seems to lie in acting out "the rime of the ancient mariner," which is to say, in pinning things down and analyzing the life out of them.
>
> (Taylor 2016:158)

Since *nomos* as custom also means something like "song," and the same is true of "mode" (which can refer to a musical mode), the transformation of wonder into analytic appreciation sounds like the transformation of human beings from political animals into political scientists. Phenomenological analyses build the experiential back into experience, but high scholarly discourse remains more visual than auditory. The more auditory it becomes the less clear it is that it is channeling something that can be acquired by skill. Herein lies my own quarrel in writing an academic book with the double entendre of satire, for the Academy lives on the noble lie that its knowledge is both formulaic and exceptional (the fusion of these two adjectives lies perilously in fashion's wheelhouse). Deliberately telling lies is another business entirely, that of fiction, of which you can only partake by first sounding an alarm bell. Rogue musing is lost on the tin ear of the high-brow. To be sure, academics go to dive bars and rock concerts—they go among *hoi polloi*—but they do so often clad in the pretension of a momentary loss of pretension. It is not so easy to tell the difference between dressing down and proving one's intellectual worth. Wherefrom did the Academy acquire its sense of its toneless tone? When did it toss aside the warfare of wit? Academics hate being teased. They are quite earnest about what they do and bothered by the jester that might sneak up and criticize them with an imperceptible smirk or tussling of the hair. The Dandy turns about, takes a drag of esoteric poetry, and blows down the house of cards that calls itself respectable discourse. How intoxicating and damning it is to think that with the tilt of a hat (or the turn of a graduation tassel) whole genres might be refuted: "Oh! You Pretty Things" (Bowie, 1971). Zeus furrows his brow. But perhaps this is not the dandy my reader is used to.

As a species of contemporary fashion, dandies are thought to be ostentatious, flamboyant, and flanked with every hue of frippery. However, "dandy" in its original sense refers to something far more obscure, where even the word itself vanishes into etymological smoke. In *Du Dandysme et de G. Brummell* (*On Dandyism and G. Brummell*), Jules-Amédée Barbey d'Aurevilly announces that the word "dandy" is decidedly not French. In truth, the word might well derive from the French verb, *dandiner*, "to waddle," but Barbey d'Aurevilly (hereafter, "Barbey") wishes to deny that the French understand the "Dandy" at all.[2] The English are dandier. This is partly because the Dandy can only be a foreigner; *hapax* that he is, he cannot be translated. Even the Dandy's sex is "undecidedly intellectual," hermaphroditic, neither man nor woman (1845/1988: 78). "He" is no noun but wit itself.[3]

The Dandy is vain. But not in the usual sense. He gathers his vanity from a rejection of vanity, annoyed as he is by appearing to have spent more than a few minutes getting dressed. In this, he seems to capture Count Baldessar's *sprezzatura*. The Dandy does not try, but springs out of the womb of the dressing room fully clothed. He is stylishly virtuous in his rejection of striving or aiming at the mean; the Dandy simply is the mean—in excess. Contrived honesty doesn't look as good as honest vanity. Anyway, why is it so desirable to look un-vain? To this, the Dandy has a clever response—no silver spoons and fine china, but an elegant fuck you, worn with elite panache of someone who bothers not with rank or status. He need not be of the elite to walk among them; he merely styles himself as such by appearing in the right place at the right time. More than anything, the Dandy is about style, curation, *la mode*. He is anti-fashion done fashionably.

As a modern movement, dandyism is supposed to have emerged from George Bryan ("Beau") Brummell, whose heyday lasted from about 1794 to 1816. But the picture will prove more mysterious. Brummell himself was like Paris Hilton, famous for being famous: an accidental star whose celebrity did not seem to hinge on any of his particular attributes. In fact, Brummell had no peculiar talent to recommend him aside from his manner of tying his cravat. He was not a literary genius. He had no political station. He was of neither noble birth nor exceeding wealth. He was not even a nice man—he traveled by sedan chair and despised "common" people. Yet, in spite of his lack of historical resume or agreeable temperament, Brummell's name adorns countless memoirs and his image has been reincarnated in every guise from Quentin Crisp to Adam Ant. For Brummell, the lack of any legitimate claim to fame seems to have been the key to the lasting power of his influence. That is to say, in being solely a man of influence, he was the essence of a man, and not a man. This made his legacy far less touchable and far less mortal.

To Wit

It is said of Brummell that he "used to stand for a few minutes at the door of the ballroom, glance round, criticize it in a sentence, and disappear, applying the famous maxim of Dandyism: 'In society, stop until you have made your impression, then go'" (48–9). In other words, stop before you become relatable, because then you can be criticized and judged. It is when people think they know you that you lose your *esprit*. *Esprit* means wit or humor or fun, or all three combined. "To have wit" can mean to have humor or to have mind. It is as untranslatable as the Dandy. Barbey does not translate *wit* into French, and Ainslie does not translate *esprit* into English, for the moment one word wears the clothes of another it loses its mystique. *Wit* is the very *je ne sais quoi*—the dandy fashion—of all speech. And yet speech, and history, too, tends to sap words and personae of wit in order to reduce them to factual and relatable threads. In the vitae of historical clothes, history misses what makes human beings breathe. Does the context in which a person lives, their birth, their career, or monuments left behind tell us who they really were? Or don't such monuments fall prey to the fate of Ozymandias?

In Quentin Crisp's preface to the 1988 edition of *Dandyism*, Crisp distinguishes Barbey as a dandy in the highest sense of the word, which is to say, by the wit of his words, which fly off the page in multi-colored ink (here, metaphorically; elsewhere, literally). Brummell and Barbey are a comic analogue to Alcibiades and Socrates, or rather, Alcibiades/Socrates and Plato. Brummell could not write; Barbey could. But Alcibiades was said to have been interested in Homer, and even to have composed a couplet as a witty repartee to the comic poet Eupolis. Alcibiades' poetic abilities may have even led him to tamper with the Homeric corpus to restore his favor with Endios, his Spartan friend whom he had tricked in order to incur favor with Athens.[4] Alcibiades was at least canny enough to rewrite a state text in order to please an opposing government.

At any rate, it is the historian's job to capture within lifeless words a life that must elude words. Barbey's words are therefore *pteroenta*, winged (17). Like the eagle of the mind and wit which hovers over life, it is Barbey's composition that captures Brummel's spirit—"Among biographies it is a dandy in the highest sense of the word" (11). It is charisma that inspires historians to make their inquiries—the song that seduces and moves people, the same sort of mode that characterized the oral tradition. The rhythm and tone with which one acts and speaks which is forced to follow the clothing of decency and grammar is not captured in words but intuited from the melody of the words strung together. Why does history always fail to capture *esprit*? In stating what has happened, almost as if it were fated and articulated as a rational process, history fails to explain the capriciousness by which the present becomes the past. The same could be said of causal accounts. But time's unceasing forward motion—fateless fate—rebels against history. Barbey thus writes to enthuse rather than recount; his charming presentation paradoxically records what cannot be recorded. As the embodiment of ahistorical caprice and seductive inspiration, the Dandy, too, defies time and place.

Dandyism was in Brummell's day a moderately audacious statement against ornate Napoleon Bonaparte fashion and English conservatism. It was dandyism's law-breaking attitude that allowed it to stay fresh. "While still respecting the conventionalities, [dandyism] plays with them. While admitting their power, it suffers from and revenges itself upon them, and pleads them as an excuse against themselves; dominates and is dominated by them in turn" (33). The Dandy breaks idols like Zarathustra with the cool indifference of Ferris Bueller. So the Dandy quietly subverts, not by means of any particular garment, but by means of his chill flare.

To see what this means we must follow Barbey's words. He presents his text as a "statuette" of a man who "does not deserve to be represented otherwise than by a statuette." He "dares not call it a book." It is "worthy a place in the bookshelf," which is to say, not perhaps worthy of being read (13). Or so Barbey announces in a dedicatory letter to his friend Monsieur César Daly at the Review of Architecture, to whom he offers the salty praise of being like Brummell in elegance, but unlike Brummell in being more intelligent. The statuette of a statuette is given as a "gift of friendship"—a reminder of "happier times" when Barbey saw Daly more often (14). It will arrive on the doorstep while Daly is traveling and his friends do not know where he is to be found. This seems to be a playful criticism of Daly's being so often away, but its tone is sharpened by the further remark that "Brummell does not belong to the political history of England, but he approaches it through his friendships of it" (13). So Barbey's friendly donation may also be of obliquely political interest. It is perhaps then no small thing that César Daly shares his name with the Roman *imperator* who transformed Rome from a republic to a dictatorship: Caesar.

The dedication, along with the format of the book itself, seems to follow the formula of Machiavelli's *The Prince*. Machiavelli, too, dedicates his expressly "brief" treatise to an unsuspecting victim with a facetiously high title, Lorenzo de' Medici (Duke of Urbino), whose family name signified the return of non-republican rule to sixteenth-century Florence. To Lorenzo, Machiavelli provides an unsolicited guidebook on how to avoid the pitfalls of princedom. Primarily, this involves not incurring the enmity of the people or the unexpected blows of fortune. However, in this "gift" of advice is the explicit warning never to take unsolicited advice. This, of course, means Machiavelli's book. The act of writing turns out to be in some way the act of ruling. From Machiavelli, one learns a dandy rule: the greatest rebels are elegantly rude. They do not raise protests or anarchist flags. If you wish your revolution to be substantial, you must command it with grace. You must write a witty text. You might be put in jail, tortured, and have your books burned, but this only confirms the pen's point.

For Barbey, the issue is not Italy but France. Dandyism is originally French, but more properly suited to the English because, "In France, originality has no country; it is deprived of fire and water, and hated like a nobiliary distinction" (50). We learn this in a footnote; and footnotes are the lifeblood of the Dandy. Barbey even dares to put a footnote within a footnote, while detailing how Brummell has a special artist for each finger of his gloves.[5] The footnotes perfectly tailor the author's hand to fit the subject. And the palace of the Dandy's body conceals a labyrinth of footnotes that lie in between the lines. The Dandy has as his most "general characteristic," the "unexpected." That is to say, his most general trait is that he defies generality. He embodies the fickleness of fortune. Brummell was "born to reign" and a "prince of his time" (75; 37); Ian Kelly deems him "once the most fashionable foreigner in France,"[6] while Barbey says that he "proved the truth of Machiavelli's maxim: 'The world belongs to the cool of head'" (45).

While Machiavelli's *Prince* ends with a call for a liberator of Italy—who, incidentally, has as his example, all of the foreign invaders of Italy—Barbey's book ends with the claim that "we may be certain that there will always be Dandies in England, whatever uniform the world may make them wear" (78). Dandies are like heroes: always needed and impossible to extinguish. But Barbey cannot mean an Englishman. The Dandy has no allegiance, except to his own dignity. He twiddles his thumbs at aristocrats with an aristocratic air. He wears convention with such an untouchable scent of perfection that he reduces it to shreds. Thus, while *Dandyism* seems to be a light book about a light man, Barbey is a Frenchman writing in French to a Frenchman, saying that "We French are not original; we ought to be more like the English." The subtext seems to have something to do with the French Revolution and its lingering aftereffects.

It is now worth quoting Benjamin more fully: "The French Revolution understood itself as Rome reincarnated. It cited ancient Rome as also fashion cites a past costume (*Tracht*). Fashion keeps to the hunt for the present-day (*das Aktuelle*), wherever it moves in the thicket of the once. It is a tiger's leap into the past" (1942/1980: 701). The "tiger's leap" is again not a leap of faith; it pounces out of the abyss at its prey, springing forth in this case to a destination that boomerangs. Fashion, sparkling in a tiger's skin, catapults into the then to trap the now. It has a revolutionary power that "carries inside it a powerful critique of historicism. It disregards the logical progression of linear time, finding a contemporaneity in the past that breaks through to the present" (Nagel 2004: 33).[7] The Dandy is then fashion's most revolutionary foil; he showcases antiquarianism with novelty, like a renovated altarpiece that conspicuously smacks of some undecipherable newness. Fashion quotes the past, and in quoting it, necessarily misquotes—for even when it brings the now into the now it cannot help but bring it into the now with exemplarity.[8]

In France, the post-Revolution dandies were called "Incroyables" or "Merveilleuses." They indulged in over-the-top luxury and frivolity as a response to the end of the Reign of Terror. The English dandy, however, was a cross between "terror and sympathy"; perhaps, the proper *incroyable*? He was less doodle and more dandy. He opposed moralism, in the form of the "horrible contagion" of Puritanism (Barbey 1845/1988: 56). Puritan morals are so tedious that they beg for a Dandy from the Underworld to surprise them, like the "hips of a dancing-girl" (34). But again, this does not mean that

France needed or needs a Brummell. The power of somebody like Brummell is not of the same stock as the power of someone who understands the power of Brummell—that is, Barbey d'Aurevilly. Dandyism is an intellectual phenomenon, and its author affects the aura of our gaze with sly missiles dispatched from just outside the doorway.

Brummell by the way was not smart. He looked smart because he had social intrigue. He only needed to stay long enough to leave his odor, since a whiff of the Dandy is like, "the finger of God acting through intelligence" (74). The Dandy acts via the disembodied aroma of the mind. As a divine medium, his non-localized potency puts him almost too easily in a position of power. He breaks the model with the model, for his enemy is the "mummy of religious feeling," even while he engenders a social piety that rivals the grace of God. Machiavelli's enemy, too, was not only the Medici rule in Florence, but also the rule of the Catholic Church in Italy. As the best prince will adapt to the times, as if he had his hand on the pulse of fate, so too is adaptability the trait of the Dandy. To elegantly displace a ruler, whether an "it" girl or a political persona, you must enlist the divine flourish of natural right. A dandy prince would never rob a Church. He would tastefully decapitate it with a blow of immortal wit. *God is dead.*

Brummell was not beautiful either. He bonded with the Prince of Wales at Eton over manners. He climbed the social ladder without struggle—"there was no rout or party where his presence was not regarded as a triumph, his absence a catastrophe" (59). In one case, Brummell was invited to a party at the Watier's Club instead of the Prince. Yet this is where the Dandy's danger lies. He has no connection to anybody and no political stakes; the extent of his power is without rational basis. Be very worried about the person who goes everywhere the prince goes and who looks princelier than the prince himself. The Dandy becomes even more influential, the fewer ties that bind him. As a free-floating entity—irrevocably foreign, and so, at home anywhere—even his clothing is wit itself. Whatever identity he puts on, he is always in fashion.

The Dandy's ability to avoid history now appears not a casualty of his air but critical to his essence. Since he has never done anything, he is never anyone's foe. Barbey characterizes the Dandy's social prowess as, "A singular tyranny without disgust"—a description that mimics the authority of the Holy Spirit (56). Even while you inhale the Dandy's transubstantial incense, he seems merely a holy wafer or neatly fashioned cravat. Is he but an outfit, destined to be scorned by the uninitiated for his ritualistic vanity? The Dandy stops at "the famous point of intersection of Pascal, between originality and eccentricity" (51). He is in between the problem of the infinite regress and the promise of solution, neither altogether naïve nor assertively tyrannical. He is not wedded to his cravat or his hat; but he is never without some accessory either. In another charming footnote, Barbey mentions that Lord Byron never wore a tie (and thank goodness, because he had a "beautiful neck"). It would be a mistake, then, to think that Dandies *had* to wear ties. Their only particular look is to overturn what's in fashion. Dandyism changes with the times, like fashion itself.

"It has been said, contemptuously enough, that the uniform must have had an irresistible attraction for Brummell. A dandy who marks everything with his personality, existing only through a kind of exquisite originality (Lord Byron), must of necessity hate uniform" (50). Here, Barbey invokes Lord Byron, and so takes on the uniform of his authority. But to appeal to Byron out of context is to challenge the function of authority. Benjamin's suggestion is that fashion makes this tiger's leap as an anti-rule rule. The Dandy is like a pun that undermines the uniformity of a word. Uniform—with its authority-soaked britches—with its partiality to a nation or group identity—tempts the Dandy's fashion all the more. This is because if you wear a uniform while not being part of the group, you can assert an indifference to the "cause" by mocking the very function of its armor. To wear a uniform like a dandy, you must divest a politically charged garment of its charge. The Dandy flies his own flag in his rude presentation of the prude; he manifests a disciplined daring. Since his independence is what makes him a dandy, there is no dandy dress code.

Nonetheless, without the Dandy's person posing in whatever uniform the world happens to legislate, his antinomianism remains dormant. Clothes cannot by themselves signify a rebel, though they are, once worn, already a foreign presence disallowing domesticity with the body. When we are feeling particularly dandy in our clothes, we may begin to take on their very air, as if they fit us exactly. But this is only an approximate apotheosis. The Dandy, too, is the impression left in his clothes, which must finally not fit, even in the face of all of his footnotes. The French could not combine tradition and rebellion into the Dandy; instead, they had a civil war. The proper response to authoritarian oppression, however, would have been to walk the line between impertinence and grace. Not to storm the Bastille but to mock its style.

> Like those philosophers, who raised up an obligation superior to the law, so the Dandies, of their own authority, make rules that shall dominate the most aristocratic and the most conservative sets, and with the help of wit, which is an acid, and of grace, which is a dissolvent, they manage to ensure the acceptance of their changeable rules, though these are in fact nothing but the outcome of their own audacious personalities.
>
> (42)

The Dandy and the philosopher share in common their seeming uselessness to society. They are both idlers, not because they do nothing, but because they do not serve any function the city can recognize. Yet concealed in their appearance of *far niente* and sweet *f.a.* lies the threat of thinking. Wit is the Dandy's greatest weapon. Its acidic grace manifests itself as bold indifference. Barbey lauds Alcibiades as the Dandy's supreme type for the most beautiful of nations, ancient Greece.

Alcibiades was notoriously handsome and unruly. In Plato's *Symposium* he appears rip-roaring drunk and wearing "a crown of thick leaves of ivy and violets" (212c–e). Violets, not Sappho's roses, are elsewhere the Muses' floral motif, and Alcibiades' erotic effects on Socrates seem a precursor for the danger he poses to the city. Unlike Brummell, who failed miserably in his attempt to become a soldier, Alcibiades embarked on a military career, however marred it was by his constant betrayal. He defected first from Athens to Sparta and then to Persia. Perhaps Socrates had no allegiance either, but his rebellious spirit was hemmed in by his pursuit of truth. The difference between Alcibiades and Socrates—the Dandy and the philosopher, beauty and the beast—seems to be equivalent to the difference between the sophist and the philosopher. Despite the Dandy's caprice, he is still infected by the puritan's dignity. His wit is easily displaced into frenzy—since wit is light, and, like *esprit*, it flies away when you try to pin it down. *Esprit* perishes "in the exile of translation. ...[It] cannot be transplanted from one language to another any more than poetry ... Like certain wines, which will not bear a voyage, it must be drunk at home" (57–8). However, since Barbey is writing in French about the inability to translate English manners into French, there must be something appropriately inappropriate about this foreign mode. Barbey's book is not just a critique of his own language; rather, it is a critique of language itself. Language will inevitably fail to apprehend the wit of its subject, and along with it, communication—which is also to say, diplomacy—is threatened. This is an irony that cannot be removed by the most puritanical of writers or oppressive of tyrants, for all speech harbors within it the dandy seed of rebellion.

The "divine ray" of the Dandy's expression lies "out of the reach of wrinkles," that genius of irony that incites mystery and trouble (54). Wit swiftly causes unconscious subjects to reveal their absurdities. It pierces "even while caressing the self-love of everyone" (55). This is Barbey's procedure on the unconscious Brummell, as was Plato's plastic surgery on Socrates. The operation must be carefully done, since "wit borders on vulgarity as the sublime verges on the ridiculous, and the least false step is fatal" (56). The danger is that the Dandy will be either too pointed or too cocky, and the double-edged sword of irony received hostilely.

Brummell's demise stemmed from a period of strained interaction with George IV. The Prince of Wales was extremely fat and Brummell used to say in his presence, "*Who is that big man?*" He referred to him as Big Ben, and to his "wife" as Benina. During that time, when the Prince encountered Brummell unexpectedly at a soirée, the Prince behaved "beneath himself," while Brummell "met the sulky attitude of His Royal Highness with that air of elegant indifference which he wore like armour, and which made him invulnerable" (64). If Brummell had made a scene, he would've looked weak; but with chainmail coolness, he made the Prince look as if he was less than a prince. The temporary strangulation of wit leaves no blood, and so, no evidence. The same might be said of Barbey's text.

When Brummell left England for France, he easily became "king of Calais." For a time, it became fashionable for the noblemen in England to go on holiday to France, simply because Brummell had gone there. Brummell had left at the height of his fame, just as "a proud beauty ... prefers leaving him she still loves to being left by him" (66). The apex of the Dandy's splendor occurs precisely at the bloom when his physical manifestation recedes. "Sometimes there came into his clever eyes a look of glacial indifference without contempt, as becomes a consummate dandy, a man who bears within him something superior to the visible world" (54). Glacial indifference without contempt resembles neutrality without malice; the Dandy is like a god polishing his shoes with champagne only to casually traipse around in the mud.[9] Godliness is the image and contagion behind the Dandy's clothes. He is "displeased too generally not to be sought after" (75). He transforms bored socialites into amateur philosophers with the mystery of his celebrity.

After Brummell's graceful fall from grace, he was given a political office but was too inept to occupy it. Of his literary legacy, Barbey says, "what he left us in the way of verses, though remarkable enough for a dandy, would not suffice for a literary reputation." So well-dressed was he that his destiny was always to become obscure. This is the cruel plight that awaits all bloggers. When their social perfume is dispelled, they will be absorbed back into the abyss out of which they rose. Brummell, too, receded into the world of dreams. He became "desperately elegant," and later, downright delusional. Eventually, he makes his textual apotheosis, where "no details are possible"— Brummell disappears literally and figuratively into Barbey's footnote (74n.).

So, this frivolous work about a frivolous man seems to entail a warning about the friction between philosophy and politics, and by extension, fashion and time. The social butterfly—a more glamorous incarnation of the social gadfly—will inevitably be chased away by its own flight. In today's literary climate, the Dandy seems to have had his winged words clipped. Where is Empedocles, clad in his purple robe and golden girdle?[10] "But I walk as an immortal god among you all now, no longer a mortal, on all sides honored, so it seems, crowned both with fillets and flowering wreaths" (Fragment 112). An obsession with looking right has sapped scholarly writing of wit (of looking good?). The sphinx of irony is no longer in fashion. Who would still deliver their insights with an air of graceful frankness or a smattering of pun(k)? Grace, perhaps. Frank, perhaps. But Grace and Frank are only friends. They are no longer lovers, married in the fever of a passion for truth. Maybe they would fall in love again, if only some rebellious spirit would throw a revolutionary wit party.

Political Interlude

"Dandyism is a sunset," wrote Baudelaire, "like the declining daystar, it is glorious, without heat and full of melancholy" (1863/1995: 28-9). Its transitional appearance is particularly ripe during moments of political unrest. As a reactionary, however, the Dandy can only remain peripheral; he is more suitably a nonchalant revolutionary, an unplanned polemic, centrally as he is on the fringe and militant in his "style of existence."[11]

In antebellum America, Black dandyism emerged from sumptuary laws, which attempted to prevent Black Americans from wearing fine clothing. These laws exposed racial injustices by way of their easy transgression: "In Charleston, the effort to prevent perceived black fashion violations was wholly ironic, for some slave masters, especially those involved in illicit relationships with their female slaves, were responsible for the distribution of finery so offensive to their fellow citizens" (Miller 2009: 92). Where livery were employed to control the looks of both masters and servants, "their efforts at doing so were undone by the very phenomenon they sought to employ—that notoriously capricious world of fashion" (54). Clothing's doubleness is here on display: it may be worn in imitation of its usual wearers, but likewise to mock and undermine them. Its function as eliciting laughter is part of an internal mutiny against its own appropriateness. What is more, as in the case of wit and speech, where freedom is limited, fashion will find a route in esotericism. It is not possible to finally oversee wit's irony or fashion's fashions, for both are fickle, and so, offer the swiftest mode of rebellion against the worst injustices, while also delivering a means to resurrect them.

Richard Thompson Ford writes of "Sunday Best Activism," the dress of the Civil Rights Movement in 1963, exemplified by the elegant style of Martin Luther King, Jr. and Coretta Scott King. "By dressing to confound racist images of Black ignorance, sloth, and slovenliness, the well-dressed

Black person used clothing to repudiate racism on the visual and visceral levels on which it operated" (2021: 207).[12] Fashion played the role of "silent orator" (Givhan 2017). It protested with style and looks. Other symbolic fashions also appeared and quickly caught on, such as denim overalls and workwear, the slick looks of the Black Panther Party, Black-is-beautiful, and Afrocentric styles. Afrocentric looks were, according to Ford, "open to the critique of inauthenticity." He quotes Robert Allen in 1969, saying that "[B]lack culture has become a badge to be worn rather than an experience to be shared. African robes, dashikis, dresses, and sandals have become standard equipment, not only for the well-dressed Black militant, but even for the middle class hipsters who have gone Afro" (183). What Allen had complained of seems to be that spirit of dress to rebel against its own claims, insofar as its authenticity is gained precisely at the moment it is worn, and in that same moment it cannot help but invite impersonators. Something remains elusive even in this, since the act of wearing is itself an imitation of the wearer's own intent, as if you only came to be at home with your expression after colonizing yourself in a moment of foreignness through clothes. Fashion helps define cultures and customs, but it can only do so retroactively, since we don't spring up autochthonously in native raiment. Everything is borrowed from somewhere else. This is fashion's mock empire—a rule that the daring and the unwitting alike can overthrow. For it is especially where fashion begins to dictate our lines, that its dandiness unfashions and refashions.

"Tell me how you knot your tie and I will tell you who you are—and even what company you keep," muses Buttologist, a Congolese dandy who is the main character of Alain Mabanckou's *Black Bazaar* (2012: 39).[13] Buttologist is a *sapeur*. That is, one who follows the fashion of la Sape, or Société des Ambianceurs et des Personnes Élégantes. Elvis G. Makouezi has written a dictionary of la Sape, in which he offers this general definition: la Sape is "a way of being, of feeling oneself (*se sentir*), of carrying oneself, and of dressing oneself" (1970: 13). La Sape is a society, complete with its own "language, habits, costumes, and rites," and even its own Messiah, André Grenard Matsoua.[14] The first *sapeurs*, says Makouezi, were "their own masters," beacons of self-control and self-discipline in their personal and social aesthetics. One thinks of Audre Lorde's remark that "Caring for myself is not self-indulgence, it is self-preservation, and that is an act of political warfare" (1988/2017: 130). Robby Gianfranco calls la Sape "a revolt movement like punk, like the Rastas" (Steinkopf-Frank 2017). Fashion is the only law in this nuanced dress club, and a mastery of appearances signifies an ascent of the individual beyond the city. In a documentary entitled *The Congo Dandies* (2015), Maxime Pilot, a *sapeur* clad in brilliant red, describes reactions to his clothing: "When I wear my bright suits, I am splendid. In my area, people start shouting, 'The God of Clothes! The God of SAPE!'"[15]

As a contemporary statement, the classy punk of the Congolese Dandies stands out in the impoverished cities of Brazzaville (Congo) and Kinshasa (Democratic Republic of the Congo); it also symbolizes a redemption from French colonization. The pilgrimage to France to buy expensive garments traces the journey and dress of the colonizers. Congolese Dandies reclaim their self-definition through this fashion wanderlust. "By taking over the signs and language of officialdom, they have been able to remythologize their conceptual universe while, in the process, turning the *commandement* into a sort of zombie" (Mbembe 2001: 87–8).[16] The Congolese Dandies have invented a species of high-brow sophistry as an antidote to the incoherence of political life.[17]

What sophistry always pretends to sell is control. It claims to give you your power back in the form of reputation, virtue, and the ability to defend yourself in any situation so that you never appear ashamed. It does this through fashion—not just the style of rhetoric, but literally through the act of dressing up. This is visible as early as the sophist Hippias of Elis, who claimed to have made all of his own clothes. For the Dandy, clothes are a holy shrine in which body falls away. So goes the saying in fashion, "own it," which really means "re-own" it. The key to being so swank is the ability to re-style: to go from *maccherone* to macaroni.[18] Once fool, now cool. So, too, the Greek word *sophos* means both "wise" and "wise guy." The Dandy coaxes you over to his particular mannerism—for example, toward wearing vermillion scarves in one way rather than another. He makes you think beyond the reigning status quo by crumpling it stylishly. He redefines words you thought you understood and makes their slang meaning the dominant usage. So the Dandy's specialty is a prowess in resignification that all fashion, perhaps especially fast fashion, pretends to be able to give to everyone.

Fast fashion, the metamorphic transience of trends, chases the constant revising of the fashion canon, where clothing, perhaps just as knowledge, is treated as detachable and disposable. This is, of course, wrapped up in consumerism; material is less important than cut, regardless of its environmental effects on our bodies or souls. The alienation of production from consumption is as piqued for fashion as it is for philosophy. You find a similar phenomenon in authors versus ghostwriters, musicians versus producers, or celebrities versus stylists, where the hidden creator is not the name on the label. Fashion is particularly expert at quoting others without acknowledgment, especially given that most of what we wear is someone else's design. The "fast" way treats people and truths as if their material did not matter, only their silhouettes (or shadows) which can be transferred seamlessly. Knowledge changes, grows, is destroyed and revamped continually. But this process loses meaning where images rule. The Dandy compels those who are chained to turn toward another flame. That there will always be dandies means the city can never close off the cave completely. The possibility of sophistry is the sign that philosophy can thrive.

The Dandy's historical maleness reveals something interesting about fashion's femininity, too. In W.E.B. Du Bois's novel *Dark Princess: A Romance* we meet Sara Andrews, whom Monica L. Miller dubs a "female dandy." Her qualifications for this title include "her personal and social grooming," and "ability to disguise politics as a game in which she always gains the advantage" (2009: 151).[19] Congolese *sapeuses* Clementine Biniakoulou and Ntsimba Marie Jeanne are also female dandies, appearing with flashy suits, tobacco pipes, and bowties. In America, Iris Apfel and Tziporah Salamon might be called dandies. The common thread is that no dandy ever plays the vulnerable ingénue. The archetype for the Dandy is a cross between Athena and Zeus: a less eroticized beauty that strikes the eye as warlike and powerful, the result of an autogenesis. Somewhere in between dandies and sophists, fashion's more modern stereotype as solely concerned with feminine frills loses all traction. For where the Dandy becomes emasculated by that absurd phrase in fashion history, "the great masculine renunciation,"[20] he/she/it/they unleashes a jar of unpleasantries, dealing as the Dandy does with a *kosmos* in which specification falls away.

> Delilah and Judith, Aspasia and Lucretia, Pandora and Athena, woman is both Eve and the Virgin Mary. She is an idol, a servant, source of life, power of darkness; she is the elementary silence of truth, she is artifice, gossip, and lies; she is the medicine woman and witch; she is man's prey; she is his downfall, she is everything he is not and wants to have, his negation and his raison d'être.
>
> (Beauvoir 1949/2011: 162)

Femininity and its disparagement, whether circling the periphery or utterly buried, captures the very traits that the savvy dandy, genderless and shrewd, seeks to exploit. Anyway, Plato knew it was those who weave in private that stand the test of time, whether political ruler or immortal poet. Glory is a trick and invisibility the truer sign of mastery. Homer, inspired by the Muses, weaves Penelope weaving on her loom by day what she unweaves at night to hoodwink the suitors (*Odyssey* 2.100–18). She rules the situation by going unnoticed in her plotless movement. In the *Iliad* Helen is also seen as Homer-like, "she was weaving a great cloth, / a crimson cloak of double thickness, and was working in the many trials of the Trojan horse-breakers and bronze-clad

Achaeans" (3.125–7). In Plato's *Statesman*, weaving is the smallest paradigm for statesmanship, "having the same business as the political"; the Stranger limits it specifically to "the weaving that concerns webs woven from wool" (279b; cp. 305eff).[21] In the *Cratylus*, weaving is a model for how language connects to the world, and it is feminine voices who safeguard it (418c). In the *Phaedo*, weaving is suggested by Cebes as the activity of the soul in connection to the body, which it weaves as if it were a cloak (87b). Outside of Greece, the cosmos itself is imagined as woven; the sun is "given the name 'Weaver' in the Talmud. An Estonian ballad represents the sky with its bright hues of sunrise and sunset as a mantle woven by Tara, the Old Father, the Old and Wise" (West 1971: 54). In the *Atharvaveda*, Night and Day weave a web as if the sky were a loom, and time and space "a thread of wind or breath" (55). And in Herodotus' Egypt, it is men who weave indoors (pushing the woof downward instead of upward), while women run the marketplace (2.35), an inversion that mirrors that of the Egyptian notions of life and death. Birth cannot be hidden when death is so controlled.

This is all to say that the feminine connotations surrounding weaving in antiquity and fashion in modernity, as a leisurely business of wiling away time in private, reveal it as a sexless paradigm for understanding language and political life from an unseen (timeless? cosmic?) vantage point. Only the foolhardy would trivialize the invisible—it is peculiarly the city's view that what is not seen is not.[22] So Shelley called the poets "the unacknowledged legislators of the world." They might as well be the dressmakers and tailors, too, both of whom go incognito sometimes by design, other times by compulsion.[23] People who fancy themselves rational dislike frills and are wary of pleasures—not because frills lack content but because they project a failure of mastery and a delight in absurdity. Where frills are cleverly wielded, the Dandy's enigma prevails, striving toward some undefined human pinnacle, a fluid other to the immortals, now floating above the sexed body with a tyranny of the toilette.[24] Perhaps it was only a matter of time before the toilette became the state. That Dandies get accused of being too femme maximizes their dominion, for they thrive on Eve's bad reputation. Where they are exiled and maligned, they are self-exiled and malign themselves—and with extraordinary etiquette, Killer Queens that they are.[25]

Dandy Demagoguery

In Plato's *Sophist* we learn that real ("non-fabricated") philosophers appear in many apparitions, which is to say, many fashions: to some, they seem to be worth nothing, to others, everything. Sometimes they appear as sophists, sometimes as statesmen, and sometimes they give the impression that they are altogether mad (216d). One might say all of this about dandies, too.

The Dandy vacillates between Alcibiades and Socrates, now tyrant-socialite, now philosopher-Siren. He has variously the looks of an opportunist, a phony, or a magician. And it is his ease at understanding how to manipulate his appearances that makes him both an outlier and a social climber. As much as England's dandy thrived on Puritanism, one might worry that a "malicious egalitarianism" (Adorno's term—1951/1981: 131) could equally magnetize and pervert a dandy force. In theory, the Dandy is an anti-fascist in his dispassionate snubbing of the norm, and even in regard to his fellow Dandies (for the Dandy hates nothing more than to appear a mere copy). But his creation of an anti-norm cannot help but draw others to him irrationally by way of his good looks. This reveals something troubling in fashion's powers.

One thinks of the indecorous suits of Prime Minister Narendra Modi, who had his name embroidered into the pinstripes of one suit that was later auctioned off for $645k. The Roman emperor Caligula, a.k.a. Basic Boots, got his name from the regular shoes he wore in order to curry favor with the common soldiers, or so Tacitus claims.[26] Fashion itself seems to flirt very dangerously with fascism in its collapse of the first and third-person in the activity of wearing. The casual identity, initially fraudulent, between the wearer and what the wearer wears speaks even when the wearer does not consent. There is no doubt that dictators or would-be dictators use fashion's erotic allure to invoke a response in their groupies. You can see the danger in the extremist symbols worn half-comically, half-earnestly by Trump supporters during the breach[27] of the US Capitol on January 6, 2021. Wearing symbolism brings the spectator into the performance in a way that is different from but related to holding a sign or a flag. The latter still bears an element of dissociation, but this is reduced to a minimum with clothing in its "Kick me" semiotics. In that unfounded identification of follower and leader, there is a spurious fashioning of the self, a pseudo-eros honed into a thumotic point, not unlike the reaction we have to someone who is dressed like us. Fashion's encoded messages can communicate feelings of eerie camaraderie or enemy vitriol.[28]

In the opening lines of Tacitus' *Annals*, *exuere*, "to strip," refers to the "stripping of power."[29] The contrary motion occurs in Protagoras' retelling of the Prometheus myth in Plato's *Protagoras*, where *kosmêsai*, "to adorn" or "order," refers to the gods' "adorning" human beings with power. Hermes is later sent to bring *kosmoi* of cities.[30] We meet a perversion of the Dandy in the tyrant of Plato's *Republic*, too. The tyrannical soul is eros incarnate, returned to the people as a twisted image of themselves. But the genuine dandy, by contrast, must always play in the space between regimes. He is the timocratic son of an aristocrat, the oligarchic son of a timocrat, the democratic son of an oligarch, the tyrannical son of a democrat, in each case rejecting the mode from which he originated in favor of the opposite fashions, straddling the boundary between angsty teen and savvy revolutionary.[31] The nascent democrat—perhaps the crucial site of the transformation—wears the Brooks Brothers suit that daddy bought him, but the pockets are empty and his jacket tastefully stained with booze. The Dandy only gives slight notice that he is about to self-destruct and rise phoenix-like from the ashes of convention. He has stitched his individuality onto and into his (*sans-*) culottes, and by way of its publicity (impossible to escape in the wearing of one's virtue), has turned himself into an accidental social demonstration. Or did he intend it? It makes all the difference. Unprepared for his fame, Brummell eventually went mad, "ceasing to take off his hat when saluted in the street lest he should disarrange his wig, and returning bows with a wave of his hand, like Charles X" (Barbey 1845/1988: 73–4).

Athleisure

What a tease the Dandy is! His transformation of bodily muscles into sartorial strength has grown together in the pervasive American fashion of wearing gym clothes everywhere but the gym. Its genus, leisurewear, seems to emanate from the heightened fantasy that the world of suits and cocktail attire is "fake" (along with the news, and perhaps reality as we know it). But strangely, in its place arises the hope of compression pants. Athleisure works within a specific dress code so that, like the Dandy's finely made suit, athleisure, done correctly, exposes the finely crafted body. This is the body that goes to the gym, that drinks green juice, that hearkens back somehow to the romance of hunter-gatherer; in high fashion, it is obscenely white trainers, luxury hoodies, and shapeless jersey fabrics, ready for a wrestling match between Alexander Wang and Saint Laurent. Athleisure would be what the professional human-in-general would wear, not as an individual, but rather as someone so ascended in down-dressing that the mere sign of jogging pants signifies a healthy body and bank account. Timberland hiking boots and armless Patagonia puffer vests are respectively the younger and older versions of outdoor fashion gone to the club or Bingo night. Dandies never wear watches, and leisurewear follows suit. The Apple watch or FitBit are not harried statements of one's dependence on time, but rather the wrist analogue to gymless gym garb.

Athleisure suggests a spectator's view on the sport of life, in which one strolls around like a retired Olympic athlete, performatively posing in one's inactivity, never encountering a drop of sweat. Athleisure one-ups comfortable clothes by making it appear as if you are not yet even in clothes but only on your way to being in them. Done correctly, it is like those Classical Greek sculptures for which Polyclitus was famous, displaying the body caught off duty in a moment of pure transition, a natural motion suspended from here to there, a leisurewear ironically called "performance wear." Athleisure is at once self-important and self-effacing, and more so than ever, first-person performance and third-person voyeurism are together in this look. Why wear your gym outfit 24/7? Because you are not defined by practical matters, such as dates, deadlines, and push-ups. Time ceases to matter. The look is of practical impracticality: to show your prowess at the mortal game. People who wear athleisure may be using their VitaMix as I write this.

It is here that the Athenian Academy, located in the gymnasium, finds new prescience. In the *Theaetetus* Socrates describes the ideal philosopher as fashionably athleisure. While he is not at all concerned about how to find his way to the courthouse, he does know how to drape his cloak, and you'll probably find him hanging out and talking in the gym (176a).[32] There are a couple of Greek words, *kalos* and *aischros*, that ring true here. *kalos* can mean both "beautiful" and "noble," while *aischros* can mean both "ugly" and "shameful." Athleisure emphasizes the beautiful as the noble—looking like a virtuous biped as one hops into a suburban vehicle in a tracksuit. But the Dandy plays on both meanings: placing every hair in its right place becomes a synonym for having one's entire life in order.

The Rational Dress Society

In 1881, The Rational Dress Society was formed in London. It called for a liberation of women's dress from oppressive constraints. According to rational dress reforms, fashion ought to follow the laws of reason and be designed for the good of the wearer, in accordance with both individual bodies and a general interest in being fit and healthy. Reformers pushed for banishing corsets and heavy skirts that limited movement, which were becoming extremely impractical for both exercise and work. An issue of *The Rational Dress Society's Gazette* from January 1889 begins,

> The Rational Dress Society protests against the introduction of any fashion in dress that either deforms the figure, impedes the movements of the body, or in any way tends to injure the health.

It protests against the wearing of tightly-fitting corsets, of high heeled or narrow-toed boots and shoes; of heavily-weighted skirts, as rendering healthy exercise impossible; and of all tie-down cloaks or other garments impeding the movements of the arms.

It protests against crinolines or crinolettes of any kind as ugly and deforming.

Below these lines is an Editorial Note that alerts readers to the Rational Dress Depot where one can get "rational corsets and bodices." No doubt Bertrand Russell would be a fan. Other dress reformers were firmly anti-corset, suspecting perhaps that rational corsets were merely less rational, something like bras. This was to champion the complete freeing of women's silhouettes from needlessly burdensome chains. For example, the enormous hallways in the Main Building at Vassar College, which were widened so that female students could exercise in their hoop skirts. After a criticism of how students dressed, on January 27, 1921, Vassar students launched a "style revolt," decking themselves out in their tackiest clothes: "[T]hose with long hair pulled it back into tight 'buns'—we made ourselves as unattractive as possible."[33]

A section of the *Gazette* entitled "Gossip about Dress Reform" worries about the artificiality implicit in fashion that serves no practical use. I must here pause to anachronously refer rational dress reformers to Eileen Chang's description of ancient Chinese clothes—

> This amassing of countless little points of interest, this continual digression, reckless and unreasonable, this dissipation of energy on irrelevant matter, marked the perennial attitude toward the life of the leisure class in China. Only the most leisured people in the most leisurely country in the world could appreciate the wonder of these details. It certainly took tremendous amounts of time and artistry to create fine distinctions between a hundred lineal designs that were similar but not the same and just as much effort to appreciate the differences among them.
>
> Chinese fashion designers of old seemed not to have understood that a woman is not a Prospect Garden.
>
> (1945/2005: 68)

Chang's interest is in how fashions reflect political transformations. With the founding of the Republic came "superficial signs of enlightenment," including "unprecedented innocence, lightness, and delight in itself" in fashion.

The Rational Dress Society, on the other hand, was certain that clothing should not celebrate the good for its own sake. Rather, "sensible shoes" were for use only as a means to "health and wellness." The Society further warns against rational dressing for the sake of fashion, where sensible fashion (e.g., the divided skirt to ride tricycles) was attracting attention because its opposition seemed cool or Parisian. Over a century later, we still don't have George Fox's all-weather suit, but the same *Gazette* ominously concludes that subsequent generations will look back with "contempt and wonder at the ignorance and obstinacy of their ancestors." Can the stubbornly irrational bent of clothing go out of style—or rather, is style itself irrational? The bewitchment of "must-haves" is mirrored by the perfect *logos* that would operate like a living animal: every word in its right place; every pleat freshly pressed.[34]

In Aristotle's *Politics*, we find that Hippodamus of Miletus "discovered the division of cities and carved out the Piraeus." Hippodamus apparently lived in an excessive manner, too much beyond work (*periergoteron*), wearing "long hair and expensive adornment (*kosmos*)," and "cheap and warm clothing not only in winter but also in summer times." Hippodamus wanted to be versed (*logios*, "rationally equipped"?) in nature as a whole, and he "was the first of those not engaged in politics to attempt to say something about the best regime" (1267b20–30). It is strange that a city-planner who wanted to look *logios* in nature as a whole, and politics in particular, should have been in his appearance tricked out in all-purpose threads that demonstrated both economy and excess. Or maybe it's not so strange? It seems important that Aristotle includes this gratuitous detail. It is a digression on an important topic, a crease in the argument's train that makes the reader wonder if rational plans demand detours.

I now return to something that will prove critical for the rest of the book: Socrates' founding of the city in speech in Plato's *Republic*. This city is brought into being as a response to the need to enlarge the fine print of justice in the soul by looking at it in the larger print of a city. Socrates begins with an account of a city that is supposedly based solely on the "most necessity"[35] (369d11); he later calls it the "true" city. But the superlative already gives away its excess.

The true city comes into being as follows: at first, four or five people get together and exchange basic necessities: food, housing, clothing, shoes. Socrates presumes these people cannot be self-sufficient but need each other. Needs are met better if one person produces a quantity of one thing for everyone else: "one <man>, one <art>." Socrates adds that "if someone lets the critical moment (*kairos*) of the work pass, it/he is destroyed" (370b8–9). The thing done, says Socrates, doesn't wait around for the "leisure" of the one who is doing it. Attention must be paid to the work at every moment, lest the critical moment be missed. The efficiency of this city at first seems to require the absence of digression.

But Socrates repeats the line in what follows with some changes, "From these things, each comes to be more, and more beautiful and easier, whenever one man according to nature and at the critical moment (*en kairôi*), does one thing, *being at leisure* from the rest" (370c4–6, my italics). The *kairos* character of the appointed deed for each now means that each is at leisure from the rest. Is a life spent baking bread a vacation from a life spent making shoes? Socrates again repeats the formula (374c), just before he introduces the need for the guardians to have more leisure time to be trained in music and gymnastic. The guardians' education will itself be purified of any leisurely byproducts that might misdirect them from their proper work. Even the tales they will be told as children will get cleansed of "embroidered" phrasing. But where everything is properly timed, leisure is already implicit in the division of tasks, for the multi-tasking or multi-tasker that determines which person does which task can only be a digression in this city.

The transformation from the so-called true into the so-called luxurious city, then, looks as if it is no transformation at all, but a realization of what is already there. Socrates calls the move "natural." But its plot is intellectual: the refinement of singular tasks demands there be craftsmen of tools to make things like plows and shuttles. But if garments are being woven, this will, in turn, require fabric and leather, which means hides and wool, which means herdsmen. Herdsmen call to mind poets like Hesiod—just the sort who embroider the tales that Socrates is about to erase from the guardians' schoolbooks.

Embroidery will itself emerge explicitly in the luxurious city as an addition to clothing—intending, I think, to mean something like "whimsical sewing (pun intended)" or "very colorful clothing." It comes with painting and poetry, gold and ivory, as well as a nebulous item entitled "the feminine *kosmos*," which either means make-up or the eugenics of Book 5. Also, since Socrates uses "painting statues" to describe his own activity of drawing up a city in words, you wonder about the precise stylistic innovation here (420c). The guardians, after all, are said to be far from needing "to have tales told and *embroidered* about battles of giants and all sorts of enmities among gods and heroes with their families and kin" (378c4–7, my italics). Just as critical timing appears to require the digression of some unseen tailor, the jack-of-all-trades will reappear when Socrates describes the democratic regime as an "embroidered cloak" (557c5). In it, many threads perform many tasks, and all patterns are depicted.

But, back in the simple city, once there are herdsmen, it will be impossible to keep out imports; with "imports" the poetic equivalence of one-to-one task masters is revealed, since a value of exchange must have already been required to determine trade (e.g., how many eggs in return for one pair of shoes, 371b).[36] No city is so perfectly situated that its land and citizenry can produce everything required (see, e.g., Thucydides' description of Attica as having poor soil, 1.2). As the healthy city begins to grow even slightly, Socrates is forced to introduce merchants and third-party retailers to help keep "idle" goods from remaining "idle" in the market; wage-earners complete the city by offering themselves for hire to work for the rest, and now suddenly everything seems to have its proper place.

Once the city is deemed complete, Socrates wonders where justice and injustice are. To look for them, he examines in what fashion (*tropos*) these people lead their lives so "outfitted." It is worth noticing that justice, *dikê*, can in its accusative form mean "way" or "custom," and function almost as *tropos* does here. "Outfitted," *skeuazesthai*, means "prepare" or "make ready," in the sense of either put on armor, get equipped, or dress up. Socrates has to look at how the city moves, and to do this requires that he jump outside of it to look it up and down—to meditate on the order of its outfit. The people of this simple city go naked and unshod in summer and "sufficiently" covered in winter. They eat in what sounds like the style of a Brooklyn hipster restaurant, with noble loaves and cakes of "barleymeal dressed up ('outfitted') from barleycorns and toasted wheat." After they've "baked (*pepsantes*) and kneaded" them, they "toss <them> out on a reed and clean leaves." They themselves are "stretched out on rushes strewn with yew and myrtle" (372a–b). And after this, they drink wine wearing wreaths and sing of the gods.

Regarding Socrates' use of the word "outfitted," I do not mean to suggest that he has tacitly used the language of clothing to describe these various preparations, but rather that the conscious fashioning or dressing up— or in this case dressing down—of life will be required for an awareness of the justice of the arrangement. This requires looking at the city from outside it, but the motive to do so can only come from someone who is inside it—something like Socrates' position on the outskirts at the Piraeus. But Socrates is not exactly at leisure. The dialogue is set in motion when Polemarchus' slave boy grabs Socrates' cloak to stop him from returning to town (*tirare la giachetta*). Cloaks on their own, with or without embroidery, seem to imply a leisure to compel. Without the cloak, the slave boy would have had to make more direct contact with Socrates' person, which would've seemed more aggressive. The cloak provides a medium of exchange, like money. So too, when Athena grabs Achilles by his hair to stop him from lunging at Agamemnon, the hair is a medium that translates a message that is untranslatable. It offers a trade, as words do, that must be slightly unfair. Even the seemingly generic term for clothing, *himation*, means not just "cloak" but "light cloak"; and the multiple words Socrates uses for baked loaves (*mazai*) and cakes (*artoi*) allude to specific grains and modes of preparation, which is to say, dressings.

Socrates will later be compelled to posit a philosopher-ruler who wipes away the memory of the citizens' "priming" and gives them the impression that they've been living their prime lives since birth, like words sprung out of the earth garbed in unambiguous meaning. This is embroidered simplicity, and by the time Socrates has woven together one-to-one production into a multi-faceted city, the analogy of city to soul demands, in turn, that the city's internal simplicity be made fraudulent in the face of the soul's complexity. Justice will be found in Book 4, "rolling around" at the feet of Socrates and his interlocutors. They are "like ones who sometimes seek what they're already holding in their hands" (432d7-e3), or the outfit they already have on. Poetry is thriving in this city the moment Socrates imagines the city as the soul's cloak.

A sense of this is present in Glaucon's immediate objection to the simple life: "As you seem to me, you're making (*poiein*) men who feast without relish (*opson*)" (372c2-3). This would be a "city for pigs." But Glaucon can only object because he imagines Socrates is stripping away the couches and tables of civilization, ideas lurking in the clean leaves and yew and myrtle on which the simple diners dine and recline.[37] It must be the yew and myrtle strewn underneath them that they use to weave the wreaths on their heads. Pastime plaiting—a simple embroidery but embroidery nonetheless—is already in the simpler city. And even if the citizens are at first vegetarians (since swineherds are only introduced in the feverish city), they already have baking, gods, and song. Perhaps most tantalizing of all is that the word for relish, *opson*, which also means "cooked" in the sense of dressing, and the word *pepsantes* (from *pessein*), also meaning "cooked" (or "ripened," "dressed"), may even be etymological relatives.[38] This city is clearly half-baked.

If, as Aristotle says, human beings are by nature political animals, and more so than other animals because they have *logos*,[39] then it is by this same nature that they are fashionable animals (1253a1-10). If we could go back before this time, then fashion could have a history and begin. But fashion's embroidered motions are already in swing well before fashion historians determine its simple beginnings. The question of its initiation does not hinge on this or that fashion but the contingency of fashion's appearance—a problem that will haunt Socrates' perfected city in the form of Socrates' and the philosopher's freak thoughts. Socrates' ugliness in the city's eyes reflects the injustice of a prefabricated arrangement. You could say, where there's fashion, deliberate attention is paid to ordering the self into a whole—to a sense of the justice of the self in relation to itself and other selves. Where there's a will there's a way. But fashion is in the same picture a threat to a perfectly working whole, like a loose button that passes judgment on a shirt, or an extra fold that casts an aporetic shadow on the wearer. Perhaps fashion attracts animosity from the plainclothes point of view precisely because of the persistent suggestion it makes, especially when it does so with a laugh: that there is no stopping time—no way to go back in time—no perfect justice.

The Carnival

The subversion of a slight sartorial folly, an allusion to some stratum beyond the norm, has a counterpoint in the overbearing caricature that is the contemporary dandy. So much does the maximal extravagance of the ultramodern riff on the Dandy shock ordinary sensibilities that the innuendo of his presentation is declawed like bleeped-out words. A peacock browsing the aisles of a corner grocery verges on clownery, on clothes as sheer costume. Those everyday sad sacks who remain uninitiated will forget an outstanding individual who seems only to be engaging in display for the sake of display—or maybe, they'll laugh at him, as when the illuminated philosopher returns to the cave.[40] The Dandy laughs back with an air reminiscent of carnival laughter, ambivalently happy and mocking. Is there anything recognizable behind the mask?

"Carnival" here means a designated time when ordinary laws of dress, discourse, and behavior are suspended (as in Carnevale or Mardi Gras). Not in the manner of the theater but rather, during carnival time, the theater is the world. "Carnival is not a spectacle seen by the people; they live in it, and everyone participates because its very idea embraces all the people" (Bakhtin 1968/1984: 7).[41] Its clowns, fools, and crass parodies of refined offices temporarily liberate the people from the mainstream mores. In medieval carnivals and their Roman predecessors (*saturnalia*), there was a degradation of the spiritual realm through bodily images, "the transfer of every high ceremonial gesture or ritual to the material sphere" (20). This involved images of what comes to be and passes away—such as bodily functions relating to food, drink, sex, and vernacular dialogue—in order to deliberately undermine the idea of the timeless and unmoving.

Laughter must lurk wherever you find rituals, since ritual invocation can only be groundlessly high, and so, low-hanging fruit for impersonation, *parodia sacra*. At the same time, in transferring the high to the low, a new ground is laid for resurrection. "To degrade is to bury, to sow, and to kill simultaneously, in order to bring forth something more and better" (21). The earth is a fertile grave, and the terms have already been set for envisioning clothing on the same zombie-like model. To the highbrow, clothing's materiality is perceived as if it were grotesque; it is grouped in with useless acquisitions, issues of sustainability, and capitalistic agendas. The Dandy seems an idol of these pagan sins, and runway fashion a kind of specialized carnival. In the Fall 2007 Christian Dior show, Michaela Kocinova paraded down the runway in a shiny pastel diamond jester suit. Of himself, Karl Lagerfeld had this to say: "I am like a caricature of myself and I like that. It's like a mask. And for me the Carnival of Venice is all year long" (2013: 66). The renovated dandy, so fashionable he becomes distorted, might be our version of a medieval clown; in antiquity, it would've been the sophist, the fool, or the double of both: Socrates.

In Plato's *Symposium*, Alcibiades describes Socrates as a Silenus figurine in a statuary shop or the satyr Marsyas. From Marsyas Socrates differs only in his having virtuosity not in the flute but in "simple *logoi*" (215b–c). At the beginning of *Gargantua*, Rabelais renovates this portrait of Socrates (here quoted from Bakhtin):

> judging by his exterior, you would not have given an onion skin for him. He was ill-shaped, ridiculous in carriage, with a nose like a knife, the gaze of a bull and the face of a fool. His ways stamped him a simpleton, his clothes a bumpkin. Poor in fortune, unlucky when it came to women, hopelessly unfit for all office in the Republic, forever laughing, forever drinking neck to neck with his friends, forever hiding his divine knowledge under a mask of mockery...
>
> Yet had you opened this box, you would have found in it all kinds of priceless, celestial drugs: immortal understanding, wondrous virtue, indomitable courage, unparalleled sobriety, unfailing serenity, perfect assurance and heroic contempt for whatever moves humanity to watch, to bustle, to toil, to sail ships overseas and to engage in warfare.
>
> (Book I, Prologue; 169)

Socrates is country-bumpkin chic, the prime backdrop to laud internal finery. His wisdom lurks in the unlikely abuse and bodily ridicule of his material failures. But this satirical costume doesn't exactly disregard the surface. Rather, it digs the grave for faux wisdom. Through it, you realize not that the truth is naked, but that it is rotten, and its fertilizer sweetened to the degree that regalia has begun to sour. Academics have long imagined that clothing is silly—its clownish formalities smugly resplendent in foul physics—but they've missed the wombs of its putrescence, which are the fruits of their own laughter.

Sound ft. Vision

Dandies, like punks, "once had a fancy for torn clothes." Barbey tells us in a footnote (torn off from the main text):

> This happened under Brummell. They had come to the end of impertinences and were at a loss how to proceed, when they hit upon this dandiesque idea, which was, to have their clothes torn, before wearing them, through the whole extent of the cloth, so that they became a sort of lace—a cloud. They wanted to walk like Gods in their clouds! The operation was difficult and tedious of execution; a piece of pointed glass was employed for the purpose. There you have a true detail of Dandyism, where clothes go for nothing, in fact they hardly exist.
>
> (1845/1988: 31n)

One thinks of McQueen's "Oyster" dress from the Spring/Summer 2003 *Irere* collection or Vivienne Westwood's shredded "God Save the Queen" t-shirt. Dandy ancestry is visible in the looks of Adam Ant, too, as a cross between Captain Hercules Vinegar and an Apache warrior (Ant's controversial war stripe declared "war on the music industry"). Is there some parallel between the intentionally frayed shoelaces of Aeschines' Telauges, or Socrates' accusation that Antisthenes' love of reputation was displayed when he deliberately revealed a tear in his cloak?[42] Family resemblances pass through Lord Chesterfield, Oscar Wilde, Marlene Dietrich, Charlie Chaplin, David Bowie, Madonna, Boy George, Tilda Swinton, Lily Gatins, and the top hats of Marc Bolan and Lux Interior. When once at a party Oscar Wilde said to James Whistler, "I wish I had said that," Whistler answered, "You will, Oscar, you will."

The word "punk," like every word and every fashion, borrows its originality from some uncredited fount. It once meant "prostitute," and is rumored to come from the word "spunk." Spunk, in turn, is (maybe) the bastard child of "funk" and "spark." The word "funk" is used to refer to the funky must that comes from incense; it is likely related to the Latin *fumus*, "smoke," the Greek *thumos*, and the Sanskrit, *dhûmâ-*. *thumos* is again equally translatable as "spirit," "will to live," or even "rage." Punk spirit seems to be that spirit of objection that is required to set any trend ablaze. It is as reactionary as its etymology, since words too, if you trace them back far enough, seem to emanate from some rogue coinage that must ultimately fracture into obscurity. Punk is fashion qua fashion, invading language and culture by consistently dismantling and redefining it. But, what punk reacts to must've once been punk itself, and so, following in the footsteps of every defiant spirit, the Dandy's *esprit* is something like that timeless thrust forward, that tiger's leap that denies status to the past by contemporizing it. Both American and British punk abounded with controversial appropriations of insignia, including the Nazi swastika, worn by both Siouxsie Sioux and Vivienne Westwood, and itself a fascistic appropriation of one of the earliest-known symbols (*svastika* is from Sanskrit, *sv-asti*, meaning "good being" or "good fortune"; the *-ka* ending is a substantive suffix). To disturb people was the point, as Siouxsie Sioux explains it to Jon Savage:

> It was always very much an anti-mums-and-dads thing … We hated older people. Not across the board, but particularly in suburbia—always harping on about Hitler, and, "We showed him," and that smug pride. It was a way of saying, "Well, I think Hitler was very good, actually": a way of watching someone like that go completely red-faced.
> (Savage 1992: 249)

Savage further suggests that the use of such imagery was meant to challenge the "threadbare fantasy of Victory, the lie of which could be seen on the most urban street corners. That this fantasy was now obsolete was obvious to a generation born after the war and witness to England's decline" (249). As a counter-culture, punk is about negating claims of legitimacy, even among its own negations. Whatever the reigning dictum, punk can undermine it. "Nazi Punks Fuck Off," sing the Dead Kennedys. In a similar vein, Poly Styrene re-appropriated the look of the skinhead. More recently, Westside Gunn, a punk not in musical genre but in spirit, released a series of "mixtapes" with the jarring title, "Hitler Wears Hermes," a riff on "The Devil Wears Prada." Maybe this was again only to make a statement. But how much making is involved in making a statement? Why not state it?

Poetry's effect is trickier than it might seem, and so too the reduction of clothes to visual phenomena. In July 2020, Vivienne Westwood, famous for her early partnership with Malcolm McLaren at SEX (later, Seditionaries), appeared suspended in a birdcage dressed as a canary (in a yellow pantsuit) to protest Julian Assange's extradition. The suit is, of course, a soundless symbol for all to witness. But it is also a visceral enactment of a call to arms. As much as Westwood appears to wear the suit, the suit likewise wears her.

Of interest are the following lines from Benjamin's *Arcades Project*:

> Each season brings, in its newest creations, various secret signals of things to come. Whoever understands how to read these semaphores

would know in advance not only about new currents in the arts but also about new legal codes, wars, and revolutions.

(1982/2002: 64)

And these lines from Wilde—

> There is not ... a single delicate line, or delightful proportion, in the dress of the Greeks, which is not echoed exquisitely in their architecture. A nation arrayed in stove-pipe hats and dress-improvers might have built the Pantechnicon possibly, but the Parthenon never.
>
> ("The Relation of Dress to Art," 1885)[43]

One can find recent semaphores and proportions, for example, in Donna Karan's 1992 ad campaign, "In Women We Trust," where a woman president is seen fashionably occupying the oval office. The model was Rosemary McGrotha, photographed by Peter Lindbergh. Since the point is apparently the clothes, the innuendo is given free reign. In William Klein's *Who Are You Polly Maggoo?* fashion appears overwhelmingly irresponsible in its surrealist role-playing. This was Klein's first feature film (1966), and likely a response to his time working as a fashion photographer for American *Vogue*. The film begins with an image of the *super*-model as pure reflection: a runway show set in a holy place, where the audience is the choir and the models are clad in sharp, reflective aluminum sheets.

While the film is obviously a satire on fashion, in being a satire on fashion, it portrays fashion in light of other, seemingly more serious things: gods, politics, art, royalty, history, psychology, philosophical observation. There are references to Borodin, Rasputin, Peter Rabbit, Alice in Wonderland, Freud, Kant, Madame Tabouis, Mussolini, Ducasse, the French Revolution, the Space Race, Polly-want-a-cracker. One begins to wonder if it is not rather fashion that is a satire on everything else. The main character, Gregoire Pecque, is a French reporter with the name of an American actor. In him, the perspective of the observer—the voyeur who watches and follows without seeming to participate—seems to recede. But the audience suddenly seems to be being watched, as actor becomes observer, and observer actor. Polly Maggoo herself becomes a metaphor for the receding "who" of self-knowledge, which mimics the constant progression of fashion. Fashion makes us aware of the fickleness of time, every model dwarfed by the next; so, too, in Rustam Khamdamov's *Vokaldy Paralelder* (*Vocal Parallels*), soprano envies soprano, and in Hesiod's *Works and Days*, potter envies potter. "Fashion is dead, long live fashion!" screams a shade of Diana Vreeland.

Outside of the fashion "world," wherein fashion's subversive powers seem almost comical, its acute punch becomes more grave. On July 9, 2016, there were protests in Baton Rouge against the police shootings of Alton Sterling and Philando Castile. In a photograph by Jonathan Bachman (published by Reuters), "Taking a Stand in Baton Rouge," Ieshia Evans is pictured calm and unarmed standing before a dense line of heavily armed police. In stark contrast to the unidentifiable policemen who wear bulletproof vests and face shields, Evans wears ballet flats and a lightweight maxi dress, which flutters elegantly in the breeze. She looks fearless and poised while two officers rush to handcuff her. From the voyeur's position, the costumes embody the customs. Also in 2016, Larycia Hawkins, a tenured professor at Wheaton College, was dismissed for wearing a hijab as a statement of Christians in solidarity with Muslims. The college found this fashion to go against its core tenets. Fashion tells us things about who we are and what we believe. It reveals what we wish we were and what we don't believe. But it sends mixed messages.

"Comrade Britney" seems to cry out for help, a clone of her former self with hip-hugging boxers and smeared eyeliner. Sir Mix-a-Lot's cheeky critique of White girl aesthetics lives on, thanks to Nicki Minaj. The absurd stylings of Jake Angeli (otherwise known as the "Q-Shaman") in war paint, furs, and a Viking helmet imitate some farcical call of the wild. Eminem predicted the entire Trump presidency in "White America," a song released in 2002 on an album that sold 27 million copies, with lyrics ironically suggesting himself as the leader of the nation's circus—democracy's hypocritical elevation of the people's own royal ordinariness. Reading (hearing) the news today about "A Day in the Life" of "Young Americans" makes you feel like you're in some kind of jungle, where no one seems to get "The Message."[44]

To be under threat is one thing, to sing about it another; but word on the street when sung, dissolves and repoints the danger. In a conversation with Cornel West and Paul Holdengräber at the New York Public Library, Jay-Z styled himself as the "Plato to Biggie's Socrates." 2Pac (alias "Makaveli"), and The Notorious B.I.G. had "hits" in a double sense. Their murders became the symbols of a rap gigantomachy in which the power of verse was at once speculative and cutting. That same duality is present in the album title *The Score* by the Fugees (short for "refugees"). Witty repartees and fatal fights blend together in a form of trap rap called "drill," which means "to attack" or "retaliate." Such warring trip hops onto something it is hard to even begin to describe. Anger and song go together like heart and break. "Sing, goddess, the wrath of Peleus' son, Achilles." Long ago, Apollo took out a hit on Marsyas for challenging him to a lyrical duel. Rhapsodes rapped in turn at the Panatheneia to see who was more in touch with the Muses; piping prowess was at stake in Vergil's Eclogue 3, ft. Menalcas and Damoetas, but also, who's the better shepherd? Fashioning threats into songs both sharpens and relaxes the blade. "The lion sleeps in the sun. / Its nose is on its paws. / It can kill a man," sings Wallace Stevens in "Poetry is a Destructive Force," "Killing Me Softly With His Song."[45]

Singing anger is not the same as saying it, but since saying is somehow not *not* singing either, so singing is not *not* acting. Wearing is importantly in between—at once acting out being acted upon. Wearing seems to say, "I'm not saying ... but just saying." Don't look at me but do. In one way it suggests; in another way it shouts. It suggests even that it is neither suggesting nor shouting. To be conflicted about clothes is already to begin to utter Hamlet's soliloquy. Dress codes and explicit lyrics are the signs that the modes of song and fashion are hardly anything *but music*. In "Take the Power Back," Rage Against the Machine makes clear the fear of the felony of the melody, which is not just reflection but also invection. The lyrics of music get away with subversion much more easily in rhyme and fashion, where the main event is not the substance but the tune. Family murders and inbreeding are a common motif in Sophocles and Aeschylus, *rapping, tapping* into unwritten verses already playing in our brainwaves (or so sung Freud in response). Euripides exacerbated the rhythmized reflection of the choral actor, pulling the audience vividly into the play.

In the Fugees' song, "Family Business," Wyclef Jean opens with a riff ranking his own dearth of ambitions below even Nostradamus' premonitions. Classicist Dan-el Padilla Peralta recalls falling in love with the Fugees (particularly, Lauryn Hill) as a teen: "The Fugees were brainy, well read, sophisticated—exactly what the popular discourse of hip-hop as vulgar and disreputable ... claimed rappers could not be" ("From Damocles to Socrates: The Classics in/of Hip Hop," 2015).When it comes to lyrics, the perception of rap and hip-hop as coarse is very odd, since "rapping" as a verb implies the "striking" or "hitting" of ruthlessly clever and slick beats, precisely the feature so much academic scholarship calling itself "literate" lacks. Ol' Dirty Bastard begins the Wu-Tang Clan's song, "Triumph," with an invocation of Osiris. Literary and cultural references are subsequently summoned with a frequency akin to James Joyce or Laurence Sterne—Inspectah Deck drops atomic bombs on Socratic psalms, a form of musical robbery, in which lyrics are weapons that can hold ideas hostage, that is, until another rapper comes along and heists the same thought with different words. Nietzsche would have called it theft; Whistler, *The Gentle Art of Making Enemies*. To take down storied "giants" can only mean to steal their clothes and become them. The video for "Triumph" begins with a killer bee swarm invading New York City—a reference to the drones of Plato's *Republic*? Jay-Z seems to be the bigger Plato buff, repurposing an argument from the *Euthyphro* in a collaboration with Kayne West, "No Church in the Wild."

The rapper, like the epic hero, is on a quest for recognition under the never-ending threat of attack. Padilla also harps on the recurring theme of the sword of Damocles in songs by The Fugees ("Zealots") and Kanye West ("Power"), and in the title of Jay-Z and Kanye's joint album *Watch the Throne*. Padilla conjectures that "Kanye *ipse*" is transfigured in paint on one of the covers for "Power" as the head of John the Baptist severed newly by Damocles' sword—perhaps a sign not just of Kanye's Jesus/Yeezus complex but also of a turn in rap toward existential crisis.[46] In 2014, Jay-Z appeared wearing a jacket bearing the title of New School professor Eugene Thacker's book on horror and nihilism, *In the Dust of This Planet* (Thacker had nothing to do with this, but the title, once released, traveled through the air, became a *nomos*, and ended up on Jay-Z's back). Kanye, on the other hand, did not seem to be playing when he ran for President nor with the religiosity of his cult shoe brand, Yeezys, through which he reaps the glory of making little Yeezuses over in his image. Gee whiz.

Rhythm is what prevents detached voyeurism, since style, like conviction, does not require that you immediately understand what you just heard; so goes the Grace Jones song, "Slave to the Rhythm." A "good," or let's say "beautiful," song will have you singing the lyrics before you process what they mean. Pop Smoke's lyrics coopted listeners not so much because of their content, but because the style in which he sang them resonated. By his own admission, he was not writing music but hearing it—"I don't write at all, to be honest. I just go in there and go crazy."[47] Pop Smoke, the new Socrates. During the Black Lives Matter protests of 2020, the invincible hook from his song, "Dior," that is, Dior, Christian Dior, broke free from its author to become the voice of the crowd. Shopping and singing turned directly into empowerment and action. Again it wasn't Pop Smoke's words but his way with words that made them so easily worn, as if they had come to be by nature in the mouths of the hearers.

In hip-hop culture, style and song, sound and vision, are intertwined, and rap's rhapsody plays equal parts Dr. Dre and Snoop Dogg, the original Idle Threat, the OG "cuff" and "crease," a metaphor for how to style khakis and beats.[48] The appropriation of prep into hip-hop fashion is another dandy smirk—this time at yacht owners with mini pineapples embroidered on their salmon-hued trousers. The best musical artists, like the best dressers, which is to say, stylists, will be able to sing almost any words or wear almost any garment. There is something in the *way* they hit the notes.[49] Nagel, again in conversation with Heti, quotes Deleuze, first pretentiously in French (he apologizes), then in translation: "'To carve out within language another foreign language and to take all of language to a musical limit—that is to have style.' That pretty well describes Jimi Hendrix playing 'The Star-Spangled Banner'" (2014: 188).

This was why the novelty of music, poetry, and clothes had to be dressed down in Socrates' perfectly just city. But arguments have style, rhythm, and melodic progression, too, to which Socrates alludes with his use of the verb *harmottein* to express the fitting together of both musical modes and verbal agreement about them. Arguments and agreements strike the ear musically, like the fit of a flossy dress that accords to the rhythm of the wearer. To be in fashion is to have good timing. But it is also to dare, to allude, to ride the wavelength of insinuation. It is these anathemas to which academics have acquired an aversion; but to fear them is hopeless, so long as there is any point to make. Points require punch, and punch requires rhythm and progression. To compose in a fever, to reverberate over and over again in inspired imitation, to write as if you were willing to die.

The chorus of *Oedipus at Colonus* sings that not to be born conquers every speech, but second best to go back from where you came as fast as possible. Richard Hell belts out the same Oedipal cry of existential horror in the first line of the song, "Blank Generation." Tom Waits quotes Solon, "Call no man happy till he dies," in "Misery Is a River of the World." Fashion cuts in when the present harmonizes with the past, and the melody begins to fade and renew its vigor in the rhythm of understanding. "If I Ruled the World (Imagine That)": what is thinking itself except a Protean prelude, homage and allude, Time's Quaalude to the Rap Gods?[50]

5

Divine Tailoring

And you yourself, old pope, how is it in accordance with you, that you adore an ass here in such a manner as God?
 —Nietzsche, *Thus Spoke Zarathustra*, Part 4, "The Ass-Festival"

nullum quod tetigit non ornavit.[1]
 —Samuel Johnson (epitaph for Oliver Goldsmith)

In 2018, the Metropolitan Museum of Art showcased a new exhibit, entitled *Heavenly Bodies: Fashion and the Catholic Imagination*. It was spread out across the Met 5th Avenue, the Cloisters, and the Anna Wintour Costume Institute, wherein spectators descended to view a collection of papal bling from the Vatican. One particular clasp of Pope Leo XII blazed with nearly seven hundred diamonds, and this in addition to gold, sapphire, and rubies. No photographs were allowed. The word *diva* springs to mind. A curiosity also springs to mind: is papal pomp piety or profanity? Shouldn't humble souls refrain from bejeweling and encrusting themselves in riches? Why doesn't the pope dress like a nun or a monk? Heavenly fashion—or, spiritual fashion—offers itself as a trompe l'oeil window into the soul. Its manifest revelation is more dramatic than the ordinary symbolism one finds in clothing. Dyed, embroidered, sewn through and through with the holy, nothing can mean what it means. Holy water is not water, wine not wine, clothes not clothes. Hollander writes of the "legless angels of Renaissance art that are buoyed up not so much by their wings as by gloriously wrought masses of bunched skirts, which do not clothe but appear to *replace* unangelic and awkward limbs." The body begins to disappear and cloth supplants it—"It is not, after all, subject to sin" (1993: 16).[2]

Pope Benedict XVI had sleek ruby red slippers, which earned him the nickname, the "Prada Pope." This made waves, since Benedict coveted certain brand names, and came scandalously close to commercial endorsements for Geox and Apple. The red shoes, however, were created by his personal cobbler, and their scarlet hue was intended to emulate the blood of martyrs, a long-standing papal tradition, perhaps related to this remark from Machiavelli's *Florentine Histories*: upon his return from exile, some citizens asked Cosimo de' Medici whether it is not an act against God to drive out so many well-to-do men from the city, to which he responded that "two bolts of red cloth would make a man well-to-do" (7.6). The pope's fashion, however, seems negative in character. There is no clear mimesis of papal style in street fashion, since the pope's fashion at least is *non sequitur*. But within the Catholic Church, red, purple, and white radiate duties and rites, not only in the earthly realm but also among ethereal entities.

Some advice from David Hume: "To imagine that the gratifying of any of the senses, or the indulging of any delicacy in meats, drinks, or apparel, is in itself a vice, can never enter into a head that is not disordered by the frenzies of enthusiasm" (from "Of the Refinement of the Arts"). Unlike the pope, nuns and monks adopt a modest habit, though they are, again, thoroughly, even enthusiastically, covered. No mitre *pretiosa* for them. Even a nun's hair must become fabric. Yet, as one gazes on the stoic black-and-white frocks—in the exhibit, these flanked the medieval wing of the Met—and the elaborate collars, it is hard not to think of Karl Lagerfeld, the mod '60s and other irreverent parallels. Indeed, the show seemed to deliberately propose a kinship between the modestly pompous and the pompously modest— between obsequiousness and fashion—though Nietzsche would probably have accessorized all priests with such sham-glam.

Clothing, regardless of its cut or color, commits itself to holiness and blasphemy quite readily, since it lords a stamp of "faux" purity whether with ornate humility or barren elevation. The pope's haute couture is in fact by dint of its very devotion coming creepily close to Cher's virtual closet. The folderol of ritual, by nature as shallow as wearing a fashion for fashion's sake, is not really meaningless so much as it derives its meaning precisely from the absence of literality. Literality, in turn, is not quite the same as materiality, but it seems destined for material. At any rate, it copies the image of revelation.

The lowly garb of a Dominican friar might be seen as the Catholic brand of normcore, enjoying its own pretension to submission. Secular normcore looks devout, too, in its piety toward ordinary people. It prowls the angelic ether, where clothes are not showy, where clothes are mere clothes, and so, everything but clothes. The ritual of putting them on is nearly an act of purification. At the Cloisters, there were several examples of the reverent turned sacrilege: Chanel wedding dresses modeled after baptismal gowns, friar's robes with unceremonious peep holes in strategic areas, and a cardinal red Dior gown adorned with a gigantic portrait of Machiavelli. So, too, the normcore elite pirate the look of the common soul, and mock its facile fashion lexicon.[3] But again, in its most simplistic form, clothing is both pope and monk, both beyond and underneath. Its heavenly ascension somehow descends. Its redemption is to tempt us to see beyond the surface. Meanwhile, the papal gems encrust a single man with the height of divine being, and so, reduce him to nothing. In his otherworldly outfit, the pope must evaporate in devotion to the Holy Spirit. He is not just wearing god's clothes; he is god's mannequin.

Sartor Resartus: Divine Nonsense

The embryo of Thomas Carlyle's *Sartor Resartus*—literally, the *Tailor Retailored*—is first mentioned in Carlyle's journal, September 1830: "I am going to write—Nonsense. It is on 'Clothes.' Heaven be my comforter!" (2008: xiii). The final product, first published as a book in 1836, shimmers with a montage of romance, history, tragedy, and, most importantly, satire. Even the most innocent reader knows immediately that the book is too explicit not to be hiding something. It is so relentlessly ironic that the question of its honesty haunts its every word.

From the first pages, Carlyle runs fashion and philosophy together against their innermost wishes. They find themselves unfortunately alike, at precisely—or really, altogether non-precisely—that point where philosophical abstraction climbs to the height of pure concepts, a.k.a. pure clothes. These conceptual shells are a transcendent remedy for the failure of British empiricists to notice the faulty vision of modern science. Science is so preoccupied with dissecting bodies into minute pieces that it misses the outermost layer. "The Editor," whom we have not yet officially met and so whom we cannot yet distinguish from Carlyle's own voice, rants that

> [S]carcely a fragment or fibre of his [Man's] Soul, Body, and Possessions, but has been probed, dissected ... and scientifically decomposed ... How, then, comes it ... that the grand Tissue of all Tissues, the only real *Tissue*, should have been quite overlooked by Science—the vestural Tissue, namely, of woolen or other Cloth; which Man's Soul wears as its outmost wrappage ... wherein his whole other Tissues are included and screened, his whole Faculties work, his whole Self lives, moves, and has its being?
> (3–4)

The obsession with insides proves a crisis of spirit, and the antidote a parody of German idealism in the form of a Professor of Things in General, or Philosopher of Clothes, called "Diogenes Teufelsdröckh." His name, again, means, "God-born Devil's Shit," or perhaps, "Holy Shit"; or perhaps, "High-end Defecator"; or "Divine Subject of Human Bodily Functions," some sort of alternative Jesus. In Teufelsdröckh, clothes will be unmasked as elitist evacuation, the hallowed bullshit of celestial satire. What Carlyle's book will say about clothes is mirrored in the clothing of the book. And what else would one expect from a book in which a book and its author are the subject?

"The Life and Opinions of Herr Teufelsdröckh," indubitably inspired by Diogenes Laertius but also by Diogenes Teufelsdröckh's "Philosophy of Clothes," prompts the illumination, firstly of the hitherto unplumbed *subject* of clothing, secondly of its obscure author. Clothing as a *sub-jectum*, as something "thrown under" when it is really thrown on top, will be difficult to locate: its origins, superficial as they must be, can only remain opaque. In a chapter entitled "Genesis," we learn that "The Name is the earliest Garment you wrap round the Earth-visiting Me; to which it thenceforth cleaves, more tenaciously (for there are Names that have lasted nigh thirty centuries) than the very skin" (67). Homer and Shakespeare may thus be considered garments, and the reader begins to wonder around what the garment of Teufelsdröckh's name is wrapped? He shares certain features with Hegel, even with Carlyle's earlier experiences of breaking from religion only to find despair. But the Editor impedes the latter parallel from working perfectly, since he is, along with Carlyle himself, playing the role of all of the characters.[4] So Carlyle invites the reader to divest the book of the very pretense that is its subject: vestment qua vestment. Tug at any thread and the whole meaning of his elaborate vulgarity is liable to unravel. If the reader is to read on, the only option is to read at face value, which is to say, on the level of clothes.

At long last, Teufelsdröckh excavates the façade: the British fascination with particulars has unwittingly missed German generics. At an unnamed University in Weissnichtwo ("Know-Not-Where"), Teufelsdröckh lectures on things in general, which lectures apparently have never been delivered, because in being so general they have no particular subject matter. Teufelsdröckh, too, remains but a name, a Thing in general (14). And his teachings, invisible as they are, are shot through with the same impenetrability as revealed doctrine. The philosopher of clothing is strangely, then, a philosopher of revelation, brought in to save godless scientists with the miracle of clothes. In the third book, the sartorial profession is elevated to divinity. "God" is merely the tailor with the greatest monopoly, and the Universe his vast woven "wonder-hiding" garment (166). *Sartor Resartus* will alter him: "What too are all poets and moral Teachers ... but a species of Metaphorical Tailors? ... Who but the poet first made Gods for men?" (219). Inasmuch as science fails to understand clothes, it fails to understand not only gods and poets, but also that "in this one pregnant subject of Clothes, rightly understood, is included all that men have thought, dreamed, done and been: the whole external Universe and what it holds is but Clothing, and the essence of all Science lies in the Philosophy of Clothes" (56–7).

Why are scientists such awful tailors? They cut things up, only to be at daggers how to stitch them back together, for they forget the whole they were seeking in the face of the parts. Even the scientist's lab coat and spectacles are overlooked, and with them, the interest in looking.[5] This is because the spectacles (provided that they are not too rosy) are designed to lose sight of the need for a lens. The danger is that science will turn us all into mere spectacles, behind which there is no "Eye" (54). Strangely, this failure to notice the activity of looking threatens to tailor the tailor into clothes. Gottfried Keller's poor tailor, Wenzel Strapinski, wields craftsmanship so fine that he unwittingly transforms himself into a nobleman with a well-tailored cape. By the end of Carlyle's tale, too, the tailor has morphed from the "I" of the self into the eye of God. It is agency that science has forgotten in its costume/custom of facts and repetition, which dampen wonder and awe by quantifying the unknown. This leads us to believe that "the Miraculous, by simple repetition, ceases to be Miraculous" (196). The inexplicable miracle of Teufelsdröckh, however, prompts the following question: is the attempt to reduce human beings to collections of fibers and tissues equivalent to an attempt to spiritually transcend? Is the highest possible abstraction in some way the same as the barest reduction? Both posit an inscrutable and irreducible unity: the one, a descent to a biological clothes-wearing organism, the other, an ascent to an abstract spirit manifested by clothes. Depth revealed is but another wondrous surface.

The Editor's project—to uncover the estranged persona that is Teufelsdröckh—to mine the depths of a man who is sheer top—to bring the spectacle qua spectacle into the spectacle—takes readers to meet their own estrangement in coming to know the unknowability of a man whose subject is nothing other than the continual alienation of cloth. The only sign Teufelsdröckh is even capable of connecting to the world is an episode where he bursts out laughing in a bar. Even in this instance, he is not a man laughing, but the very essence of laughter (26). When the laughing ceases, he is as dense as ever. Teufelsdröckh's writing, too, is completely disorganized, arranged in paper sacks with cosmological labels and references to himself in the third-person. His "I" appears to have already disappeared behind his spectacles. But is Teufelsdröckh the Editor of his own obscurity, estranged in Editor form from himself?

He comes out of nowhere and disappears in an equally mysterious manner. He is left on the doorstep of a soldier-turned-farmer and a housewife whom he compares to Desdemona. He doesn't know who truly authored him but he conjectures that it was an "ill-starred parent" who had his head in the sand because of misconduct. So born from an unnamed criminal, he imagines he is Adam and Eve's son with a singular name that prefigures his destiny.[6]

Teufelsdröckh almost immediately begins to speak—that is, to name, that is, to clothe. From childhood onward he is an observer, and he comes to see the whole universe in a Duck-Pond (74).[7] His shallow origin, along with his esoteric philosophy, threatens to render him imaginary. But there is a metamorphic event that guides the story of his life and times: his falling in love with a woman named Blumine who rejects him for his friend, Towgood. This plunges him into a deep depression which causes him to have a threefold dialectical experience while he is walking down St. Thomas Hell Street— an infernal journey of rejection, restless doubt, and openness to new belief. In a cursing conversion from nay to yea through a center of indifference, Teufelsdröckh discovers Clothes. The result is neither erotic shame nor absolute clothedness.

Goodbye, Eden—language is the flesh garment and body of thought and "Metaphors its muscles and tissues and living integuments." We can as quickly strip human beings of clothes as we can rid them of words. Silence is pregnant; ignorance never blissful. "An unmetaphorical style you shall in vain seek for: is not your very *Attention* a *Stretching-to*?" (57). Attention is a carrying beyond, a *meta-phorê*. Beyond what? Clothes were neither discovered nor invented: we only come to realize they are on us after they already are. And if Carlyle's text is itself a Flesh-garment, the unutterable mystery of its spirit would be the author, the *subjectum*, cast underneath the words. It does not then seem possible to separate the book's irony from its honesty, by virtue of its own ironic claims.[8] Speech works in patterns, weaving together meaning and saying, yet never quite saying what it means. If meaning could be captured just so by speech, it would collide with reality. But reality would then be unspeakable, like the exposed rooms of a dollhouse seen from the back. Religious and political orders follow suit. Body and clothing are the site and materials whereon and whereby the patterns of our persons are woven. Cut and color—whether Grecian, Gothic, or altogether Modern—betoken spiritual idiosyncrasies (28). Becoming aware of the domestic conditions of experience will have nothing to do with returning human beings to paradise, but rather, enrolling them in a foreign exchange program. Self-awareness requires a certain othering from oneself. Without clothing the self could not travel, and so, could not think of itself as having a home. But Genesis begins when clothes have already become a second skin.

Teufelsdröckh claims that the first spiritual want of human beings was not for decency but decoration. Underneath decoration, shame mysteriously arose. Clothing provided a breeding ground for the holy. It created a passage for the unutterable with its colorful spectrum of perplexities. If we are ashamed when we wear clothes, it is not because we are really naked underneath, but because clothes are so endlessly revealing of our souls. Teufelsdröckh

muses that, there does not live a man who can imagine "a naked Duke of Windlestraw addressing a naked House of Lords … Imagination, choked in a mephitic air, recoils on itself and will not forward with the picture" (49). Society naked and unfiltered means either human beings in the state of nature, savage, and anarchical, or human beings divinized.[9] To denude is to be "dressed in the one remarkable way that said 'civilization at its best' and also feigned ignorance of civilization" (Pappas 2016: 224). This is the nightmare or pleasure trip that is chased by philosophers, scientists, and religious fanatics alike. The goal is to divest human beings not of their investment, but of their impetus to invest.

So *Sartor Resartus* demands bawdy humor on a lofty theme. An entire chapter is devoted to the Laystall's apron, which is used as a shield for bull shit. The "rags" get discarded with dung on them and then pressed and turned into printed paper, onto which books are printed (34–5).[10] Clothes-rubbish, then, conceals and defends us first from literal shit (in the form of an Apron worn to prevent being soiled by the defecation of cows), only to itself become an apron for literary shit. The question of whether clothes are somehow concealing us from human crap is the same as the question of whether they are likewise the vessel for it, as is the paper onto which words are newly vomited. Clothes would then be civilized shit as bullshit is metaphorical shit. Already, profanity is the height of pregnant expression: investment without an actualized referent.[11] It is a stand-in for we-know-not-what from we-know-not-where, an intercourse between shallow and profound, the ineffable precursor of poetry.[12] Its excrement fertilizes as it decays, every word a tomb and womb regurgitating repulsive subjects in a "meadow of asphodel," or tilling the beautiful till it becomes "hell-on-earth" (55).

> While I—Good Heaven!—have thatched myself over with the dead fleeces of sheep, the bark of vegetables, the entrails of worms, the hides of oxen or seals, the felt of furred beasts; and walk abroad a moving Rag-screen, overheaped with shreds and tatters raked from the Charnel-house of nature, where they would have rotted, to rot on me more slowly!
>
> (44–5)

Human beings move on from being oblivious animals who do not know that time will slaughter them into tamed animals who fashion decay on their persons. This is to begin to see everything in clothes, even Dutch cows with their striped petticoats. Clothes are the author's giant diaper and God's, too: we are the holy shit, the thumotic excrement of some erotic designer. Since the universe is woven, its primary fabric is that of space and time.

The obscurity of clothes seems to be the precondition for the possibility of any scientific (or maybe any) inquiry. Obscurity is born through clothes, as literality through metaphor. In one way, then, covering ourselves appears to be a consequence of our ascent from barrenness; but, in another way, it is an elevation of our ignorance. George Fox's perennial leather suit spuriously puts forth a solution—hand-stitched breeches for every season, a second nakedness, revised for a pilgrimage immune to bodily plights. The scientist and the phenomenologist meet here, which is to say, nowhere, for the one is heading toward the most naked particle, the other toward a reimagining of the surface as undressed.

Spiritually restless fast fashion strives toward the same nowhere: it comes to be and passes away with an air of ritualism. This is the atheist's dress, wherein you can no longer have faith in the holy power of covering. The body now sheds its skin and replaces it at a godlessly rapid pace. But, in Carlyle's characterization of God-born-Devil's-shit, underneath clothes an awareness of the self is born, and this tacitly suggests that clothes stop human beings from cannibalism. Fast fashion, on the other hand, reconnects us with our animality. We consume without the thought of what we are consuming, without the distinctive otherness of clothes cutting in. In this regard, the voracious appetite of fast fashion is not so different from high fashion: fashion immortals go down the runway as if they were impenetrable, disembodied clothes, and we greedily devour their souls, breathing them in with our eyes. As materialism acquires new symbolism, and fabric becomes a simulacrum of what it means to be embodied in space and time, everything turns vestment, and it does not seem that we can be *in* anything when we are in clothes.

What then of being in "body"? It means being in life, but can we get "out of it" in order to understand its materiality? Or is this itself the apex of the immaterial? We are comfortable relegating truth to the beyond, but in doing so we take for granted the idea of our own nudity. The fashion of inquiry fabricates our discoveries: it coats what is there with our gaze. To consider ourselves subjects we must already have tacitly assumed that we are clothed. If thereafter we consider ourselves bodies in the buff, this only reaffirms our ignorance.

Clotho

In Pindar's *Olympian I*, composed to celebrate the Syracusan tyrant Hieron, Pindar sings about Pelops, the son of Tantalus. Tantalus, again, was an ancestor in the house of Atreus, a half-mortal, half-god who chopped up

Pelops and served him to the gods to test their power. After depressed Demeter accidentally ate a piece of Pelops' shoulder, not realizing it was a human sacrifice, the gods punished Tantalus with eternal thirst but the inability to drink (which is where we get the word "tantalize"). Meanwhile, Clotho, a fateful plastic surgeon, or, as Bari characterizes her, the original "spinster" (along with Lachesis and Atropos), fashions Pelops a new shoulder, and he reappears as good as new. In Clotho's cauldron Pelops emerges, dazzling with a false shoulder that deceives as if it were the true original. Clotho reverses Pelops' fate, his gleaming shoulder now furnished with ivory. These words of caution swiftly follow:

> Indeed many <are> the wonders,
> And to some extent the rumor
> of mortals, over and above
> the true *logos*, may deceive, as
> stories wrought (*dedaidalmenoi*) with embroidered falsehoods
> But Grace, who readies altogether
> everything soothing to mortals,
> bringing honor, she too has designed
> unbelievable to be believable
> often
>
> (28–32)

From Clotho, Pelops gets a cunning repro shoulder made out of ivory. Although it isn't flesh and bone, it bears a deceptive likeness to the original. Pindar goes on to tell us what a wonder this is. It is similar to how the Daedalean speeches of mortals sometimes trick us into believing false things are true. Grace has a similar power. She is the half-sister of the Muses who inspire the poets, and she contrives, as Pindar says, soothing things that make you believe the unbelievable. Still, Clotho, not Grace, makes the fake shoulder.

Clotho is one of the three Fates (*Moirai*) who fashion souls in the underworld. They are described in this way in the Myth of Er in Plato's *Republic*—"Fates—clad in white with wreaths on their heads, they sing to the Sirens' harmony, Lachesis of what has been, Clotho of what is ('being'), and Atropos of what is going to be" (617c1–5). To clothe is to fashion reality like playdough. In *Olympian I*, Pelops' new shoulder implant, a fate-spun garment, lies as if it were a true body part. It is perfectly assimilated to him, just as an impeccable outfit would be an eerily realistic prosthetic limb of character. Yet as much as this seems to be an image of clothing shaping *us*, the deception that mortals undergo seems an argument for the way *we* shape our clothing. Like a bandage that begins to fuse to your skin or a precious ring that you never remove, clothing can become part of us without us even realizing we have spun it so. So the Muses tell Hesiod, "We know how to speak many falsehoods like to genuine things / and we know how to sing out true things whenever we wish" (*Theogony* 26–7). This is perhaps the most frighteningly poetic aspect of clothing, since it can come to infiltrate us like a true lie.

Many years ago now, I had an argument with a colleague of mine, the late Karl Maurer (dearly missed), who didn't believe fashion was of any great importance. Karl would never have claimed to care about something so trite as mere looks, though he had impeccable style. About Pindar in relation to fashion, he wrote to me:

> Like Pindar's poems themselves—all "occasional verse," each composed for an occasion as flimsy, as nearly nothing, as some chariot victory; yet once they exist, radiant, and able even to be torn from context (so that if I quote even a bit of one, I burn a hole in my own page)—so beauty is. Fashion is the opposite. Fashion is like someone chasing Beauty's shadow, in a futile attempt to catch it as it flits along the ground. Some clothes do rise above fashion even if perhaps they arose from it. But it's a terribly minor art because all clothes depend on context, far more heavily than beauty does.

Yet, though "fashion" is fashioned for an occasion, just as Pindar's poems, it seems to *want* to be, even if it doesn't become, more. Karl knit together words without a moment's thought, but the result seemed carefully embroidered. There was something elegant about the way he carried himself that bled not only into his writing, but also into the fibers of his dress suit (and he always wore a dress suit—at least to school—suits that he had tailor-made for his lanky, irregular body). Almost by accident, this gave him a meticulous look, even though he insisted that the reverse was in play. When I pointed this out to him, he relented a bit.

> Yes, nearly all people are slaves to fashion; and most are not aware of it—you're quite right. We could even divide all people into two kinds: the wise, who know they're wearing costumes, and the fools who don't. Many imagine that they're ignoring fashion, or even disdaining it, when in fact they're locked in the most rigid and ugly uniforms of all—as ugly and monotonous as a prison uniform.

Fashion of earlier times—such as nineteenth-century costumes—Karl deemed "saner":

They knew that their costumes were costumes and just accepted it. They saw that the object of the game is not to be "above fashion" (for they knew that no one is), but just to make oneself as pretty as possible! (Whereas our present-day slaves cannot make themselves pretty—they don't dare! They're too afraid that if they do, they'll look a little strange.)

Karl's words now seem as striking as Pelops' prosthetically perfect shoulder: I can see in the words the shape of his emphasis, the silhouette of his gestures, the contorted way he used to sit. But even without the character of Karl, one can sense his sense that he'd hit the nail on the head or put the shoulder in the joint—strange, because, where we are dead right, our opinion ought not to seem so outstanding or borne by the carriage of our very words. In the same way, so-called truths strike us powerfully when we suddenly notice what we have failed to notice: we are ecstatic to learn what was already there. I feel sure Karl would not have liked my drawing attention to poetry's fashioning (he was deeply suspicious of philosophy for this very reason), but I smile to think of his admitting a beauty to the argument.

The flawless speech is as elusive as the flawless outfit—so well-tailored to us and to the world that upon its delivery it would cease to be noteworthy, because it would be so seamlessly in sync. We delight in capturing something that is in the air and cannot be pinpointed by any particular word or article (of clothing). But this *something*—culture, character, life, or what the Greeks would have called "soul"—lurks eccentrically in clothing. There is in clothes as in words the residue of human movement, some bleed between the soul of a person, their carriage, and their dress. Clothes gain their significance not from their own substance alone, but because they embroider themselves cannily after the substance that wears them, again, as words and speeches do.

Words may not fit in the mouth, as clothes may not fit on the body, though certain sophists can make it seem that they can know or wear anything. Like the soul in conjunction with the body, the clothes in conjunction with the self create a symbiosis that cannot be reduced to either self or clothes. Clothes are an alien possession, like hearing a song on the radio that reminds us of times past, or entering a vintage clothing store or your grandmother's attic, where there are stories and scents embedded in threads, as if there were still human beings inside of them. Styles of writing are this way too. Syrupy prose might remind us of a bad Hallmark card, while perfunctory phrases have the double meaning of being "short." The way clothes spin realities is, of course, never as successful as Clotho's shoulder surgery. Clothes never perfectly bleed into the person who wears them. But it is this flicker of imperfection, the chip on beauty's shoulder, that is so very telling.

Hephaestus

Hephaestus commits forgery like Clotho, but it is of a slightly different ilk. On two elaborate shields created for Achilles and Aeneas, respectively, we find an *imago mundi*. Aeneas' shield is given to him by his mother Venus; it tells a future that only the poet Vergil knows ("Aeneas loved these scenes on Vulcan's shield / His mother's gift—but he didn't know the stories," 8.729-30[13]). Achilles, on the other hand, is none too impressed by the looks of his shield. It is also given to him by his mother, Thetis. It has the entirety of the *kosmos* on it, and it offers a particularly striking image of the problem of both gods and clothes.

First, gods. In the *Iliad* the Olympian gods present themselves as if they were unproblematic contradictions: Aphrodite bleeds bloodless blood (5.339). Hebe is a wine-pourer of nectar (4.3). Zeus gets the wool pulled over his eyes by Desire, Delusion, and Sleep (14.160ff, 19.110ff). His plans are foiled by Hera, Athena, and Poseidon. Yet he is also supposed to be the sky that cannot be pulled down (8.68). On the outside the gods appear as what they want to be taken as on the inside—a prophet (13.111), a confidante (3.386), or Nestor (2.20). In other ways their motion is motionless. Hera speeds from Ida to Olympus, "As when a man's thought flashes, after he has traveled / much land, and in his sharp mind he thinks, / "Would that I were in this place or that" (15.80).[14] Elsewhere, Ocean claims to fly birds with his mind (Aesch., *PV* 286-7). But for beings for which thinking and acting are one motion, is there any possibility of intention? What forethought could push thinking one way rather than another? The gods need mortal desires for their own intelligibility. They are somehow both common nouns (war, fire, strife) and proper nouns (Ares, Hephaestus, Eris). They combine a universality of domain with mock soul. They are pure poetry.

Ocean is perhaps the strangest. He is the end of the earth and the place where the sun sets and rises: the measure of time in terms of a mirage of space. Ocean is the only river that does not attend Zeus' assembly at *Iliad* 20.7 (how could he appear and yet continue to encircle?). But Ocean is also the image for Achilles' immortal glory: an extension of the ephemeral character of human life to the boundaries of the cosmos. It is Achilles' peculiar fate that he can only have this glory in the form of a shield. Ocean's river flows around the entirety of the rim. The representation defies conception and Achilles seems, at least deep down, to know it. In Book 23, Patroclus visits him in a dream with instructions about how he wants to be buried. Upon awakening, Achilles remarks, "See now! There is after all even in the house of Hades / some kind of soul and image (*eidôlon*), though the power of life (*phrenes*) is not altogether there; / for night long the shade of poor Patroclus /

stood by shedding tears and weeping, / and enjoined on me each thing to do; wonderful was the likeness to him" (23.103-7).[15]

Achilles discovers a distinction between the shade of Patroclus and his person. But the wonder he has just witnessed is already the principle of all his actions. As Achilles had believed in the image of his armor, so too he does what Patroclus' shade orders him. He himself will become a blur of unbridled vengeance. He will have no qualms about beheading twelve Trojan children or making the river Xanthus run red with blood (21.20). He becomes a brutal killing machine with no apparent reflection (*phrên*). Nor can Achilles recognize that Patroclus' corpse is not the man, and so he laments to his mother that the body will rot away or be eaten (Thetis obliges to keep Patroclus' corpse firm with ambrosial nectar). Achilles seeks revenge for a symbol (*sêma*) of what once was Patroclus, a corpse and a dream. He idealizes Hector as a villain, too, though Hector played a very small role in Patroclus' death—Apollo disarmed Patroclus and Euphorbos, whom Menelaus kills, wounded him (16.850). But Achilles needs the excuse to fight out his own guilt. It is a fight that, like Ocean, cannot end. The story is sewn into Homer's *Iliad* as it is etched onto Achilles' new shield. But the shield's false impression casts doubt on the tale within which it is lodged.

The making of the shield occurs as follows: Hector had plundered Achilles' former shield from Patroclus' corpse; so Thetis goes to Hephaestus to commission a new one. As intriguing as the shield itself will be, its creator god is no less remarkable. Hephaestus is a crooked-legged divinity, either by birth or by Hera's hatred (when she threw him off Olympus). The oddity of his limp is a tragic-comic oxymoron that hovers over all the deathless immortals: how can they be invulnerable, yet concerned with human life?

When Thetis arrives at Hephaestus' workshop, it is described as containing *automata*—the sorts of products that Daedalus is also said to make. Hephaestus laments to Thetis: "Would that I were so surely able to hide him away from death and its hard sorrow / when dread fate comes upon him, / as he will have his splendid (*kala*) armor, such as many a man / of the many men to come shall hold in wonder, whoever sees it" (18.462-7). The shield's defense consists in its *stunning* appearance. It takes almost 130 lines to describe, from 481-608. It has five layers in which are figured: the earth, heaven, sea, sun, moon, the constellations, a city at peace, a city at war, a three-part description of farming (sowing [spring], reaping [summer], harvesting of grapes [fall][16]), the herding of cattle and sheep (with an intrusion of warring lions), a long section on dance, and two lines about Ocean, one that speaks of the constellations as having no part of him and another that deems him as encircling the shield's triple rim. The dance floor depicted on the shield is compared to the dance floor that Daedalus made for Ariadne.

The substantive adjective *daidala*, "cunningly wrought things," or "intricacies," and the namesake of Daedalus, is used six times in the *Iliad*.[17] All the occurrences describe objects made by gods or objects made with the skill or intricacy of gods, and the last three have to do with Achilles' shield.[18] At 18.482 *daidala* describes what is placed on the shield; at 19.13 *daidala* describes the shield as a whole; and at 19.19, *daidala* ambiguously refers both to the shield and to what is on it. That is to say, the shield as an image and the details on it are univocal in the adjective used to describe both it and them. As a poetic description, the whole and constituent parts are a single word. Attempts to recreate the shield in real space reveal interesting problems, such as the color of death's blood-stained cloak,[19] the placement of each stratum in between Ocean and the heavens, the double adjectives that describe both golden Athena and her golden cloak, and the fine linen garments, "soft shining with oil," that maidens wear while dancing (how exactly is the sheen of oil differentiated in metal?). Athena is made of gold and she is wearing gold. But how do we see the difference except when we hear it described? Golden must stand for Athena's fabric and her image. The goddess is subject and object, a distortion that is itself an image for poetic composition. The power of the shield's poetry becomes explicit in the description of farming, where the earth "was *blackening* from behind, as if it were ploughed, *though it was golden*, and this was the wonder that was wrought" (549–50).[20]

The shield contains both the entirety of the earth and the human place within it, both the poetic image of the cosmos and the cosmos as it is seen from the human perspective.[21] From the perspective of the whole, the two cities depicted on it can only be a univocal image of human life divided into separate scenes. In the city at peace, there is marriage and feasting, dancing and singing. A blood price is resolved by way of a judgment. In a later scene, an ox is sacrificed, but no gods are invoked before feasting commences. In the city at war, meanwhile, two besieging armies are divided about whether to utterly sack the besieged city or to divide up its goods; the doubling makes it unclear whether the two are allies from different cities or the same, but either way they are split. The besieged, however, are preparing for an ambush; two herdsmen follow, playing pipes and not perceiving the trick (are these the poets in the picture?). Led by Ares and Athena the ambushers slaughter both herded and herders.[22] The men are called small; the gods great. But their ambush is ambushed in turn by the besiegers (yet another doubling that increases the sense of the inseparability of the quarreling parties, and perhaps, too, immortals and mortals) and the account ends in an inconclusive battle by the river.

The subsequent scenes of farming and herding seem to correspond to peacetime and wartime, respectively. In the herding scene, two lions fight with each another, pursued feebly by herdsmen and their dogs; this seems to be an image within the image of the earlier scene of internal and external division. Do poets only feebly chase the reality of war? Even while you might be able to imagine the shield flashing impossible metallics, the latter sort of double entendre can only be captured through its working out. In other words, the plot of Hephaestus' making unfolds the shield as if it were a story rather than a "map of the finished product" (Taplin, in reference to a remark by Lessing, 1980: 5). By the end of the description, an *Iliad* forged in miniature makes human life look as though it can be self-sufficient, as if the whole world and its interworking could be figured on a screen. But the shield is wrought by a limping god and carried by a divine mortal. Hephaestus warns Thetis that the armor won't protect Achilles from death. It only creates an image of the world that leaves onlookers in awe of its wondrousness. In this way, its power and powerlessness offers a reading of the significance of the poem itself.

If it is not possible for Achilles to escape even with this divinely made icon, the shield's hopeful *Iliad* reflects the tragedy of Homer's *Iliad*. Zeus remarks, "there is nothing more wretched than mankind / of all things that breathe and creep on earth" (17.446–7). Zeus thinks he can see the human plight. But "Zeus" likewise signifies the impossible attempts of men to understand their own dismal position, since the god's perspective is also the ruse of our inability to see our own fates. "Oh how wretched human beings are!" says the human poet, as if Zeus. Poetry erases the distinction between the outward form of a thing and its inward nature by dividing human beings from gods. Hephaestus' shield is a metaphor for the whole that Achilles cannot see, for it will face only his enemy.

When Thetis retrieves the finished shield, she flies down "like a hawk" into Achilles' midst. The armor makes a loud crash as she sets it down on the ground. The other Myrmidons shudder, "nor did any dare / to look upon it straight, and they shrank afraid; but Achilles / as he gazed upon it, so anger (*cholos*) entered him all the more, and his eyes / terribly (*deinon*) shone out beneath his lids like fire flare" (19.12–17).[23] Clothing, here in the form of the shield as poetry and poetry as shield, collapses the particular and the general in such a way that it seems to be tending toward gutless metaphor: clothes are the fashionista's ultimate defense against time, against flux, against choosing between life and death. But something stops it—material or "material"—what are the clothes without the subject, and yet, how can the subject be known without being sewn from clothes?

If we were sewn completely into our clothes this would mean we could not imagine ourselves as anything beyond them; we could not loosen the spin of fate. Achilles' rage at the inevitability of death (both his own and that of Patroclus) causes him an unrest that looks comically similar to the dyspeptic flippancy felt against those who spin clothes with special meaning. If Clotho could tightly twirl us in her trap, our personalities would be suffocated by fabric, and we could no long breathe. This is ironically the dream and dread of clothing. Fashion is the sign of our mortality. To get rid of it, we would have to die. The alternative, to attempt to control our fate by tailoring it into a seamless whole, gives the impression that the body might make an apotheosis. "The dressmaker that can fabricate the gown that is right, that fits us just so, is, then, like some divine being" (Bari 2019: 76). And yet, if the gown were just right, we would find ourselves renewed in fate's web, which is to say, the poetic shield against the unpredictable. Gods and gowns alike are the straightjackets of the unknown.

6

The Beauty of Ugliness

For we delight in observing the most exacting images of things which themselves we see with pain, for example, the shapes both of the least honorable beasts and of corpses.
—Aristotle, *Poetics* 1448b10-13

For the one is beautiful who is <beautiful> to see,
but the one who is also good will be at once beautiful too.
—Sappho, Fragment 50

Beauty—sublime, not street—will relieve those readers who are getting tired of the F-word. Back in her 1991 essay by the same name, Valerie Steele tells a story about being a graduate student at Yale, when a history professor asked her about her dissertation:

> "I'm writing about fashion," I said.
> "That's interesting. Italian or German?"
> It took me a couple of minutes, as thoughts of Armani flashed through my mind, but finally I realized what he meant.
> "Not *fascism*," I said. "*Fashion*. As in Paris."
> "Oh." There was a long silence, and then, without another word, he turned and walked away.

The B-word, on the other hand, has artsy and grandiose connotations. Beauty sounds as if it might pass respectably in the company of Truth, both with capital-letter lapels. Fashion, meanwhile, is not a requisite in courses on aesthetics, besotted as it is with industry. Fashion brings with it the ghastly sins of consumption, while beauty perms its hairs primly from the rafters, spouting eternities onto the changeable filth below. But I wonder: is beauty fashion by another name? Or, to put it more demurely: is fashion's ugliness more necessary to beauty than either makes out? Even if beauty seems a more legitimate scholarly object, it hits the eye differently when those who study it venture to engage in it.

The effect of beauty's "truth" seems to increase in the absence of any fanfare, when it pops up unannounced or where we previously did not notice it, as if a sudden insight that illuminates the whole. Still, in order for us to see beauty, it must appear. And its appearance, however close it comes to sheer invisibility, is at odds with its being "true" beauty, since appearances are dependent upon circumstance and perception. Beauty's appearance thus threatens to render it merely apparent beauty—merely fashion. But, like truth, beauty aspires to be more than just opinion; it seeks to rise above fashion's ebb and flow, to be no trick of the eye or cosmetic facsimile. "The question of Beauty takes us out of surfaces, to thinking of the foundations of things" (R.W. Emerson, *The Conduct of Life*, 1860). At its least conflicted, beauty would so channel the Zeitgeist that it could grant a beautiful person or thing the impression of effortless iconography—of having captured a transcendent moment, neither a rigidified corpse of past ideals nor subject to a watery fifteen minutes of fame.

khalepa ta kala, "the beautiful things <are> difficult." So ends Plato's *Hippias Major*, a dialogue about the beautiful. As a simple gloss on a knotty issue, the proverb itself is an example of vexing beautification. In its apparent simplicity, beauty reveals itself to be hard. When it hits us with its polished surface we find it is laughably distant from reality, almost ugly in its distance from everyday experience. But behind beauty's ugliness is the keenness of sight that is requisite for the recognition of the beautiful. And herein beautiful things get complicated.

Bernie's Mittens[1]

The image of Bernie Sanders at the 2021 presidential inauguration launched more ships than Helen of Troy. Senator Sanders, or more casually chic, "Bernie," appeared wearing Fair Isle mittens made by a Vermont school teacher, Jen Ellis, and a very practical coat from the Vermont-based company, Burton Snowboards. He was photographed in this locally sourced utilitarian outfit, carrying pieces of mail, and seated in a pose that resembled Gru from *Despicable Me*. He looked curmudgeonly and cold but comfortable. This stood in stark contrast to the rainbow of elegance painted by Michelle Obama, Amanda Gorman, and Jill Biden. But it was Bernie who became an overnight fashion phenomenon. Bernie's portrait graced countless memes and products; he was featured on digital *Vogue* and *The Cut*. There was even a "Be Bernie" filter on social media. And while reactions ranged from fond admiration of Bernie's grumpy-grandpa threads to gushing over his inconspicuousness, there is something lurking not so much in Bernie's outfit, but in the reaction to it, that deserves attention. This, we imagine, is how Bernie really is (or at least *looks*) no matter where he is, and this image of reality strikes us and amuses us like a common dandelion growing amidst a swathe of bougainvillea.

Unassuming, mittened up, arms crossed, Bernie Sanders appears as if he does not appear. He is the transient Everyman, as emblematic as Baudelaire's Monsieur G., the anonymous sketcher of the manners of the time, the painter of modern life, a lover of its subtle changes of outfit. Bernie, too, has a pulse on change. Like Monsieur G., in his anonymity he appears somehow distinctive. He happened to be there at just the right time, like a Kate Moss or a Grace Jones, so perfectly embodying the era that his image appears beyond the era. In Bernie's natural beauty, one finds the height of that art of contingency that every serious fashionista and politician covets, the point at which the trendy becomes classic. Will Bernie's look of the moment live beyond the moment? Already, Bernie has teleported to more places and times than Amélie's gnome. Already, he signs his signature in disappearing ink:

> In the window of a coffee-house there sits a convalescent, pleasurably absorbed in gazing at the crowd, and mingling, through the medium of thought, in the turmoil of thought that surrounds him ....
>
> He is a master of that only too difficult art—sensitive spirits will understand me—of being sincere without being absurd ....
>
> The crowd is his element, as the air is that of birds and water of fishes ...
>
> (Baudelaire 1863/1995: 7–9)

In this way, Bernie Sanders, not unlike Baudelaire's *flaneur*, appears arrestingly human and unsurprisingly popular. He has struck an elusive mean between the capriciously untrendy and the deliberately anti-trendy. There is an effortless twinkle in Bernie's eye—or is it a wink?

Anti-fashion fashion—the beautiful ugly—has long been attractive to those of us who fancy ourselves engaged in higher pursuits. Too much looking in the mirror seems at its worst narcissism, at its best philosophical self-reflection. Especially in times of political, social, and economic despair, dressing up seems almost as mad as metaphysics, even or perhaps especially when the world is watching. Fashion in hard times is seen as excessive. We don't want to look like insensitive idlers, even if we are. We contrive to be real. But having discarded fashion in favor of anti-fashion, the specter of effortless beauty haunts our desire for exposed truths. So, there is Bernie Sanders, who looks somehow more "authentic" than the rest, as if authenticity could admit of degrees or even publicity. Either way, we're impressed and want to stare at him: the absence of frills, the eschewing of capitalist consumption, that no-time-for-fun-and-games-anti-fashion-statement that says, "don't look at me"—all of it transfixes our gaze with inexplicable magnetism. But before Bernie and stodgy academics, Plato knew the power of anti-fashion, or, let's say, the extraordinariness of the ordinary.

No doubt if Socrates were to appear in the twenty-first century he would wear repurposed wooly mittens, the very symbol of homespun realness that at once warms our hearts and refutes our [fashion] statements. But Socrates' ability to draw people to him without superficial looks was part of what led Athens to suspect him of concealing his vanity under a mask of ignorance.[2]

Bernie, of course, does not and cannot seem at all vain or cynical to us in his practical garb. His response to the flattery said as much: "Fashion? Let's get to work"; "We [in Vermont] know something about the cold. And we're not so concerned about good fashion, we want to keep warm, and that's what I did today." It's-cold-let's-get-to-work fashion wants to be and to look "comfortable," so that we can get the job done. When people look comfortable, it comforts us and makes us feel warm, as does the fact that Bernie, the inaugural Madonna, graced a sweatshirt to fundraise for Meals on Wheels in Vermont. The mittens, too, went to auction for a good cause, and all over Bernie-style envelops fuzzy feelings and good intentions. Yet the initial craze over Bernie's grumpy carriage remains the curiosity. Bernie looks so genuine it makes us burst out laughing. He is just *so perfectly* himself—too perfectly, in fact, to be real, as he in fact really is, which is what makes him so funny. Authenticity seems to give way immediately to a comic caricature, where at once Bernie in being so Bernie ceases to be Bernie and becomes a starter pack meme. Is the perfectly paradigmatic instance akin to a perfectly timed joke?[3] The more Bernie seems to be seamlessly portraying himself, the more self-mockery he appears to admit. And so we delight in how true he is—or looks. It is not his substance but the appearance of substance on the surface that charms us.

Bernie Sanders does not have a stylist like the impeccably dressed Michelle Obama. Clad in a magnificent outfit designed by Sergio Hudson, the former First Lady turned heads until Bernie appeared. By comparison, she suddenly seemed too put together. But isn't this fashion's greatest trick? Isn't Bernie in this instance a mitten-wearing dandy? The Dandy, we remember, has no uniform; he is an individual, an independent, an original. He could, for example, appear during a pandemic at a presidential inauguration wearing a plain jacket and snug mittens. The peculiarity of Bernie's everyday looks is not, then, in the specifics of his outfit but rather in that poetical fashion of his disposition. He appears artfully uncontrived, as we imagine we'd witness a Bernie in the wild on the way to the post office or the DMV. This is the irony without which beauty cannot do—for, while one can condemn this or that fashion as a vain display, to condemn fashion as such will inevitably appear itself a fashion. The fandom surrounding Bernie's image appears to be generated out of an attraction to a genuine "article," which is perhaps, underneath it all, a longing to be laid bare as who we are when no one is looking. But the naked truth, like true beauty, is an oxymoron. In our eagerness to see past surfaces, we neglect to notice the superficiality of depth. Why are we so attracted to the look of truth? Fair isle mittens are all the rage. Fashion rules us, even when it seems to least.

Hippias of Elis

As Bernie is the copper button in an endless sea of diamonds, so Karl Lagerfeld is the overdone fashion plate who shuns us from his inner sanctum. Lagerfeld was known for his herm-like quips and comically static uniform. On fashion and philosophy, he had this to say: "Designers who get all serious. I find that mind numbing and ridiculous ... You're not Kierkegaard after all" (2013: 110). But Adolf Loos gets a word in too, "What use is a brain if one doesn't have the decent clothes to set it off?" (1931/1998: 39). Lagerfeld was judgmental, elitist, and apparently aware of his own absurdity—"Normal people think I'm insane" (2013: 64). His grandiose wit made most people laugh, even while some found themselves unhappily reflected in the objects of his derision. As an exaggerated portrait of himself he was funny in the sense of both being strange and laughable.

"Le beau est toujours bizarre."[4] Its bizarreness seems to come from its being a standard for itself—for the moment it is compared with anything else, even the eye that discovers it, it finds itself only relatively occupying its position of being beautiful. Our attraction to beauty hurts us and it; it throws the injustices of the world in our face: first, because beauty seems beyond us, second because of our inability to do it justice. Yet beauty's self-justifying looks have to be just a little off. Elaine Scarry's words ring true—

> that beauty and truth are allied is not a claim that the two are identical. It is not that a poem or a painting or a palm tree or a person is "true," but rather that it ignites the desire for truth by giving us, with an electric brightness shared by almost no other uninvited, freely arriving perceptual event, the experience of conviction and the experience as well, of error ... our very aspiration for truth is its legacy.
>
> (2013: 52–3)

Like beauty, fashion deceives, beguiles, and tricks. It coerces us to favor exteriors over interiors. But even when it is brought down to earth and newly unfashioned, fashion serves itself back up mutilated and beautified as an anti-aesthetical corrective. It uses beauty to enhance its lure, and contrives all the more to exert its enchantment by presenting itself as not beautiful, whether by means of elegant, plain, or monstrous style.[5]

The ancient Karl Lagerfeld is Hippias of Elis, and he is the subject of two extant Platonic dialogues—the *Hippias Major* (again, about the beautiful) and the *Hippias Minor* (about lying).[6] At the start of the *Hippias Major*, Socrates remarks to Hippias, "Hippias, the beautiful and wise, how after a time you've swooped down on us at Athens!" (281a1–2). Hippias is apparently pretty (*kalos*) and smart (*sophos*), *not* the more classic combo of beautiful and good (*kalos kagathos*). The good by contrast could never be a mere surface phenomenon. If you are hungry, and you see a beautiful display of fruit in a still-life painting, you might marvel at its beauty, but it would not satisfy your longing to bite into a piece of fruit. Goodness is tied in some way to realness. And yet, where the literal enjoyment of the fruit is forbidden, the imaginary consumption of the fruit grows—a vicarious pleasure we get from the mediation of forks and plates (or reeds and clean leaves) that put our hunger in courts of leisure. We ravenously feast our eyes on a painting, and experience the pleasure of observation, laced with a pleasure taken in observing our own act of seeing.

There is a story told by Pliny the Elder about a painting competition between Zeuxis and his rival Parrhasius. Zeuxis had painted a bunch of grapes so realistic that birds tried to peck at them. Certain that he had won, he asked Parrhasius to draw back the curtain on his picture. But Parrhasius' picture was the curtain itself. So Zeuxis had tricked the birds, but Parrhasius had tricked Zeuxis (*Nat.* 35.36). This deceit of a painting as depicting drapery on a painting serves as a metaphor for looking in general. In the pleasure of taking in the *Mona Lisa* is also the pleasure of fancying yourself the sort of person who takes in the *Mona Lisa*. Such a person, says Baudelaire, glazes over "secondary paintings" and, "having once read Bossuet or Racine," imagines they have "mastered the history of literature" (1863/1995: 1). Delight in a composition is already transfixed by the notion that you have understood something in it—that there is a sympathy between you and the artist. To reach this level of civilized appreciation requires that you believe you know what justly deserves your looks. It is this beauty of looking intelligent—being admired for your admiration of admirable things—that unexpectedly moderates the beautiful with morality. Beautiful objects are inseparable from a subject's recognition, and so, the virtue of knowing what is beautiful is among the beautiful things. In this, too, "one" must know the beautiful things *effortlessly*—or rather, beautifully. Effortless beauty is the only sort that does not overcompensate or underperform. Beauty is a *kosmos*, perfectly knit without struggle. But there is another Greek proverb, "the beautiful twice and even thrice." The presentation of beauty's levity is at odds with the oomph it engenders in its onlookers. The true aesthete continually returns to the site of admiration without pretense or ritualistic ignorance. But if, again and again our attractions strike us as irrational, the beautiful offers us pseudo-rational justification too. It supervenes when we say, "Wow, that's a vision," meaning "I see it as if it were the whole of my range of sight." Beauty's primary illusion is to foster in the audience a partisan belief that its sight is nonpartisan. In this it paves the way for our experience of conviction, and so, as Scarry suggests, the inevitability of error. In a world in which you cannot make mistakes about the beautiful, you cannot desire to know either.

In the *Hippias Minor*, we learn from Socrates that Hippias comes to Olympia boasting about his wisdom, bedazzled with signet rings and other items of clothing, all of which he has made himself, including a foreign belt and hygiene products and poems, which he carries around on his person as if they were part of his outfit. Hippias is quite literally a self-made man; he is beautiful on the inside and the outside. Of a piece with his claim to this look is Hippias' assertion in the *Hippias Major* that beautiful things are beautiful by the beautiful as "something that exists," which is to say, as something real (287d1–2). To be sure, perhaps the beautiful elicits real feeling from its spectators, but Hippias' view seems truer of the ugly. The ugly conjures feelings of pain, misery, and embarrassment. In English, we have phrases such as, "brutal honesty," "reality bites," and "the ugly truth," which suggest that we cast the real in with the hideous and unpleasant. What tickles our fancy we are more likely to doubt as a dream or even deleterious to our sanity. Is there, then, something self-effacing in the presence of beauty? Or do we bring this with us while beauty remains untarnished?

There is a marked contrast between Socrates and Hippias in this regard. Socrates comments on how beautifully Hippias is dressed: he is wearing pretty shoes and he is "so well-reputed for wisdom among all the Greeks" (291a7–8). Socrates, on the other hand, is ugly and probably barefoot. We enter the *Hippias Major* believing in Plato's stereotypes. We think: there is something about Hippias that is false and something about Socrates that is true. But the plot is as follows: Socrates tries to get beautiful Hippias to tell him what the beautiful is on behalf of a super-critical unnamed friend, whose identity is later revealed (though Hippias does not seem to notice) to be Socrates himself. Socrates apparently doesn't think Hippias can handle direct objections, so he mediates his critique through an obnoxious "friend" whose coarseness shocks Hippias ("I at least wouldn't converse with the fellow who asks such things," 291a3-4); Socrates attributes Hippias' repulsion to the fact that he is so dolled up, and so, not fit to associate with the common lot. No matter the true identity of Socrates' evil twin, by the end of the dialogue, Hippias remains annoyed with Socrates—so much so that at the beginning of the *Hippias Minor* the two of them are not speaking to each other. But it is peculiar: Socrates is only able to converse with Hippias in the *Hippias Major* by dividing himself against himself. Yet it is to Hippias himself that Socrates appeals to repair his self-division. He has therefore asked Hippias to perform an insoluble task. Hippias is all too eager to do the impossible; he will pin his failure on Socrates' deafness to beautiful arguments about the whole.

But before Socrates turns to the question of the beautiful, he comments on Hippias' unexpected presence—"how long a time it's been for us since you have alighted at Athens!" The reason for this is clear: the Peloponnesian War lasted from 431-404 BC. The supposed dramatic date of the dialogue is, accordingly, around 420 BC,[7] when Elis, previously allied with Sparta, defected to Athens. Hippias' answer, however, does not mention the war—"I've had no leisure," he tells Socrates, because Elis has kept him busy as an envoy for judging and reporting "whatever speeches are made by each of the cities," most often in Sparta. While this is clearly because he was constrained by internal division among the Greeks, Hippias makes his business seem as if it is not governed by war, but rather the demand for his beauty and wisdom.

Conceptual Cash

Hippias exaggerates. His response to Socrates is adorned with a plethora of alliterations, superlatives, and prepositions—one among them is *eis*, which means "into," "among," "with respect to"; in the absence of diacritical marks, however, it appears identical to *heis,* which means "one." In Plato's time, diacritical marks were not yet in use; he would have been free to play on words, as we do with homonyms. In *heis* and *eis*, there is a linguistic intersection between an absolute singularity and a relative connection. The vacillation between the relative and the absolute seems to be present in Hippias' superlatives, too, since superlatives can only stand in their topmost position by actively promoting themselves in relation to some lower level. Hippias claims to be first, eldest, most sufficient, many times eldest, most and about the most and greatest in Sparta, which is why he doesn't "oftenize" Athens.

Socrates is surprised. Hippias seems to be able both to earn a lot of money (*chrêmata*) in private *and* to offer public benefits. For the wise men of the past, however—Pittacus, Bias, and the associates of Thales, and those still later all the way down to Anaxagoras—"either all or the majority appear to keep away from political affairs" (281c7–8). Socrates may have a special interest, given his impending fate, in whether wisdom and politics, truth and beauty, can go together. Where Protagoras had said in the *Protagoras* that he didn't need a "cloak," Hippias is presented in the same dialogue as engaged in thinking about *ta meteôra*, "the lofty things" (315c5). Protagoras' flaunting of openness and honesty is recycled by Hippias in the dialogues that bear his name—he will argue that beauty is simple, honest, true, and good. But is it possible, especially for the beautiful and smart, not to need a cloak?

Socrates wonders, "Therefore, Hippias, if Bias should come to life for us again now, he would owe laughter to you all, just as also the sculptors claim that Daedalus, if he were born now and produced works such as those from which he held his name, would be ridiculous" (281d9–282a3). Since Daedalus produced moving statues (and it's hard to know how you could progress beyond that), the phrase, "if Bias should come to life," seems to be the sign of Hippias' novelty. Hippias can count a lot of names by memory ("if I hear fifty names just once, I recollect them," 285e7–8), but his real power lies in his ability to give performances of "in sum, the entire account of ancient things" (285d8). He can re-count stories of beautiful heroes, which lead young men to want to become virtuous. The force of his performance is in his beautiful delivery. One senses such method acting when he begins to recite an exchange between Neoptolemus and Nestor, saying that "Indeed, this speech I exhibited there, too, and I'm going to exhibit it here on the third day in Pheidostratus' school, and many other things worth hearing, for Eudicus the son of Apemantus has begged me to" (286b4–7).[8] The words "on the third day" recall the speech of Achilles to Odysseus in the *Iliad*: "on the third day, I would come to fertile Phthia" (9.363). Socrates quotes the same speech in the *Hippias Minor* to refute Hippias' claim that Achilles never lies (370b–d).

Hippias here uses the oomph of rhetoric to convince us we are beholding a live truth. He sells this as if it were his own performance (a one-up on Homer's copycats, the rhapsodes). While Hippias initially doesn't want to brag, since he fears the wrath of the dead and the envy of the living—a reference to his having counterfeited Protagoras' nuance?—Socrates baits Hippias with a long speech filled with name-dropping. Gorgias, Prodicus, Protagoras all earned wondrous sums of "silver" (282d2). Hippias is immediately triggered— "Socrates, you know none of the beautiful things about this. For if you knew how much silver I have made, you would wonder" (282d6–7). Hippias cites as an example when he went to Sicily, and Protagoras was also there and much older than Hippias,[9] but nonetheless Hippias earned more than 150 minas,[10] and 20 of them from the very small town of Inycum. Apparently, Hippias profits from the "young genius" look over the trope of the old wise man. At any rate, one wonders what the two of them are doing in Sicily ....

Comparisons of size and value seem to be the sole basis upon which Hippias places his vaunting. "And coming home, bringing this, I gave it to my father, so that he and the other citizens wondered and had their minds blown. And I almost suppose that I've made more money (*chrêmata*) than any other pair (*sunduo*) of sophists, whichever ones you wish" (282e4–8). Money is good not to buy other goods but to show off.[11] Hippias treats it as if it could stand on its own, just as his performances apparently occur without the aid of the Muses and Memory.[12] Where money is the potentiality to deliver the promise of substance, its values are always poetically standing for something else, as a "buck" once meant "one deer" but now means "a potential deer" or "a poetic deer." Hippias, in Midas fashion, treats money's medium as a possession in its own right, and this is roughly equivalent to treating concepts as if they were detachable from the things that give rise to them. This already glosses the paradigmatic and the generic, since a concept—for example, Cat—may signify the model cat, which all other cats aspire to be, or the generic cat, which all other cats have in common. But the tension in the moniker "cat" between the copycat and the archetypal, supermodel cat (neither of which is a real cat) lies dormant in Hippias' financial accounting. He is only interested in the exceptional art of understanding exceptional cats. In the *Cratylus*, naming as calling, *kalein*, is said to be etymologically connected to the beautiful, *kalon* (416d–e). Whether this is true or not, Socrates has in mind that identification implies beautification. Hippias displays this in summing things up and in his display of his great sums.

Socrates concludes that if Hippias is so valuable and in demand in cities, he must be making people better with his education toward virtue. By extension, Hippias' frequent business in Sparta must mean that he benefits the Spartans most and makes the most money there. When Hippias reveals that he makes no money in Sparta, Socrates is taken aback. Hippias clarifies that the Spartans do not allow either foreign education or the changing of their laws (284c5–9); this is clearly in contrast to the Athenians. The Spartans like to listen to Hippias talk and they praise him for it, but in regard to their own betterment, Hippias has no effect. Socrates uses this to conclude that they must be lawbreakers, since law exists to help not harm, and if Hippias helps, and if the Spartan laws are good, "the Spartans therefore break the law in not giving you gold and turning their own sons over to you" (285b1–3). Socrates' earlier use of silver, and here gold, both present money with a less abstract terminology than *chrêmata*, which literally means, "things of use," but has a colloquial meaning of "money," something like "cash." While all three are still conventional, since on Mars, silver and gold would lack as much luster as the concept of money, *chrêmata* is relentlessly abstract. Silver and gold, on the other hand, double as adornment. This is soon explicit, when Socrates introduces Phidias' statue of Athena, which also happens to be Athens' monetary reserve.[13]

But back in Sparta, Hippias finds an audience like no other. In Sparta, Hippias gets wonder directly in exchange for his performance. There, Hippias *is* money. As a metaphor for being without resource, wonder (like *chaos* or "gaping") implies poverty (literally, being bereft of money after giving it to Hippias), but also perplexity (being, metaphorically, without means). Wondering is proposed variously in Plato and Aristotle as potentially the beginning or a beginning of philosophy. Does this mean that emptying out your pockets to Hippias makes you philosophical? Hippias quantifies his own "wow" factor with intensifiers and superlatives, which suggest but do not quite pinpoint what it is that takes people's money and breath away. Socrates does the latter but for free.[14] Hippias' summaries are happily received by the Spartans, "just as children use old women to tell them stories in a pleasant way" (286a1–2). Years earlier, Hippias was talking meteorological events at Callias' salon, but he has changed his expertise with times and places. The Spartans don't like to hear about "the stars and heavenly happenings" or geometry and calculations, because the majority of them can't count (285c5–6). This goes together with the Spartan law against foreign education. In Sparta, there is no common standard of value; no "one" for which one can exchange an "other." Foreignness only makes sense if there is something familiar against which to understand it. So only in Sparta is Hippias a priceless exotic, for only there is Hippias beautiful relative to nothing and no one else.

Partial Wholes and Evil Twinning

All Hippias' talk about his ability to compose beautiful speeches reminds Socrates to pop the question:

> Recently, best one, someone cast me into perplexity in some speeches, when I was blaming some things as ugly (shameful) and praising others as beautiful (noble), asking somewhat in this way, and very hubristically: "So, from where, Socrates," he said, "do you know what sorts of things are beautiful (noble) and ugly (shameful)? Come now, could you say what the beautiful is?" And I, because of my poverty, was perplexed and was not able to answer him in an apt fashion (*tropos*).
>
> (286c5–d3)

Socrates hopes that Hippias can teach him what the beautiful is to save him from *both* being refuted *and* looking laughable in the face of his critic's insolence (286e1-2). But if this is Socrates splitting himself off into his own evil twin, then solving the perplexity, "what is beauty?," and preserving his dignity (not looking laughable) are the same question.[15] Truth and beauty seem to be together in Socrates' request. Hippias, asserts Socrates, will know more beautifully what the beautiful is; he'll know just how to say just what to say.

Hippias discounts the question as "worth nothing," and offers to answer it, plus a bonus: he can make Socrates irrefutable in things much more difficult. But in what follows Hippias hardly seems to have understood what Socrates asked. Socrates wants to know what the *genus* is that makes all of the particular *species* of beauty beautiful, but Hippias gives only particulars in response. He answers first that "a beautiful maiden is beautiful" (287e4). Socrates responds with an oath to an Egyptian animal god, "by the dog" (e5). He then wonders about beautiful mares (*hippoi*), which is amusing because Hippias' name means "horse." Hippias agrees, "For among us there are very beautiful *hippoi*." Socrates proposes beautiful lyres; Hippias agrees on this point, too. But when Socrates asks about a "beautiful pot," Hippias draws the line—"Socrates, who is the fellow? How uneducated is he who dares in this way to name trivial names (or, 'use base words') in a revered business!" (288d1-3). Pots are mere objects of use, not objects of admiration: "What do we understand by beauty? Complete perfection ... being functional alone does not make it beautiful" (Loos 1931/1998: 63).

But, suppose, continues Socrates, the pot was molded by a good potter, "smooth and round and beautifully fired," like those pretty pots with two handles that hold six choes,[16] "completely-beautiful ones" (288d6-9). That is, not just any old pot, but a *model* pot. Hippias consents that if a utensil is beautifully made, perhaps it is beautiful, but only relatively so. Compared to maidens, mares, and all the other beautiful things, it could not be called beautiful. In contrast to the other examples, which are all feminine in Greek, pots are neuter. Hippias seems to be uninterested in *things*. He is into model style, not common fashion. A model maiden is the *quintessential* maiden, the maiden in light of which all other maidens become imposters. The quintessential maiden symbolizes every maiden—for this is what makes her so maidenly— and yet in being so exemplary she defies every other instance of her class: she is no mere maiden. This is already evident in the Greek word for "maiden" or "virgin," *parthenos*, which is also an epithet of the goddess Athena. Achilles, too, outstrips the class of fighters in being the model fighter; he is at once the standard and the caricature. Or consider the "standard poodle," which means either the common poodle or the poodle that outstrips all other poodles: the Achilles of poodles. The standard is both the common denominator and the bar. So goes Lagerfeld's saying, "I am like those bidets and sinks: Ideal Standard"

(2013: 97). Fashion models, too, while they are supposed to seem neutral and anonymous, from another perspective appear to stand out as misfits; they must be simultaneously beauty in motion and at rest, supermodels and sales models. How could the model of everything look like everything? The model of models that unites them all as models can have no name and no look. Yet Hippias claims to have *that* look in thinking beautiful things are easy and high: he defies classification. He thinks he has what it takes at least to be Sparta's sole top model.

Hippias' claim that pots are only relatively beautiful prompts a laugh from Socrates' adversary. Luckily, it is directed at Socrates, since Hippias couldn't stand to be mocked. Hippias' willingness to talk to Socrates seems to have to do with the fact that Socrates has not appealed to Hippias to answer a question, but to give him advice on how to answer someone else's question (Socrates commends him for speaking "worthily of himself," 291e4). At 289a, Socrates gives a performative summary of the projected reply:

> Okay, gotcha. I understand, Hippias, that it's therefore necessary to contradict the one asking these things in the following way: "O human being, you're ignorant that the saying of Heraclitus holds well here, that therefore, 'the most beautiful of apes <is> ugly in comparison with the class (*genos*) of humans,[17] and the most beautiful of pots <is> ugly in comparison with the class of maidens, as Hippias [the horse] the wise claims." Isn't it so, Hippias?

Hippias assents, and Socrates goes on to say that his adversary will say that this means that the most beautiful maiden will appear ugly in comparison to the class of gods—"'Or doesn't Heraclitus, whom you brought in, say this very thing too, that "the wisest of human beings, in comparison with a god, appears an ape both in wisdom and in beauty and in all other respects?" Shall we agree, Hippias, that the most beautiful maiden is ugly in comparison with the class of gods?'" (289b3–7). Hippias again agrees. Apes are second-rate humans and pots are second-rate maidens and maidens are second-rate gods, "as the wise horse asserts." But Heraclitus also says that the wisest human being is an ape in comparison to a god in respect to everything. So gods make monkeys of humans, since humans are the apes of gods' wisdom and maidens the apes of gods' beauty (heroes and Athena Parthenos are a problem in this hierarchy), apes are the apes of humans, and so, then, are pots the apes of apes?

But what about Socrates who is aping himself aping Heraclitus? Isn't Heraclitus, who can see this ranking, aping all the rest? Still, Socrates-2 apes Heraclitus (and Hippias aping Heraclitus), and Socrates-1 apes Socrates-2, and Plato apes them all. If this hierarchy is going to work, there has to be some instance that isn't defined in light of its insufficiency to another class. It is hard to resist cracking a joke that must be lurking here—in the *Phaedrus* Socrates says that asses are just another version of a horse (260b). If horses had been included in this chart, Socrates would have introduced the problem of "asses," and potentially made an ass out of Hippias. He tiptoes around the issue. But Socrates has been mocking himself this whole time and forcing Hippias to reflect on it. This seems to exemplify the self-undermining character of beauty's appearance. As a standard, it must and cannot take itself seriously. We wouldn't say to a beautiful maiden, "You're pretty in comparison to this bowl, but next to Aphrodite you're hideous." Beauty is not self-confidence, as Hippias thinks, but self-mockery. Its mystique is to make itself seem serious. At a fashion show, no one laughs, but maybe they should? The somber attitude seems a bit too religious. It is easy to find high comic elements in Leigh Bowery's exaggerated makeup, Elsa Schiaparelli's shoe hat, or McQueen's Armadillo boots (for his collection, *Plato's Atlantis*). Surrealist fashion mocks itself in an elevated way, the nexus of the funny as funny and the funny as strange. The couture runway teems with garments that poke fun at the very function of clothing by either rejecting the human shape or revealing its inner monstrosities.

Alchemy is Hippias' next response. If we gild anything, which is to say, *kosmein* (adorn it) with gold (which we remember is also money), this will make it beautiful. Marcel Duchamp gilded a urinal and called it, "Fountain"; Ai Weiwei gilded everyday wooden stools ("Bang"). Gilding an object of use freezes it, and puts it to a different (higher?) use. The person who would not agree to this self-evident claim, imagines hip Hippias, would again be ridiculous. But Socrates claims that his evil twin will mock him, and the proof is in Phidias. Phidias did not exclusively use gold for his statue of Athena. He used gold for her dress (again Athens' monetary reserve), ivory for her skin, and stone for her pupils. Socrates' adversary would thus argue that, while her stone pupils are not beautiful when removed from context, in the statue they appear appropriate, and so, beautiful. In order to be part of Phidias' beautiful whole, stone has to *prepein*, "to fit," the statue to create a fitting likeness. This would work splendidly if only Athena were not depicted as enormous, and if there weren't already a problem with depicting a goddess at all. But, if we ignore that, perhaps it is "the fitting" that makes things beautiful; "the fitting" is Phidias' perception of which stone suits the statue, mirrored in the judgment of those who perceive the statue as fitting together. In neither case is the beautiful in the stone—the critical eye here, in other words, is not Athena's but Phidias', which is not in the statue per se, but rather the synapse of its composition.

Socrates' adversary then asks, "'So, which of the two is fitting for it, whenever someone boils the pot that we were just speaking of, the beautiful one, full of beautiful <pea> soup (*etnos*)—a golden ladle or fig wood?'" (290d7-9). Hippias is again amazed and wants to know who this guy is. Socrates won't tell him, because despite Hippias' expertise in naming, he doesn't think he'll recognize the name. When he tells him that it's "the son of Sophroniscus," a.k.a. some cognate shade of Socrates, he gets no reaction, as if Hippias' conflation of genus and species has made it impossible for him to understand one who is both the same and other (298b11). That the pot is full of a possibly pea-based soup recalls this passage from Aristophanes' *Knights*:[18]

> SAUSAGE-SELLER: Here, bread-crusts, scooped out by the goddess with an ivory hand.
> DEMOS: Oh queen! What large fingers you have!
> CLEON: Here, soup (*etnos*) made of peas, with a good complexion and beautiful; Pallas Athena, victorious at Pylos, ladled it herself.
> SAUSAGE-SELLER: Oh Demos! The goddess manifestly watches over you; and now she holds over you a pot full of broth.
>
> (1168-74)

Cleon and the Sausage-seller are here competing to flatter Demos with food and clothing. But the critical feature for Socrates' account seems to be that comedy is a lowbrow exaggeration of the high; it puts images together in a fittingly unfitting fashion. So, while Phidias places ugly stone eyes fittingly into a beautiful whole, Aristophanes makes the statue comical by having her ladle out pea-soup. The transformation of Athena into a chef is a parody of Athenian democracy with its bad taste for serving up the whole in a partial, cooked-up way (216). Seth Benardete envisions Plato casting Socrates in the role of the Sausage-Seller here; "Hippias' indignation, therefore, is misplaced, for beautiful dress and reputation for wisdom make him the equivalent of Athena Parthenos, who did not disdain to dip her ivory finger in the lowly fare of her people" (1984: xxxi).

In Socrates' hands, the pot seems to be an image for the activity of thinking, which ladles out mind-soup. The ladle is equivalent to Phidias. What happens if you try to spoon out soup with a gilded ladle? It will get really hot, and cause you to drop the pot and spill the soup. By analogy, if you try to gild the organ of thinking (the artist, the observer, or the knower), you will be unable to ladle out your thoughts. The ladle is the thing that makes it possible to serve up various particulars. But to sum up the ladle itself with a gilded flourish will cause the activity of knowing to freeze. Beautiful things can only be ladled out by a presence that cannot be likewise beautified. The wooden ladle is a Bill-Cunningham ladle or a poorly dressed designer emerging at the end of a fashion show, unembellished, yet responsible for the entire gilded affair. Fig-wood enters as a standard for the reality against which the "good taste" of the soup takes its bearings.

The double standard of the pot perplexes Hippias, because it requires that you take the interior utility as a reality that affects the gild. Hippias only seems to want useless items of use: an incredible dress in which one cannot sit down, platform shoes that are so high it is impossible to walk, or money for the sake of showing that one has money. Hippias adopts a hyperbolically philosophical view that everything is to be looked at, not touched. To touch would be to introduce the impurity of partiality, but with partiality comes interest, and so the perspective of the good. But if touch and sight are connected, this spells trouble for beauty, which without realizing it must collapse the particular and the whole. This *is* the standard *kalon*, where the beautiful presents itself to us as the *one* particular that serves up a complete paradigm. At 291c4, Hippias changes Socrates' "fig-wood" to "fig-tree." He gilds that which is like fig into its upper-class parent, "tree." But this too will prove insufficient: generation—all parents—must be buried.

Apparent Beauty

Hippias subsequently introduces a third argument about the beautiful: the beautiful is a life well-lived with health and wealth, and well-ended in a beautiful grave for your parents and then, for you yourself to be buried "beautifully and magnificently" by your own offspring (291e1–2). Heroes and parents like Tantalus who chop up their own children will present problems for Hippias, as well as the trouble that in order to undergo a beautiful burial of yourself by your products, you will have to be gilded and ladled into some afterlife (Hippias' outfit offers a material solution in the *Hippias Minor*).

For this answer, Socrates (and vicariously, though distantly enough, Hippias) earns a response of laughter that is so intense the conversation stops and there is a trial of whether Socrates will be beaten, and if this is legal, and the Athenians therefore barbaric. Socrates-2 says of Socrates-1 that he's like a millstone statue: all stone, "having neither ears nor a brain" (292d5–6).[19] Socrates-1 is dull as a post and needs sense knocked into him: an appropriately inappropriate characterization of Socrates as both the son of a stonemason and a book. Don't all inscribed books need to have the sense of the reader knocked in? Hippias actually agrees to the beating simply because Socrates does. Socrates is his own worst critic; Hippias is his own biggest fan. But the self-abuse Socrates undergoes at his own hands seems to be again an image for the beautiful as self-mocking, as in some way demanding laughter for its absurdity.

You could level the same judgment at fashion by asking if there is some sign of life in it. This seems to be the impetus behind fashionable flaws (e.g., wabi-sabi), which celebrate internal imperfections as if they could be whittled and externalized, both trend and outlier, relative and absolute. Imagined reality pretends to put sense into a statue. So Gucci's paradigmatic bad teeth idealize the crooked smile of the *real* real (ironically, also the name of an online consignment store). The individual has not challenged but become the beauty standard, a way of inclusive-looking that appears an exclusive look. Where the glossy patinas of fashion magazines make us think—"it must've been doctored," "it must've been retouched"—beauty seems to merely appear and not to actually be. "Merely" by the way also means "purely"; its root may be *mer-*, which means "glimmer," "gleam," or "sparkle." Mere appearance redundantly draws attention to appearance's insufficiency, and so to its suggestion of implicit reality. Instead of aspiring to unreality, we aspire to the reality of unreality, the real unreal, which is supposedly a more reachable look. But it brings with it an air of resentment at our prior ideals. This caters to something in us that does not reject the beautiful but rather hopes that it will manifest itself realistically—hopes that it will be less ostentatious and more … truthful. Our attraction to beauty is an attraction to the look of truth. How does real beauty become apparent? Beware of the Gucci teeth, which seem to say, *apparent* true beauty is also an appearance. "We are perfectly imperfect," bad teeth say. "We have self-reflection built into us." "We are the knowledge of the ignorance of perfect teeth."

At any rate, the beautiful, according to Hippias, is for the effect to completely bury the cause. In doing this, it appears self-produced. The beautiful gives you the illusion of an *ex nihilo* parent without origins. Fore-bear (*pro-gonos*) and off-spring (*ek-gonos*) are treated as if they were absolute and not relative terms. When Socrates' adversary casually offers the "fitting" as a new standard (293e)—now proposed more fittingly apart from Phidias—Hippias takes this to mean the same old gild: when an unseemly person puts on beautiful shoes, it makes him appear beautiful, because the shoes are "fitting." Lurking within Hippias' prejudice for luxury shoes is the "self" as a stylist who can transform, let's say, a utility pot or a fig-wood ladle, into a sexy item, just as Plato has transformed a trolling Socrates into an anti-fashion plate. But the standard of the "fit" is *very* strange, since certain shoes *fit*, not in the physical sense, but in the sense of their being *so you*. At 295a, Hippias says he will need to go into complete seclusion in order to achieve more than total precision about this argument. Complete seclusion is something like Sparta: a place in which there is no real audience and no questions are asked.

After the fitting is proposed, Hippias and Socrates finally directly talk to one another, and Socrates' mockery and fear of himself become a fear that the argument might be tricking them. It threatens to run away, and Socrates warns Hippias to remain still. The elusiveness of beauty now becomes the subject of the dialogue. Does the fitting create an appearance of beauty or a reality? Apparently it is not allowed to do both. Either beauty is real and unrecognized (like lawful things and pursuits) or it is apparent and then it makes things look better than they really are. Socrates wants the output to be zero, since if the beautiful is what makes something *more* beautiful, it is somehow imperfect. Likewise, for there to be a good fit one must not experience the fitting-together of the joint. Once Phidias (the parent) has been revealed, the statue (his offspring), no longer convinces us of its self-sufficiency. The thing that fits everything else together won't itself now fit. This is both the problem of evil and of fashion designers.

The tension between beauty's appearance and its reality will lead Socrates and Hippias to argue that beauty's reality must be grounded in some power. That is, the beautiful must in some way be good; it cannot be useless. For if beauty requires reflection in order to be seen, it likewise requires that the thing identified as beautiful contain reflection in it—otherwise, it could not be identified. The eye must have the power to see in order to be beautiful (295c). In the stone eyes of Phidias' statue are the sharp eyes of Phidias, just as in the millstone brain of Socrates is the sharp wit of Plato. Yet, power is neutral to good and bad. And the beautiful could not have powers to produce bad things, only beneficial things (here, Hippias' own beautiful demonstrations seem to be influencing his answers to Socrates' questions). But if those who are beautiful have the power to produce the good, and if they are *good* for such productions, this is already to confuse where the argument is heading, namely that "The beautiful is the cause of the good."

This is the sticking point that will lead Socrates to be at a loss for answers— "So the cause is not a cause of a cause but of what comes into being because of it?" (297a11-12). But why can't a cause cause a cause? Fathers and sons will be Socrates' further example, but this is easily contradicted, since fathers were once sons, and sons have the potentiality to become fathers. For the metaphor to work, father and son must be treated as ideas, and genetic parents beautifully buried. Socrates speaks of causes as doing (*poiein*) something, while effects come into being (*gignesthai*) (297a5-6). Causes appear to be poetic, effects genetic. But if the beautiful is the father of the good, and the cause cannot be the effect, the beautiful cannot be good. This is the father that was never the son, and the son that can never be a father. Yet to say that the beautiful is not good is no good ("least satisfactory"), and so the pleasure of the argument will now dictate how the beautiful is defined.[20] The pleasure attached to the argument in turn seems unwittingly to lead to the next move, which comes over Socrates all of a sudden: the beautiful is perhaps some appreciation of the beautiful. Aren't beautiful pursuits and laws beautiful by a pleasure through seeing or hearing? Although Hippias does not realize it, on this reading of the beautiful, his pleasurable performances in Sparta are saved from becoming un-beautiful in their uselessness.

Socrates does not acknowledge an overlap between sight, hearing, and knowing, but it is implied by the language.[21] Even in the case of the supposedly non-voyeuristic pleasures like eating, drinking, and sex, pleasure will be dependent upon the acknowledgment of the experience from the outside. Socrates says that everyone knows that sex is "most ugly to be seen" and even "shameful to assert" as beautiful (299a3–8). But this negative voyeurism seems to have some pleasure attached to it, and it is of a piece with what Socrates has been pointing out about beauty, namely, that its appearance is at odds with its perfection. Perfection would be at its most powerful when it appears to have no source. But this requires editing out the viewer, too. As a cause that doesn't admit of being traced to another cause, beauty cannot appear to be affected, which likewise severs it from producing an effect on you with its agency. The attraction that pulls the onlooker's gaze is the sign that beauty is not itself unaffected.

The way that Socrates has set it up, the power to see cannot fail to see, that is, be bad at seeing. It must be successful, and so, good, and this success in its accuracy (fitness?) has bled into the moral terms of its being beneficial (now under the coding of the "pleasant"). True beauty cannot be erroneous, failed, or bad beauty. If it appears fitting, its fit must be verified by some further confirmation. Once again the beautiful and the noble, in one word, *kalon*, appear to be inseparable. Beauty is, on the one hand, excess; on the other hand, the mean. Or, rather, beauty seems to be ideal, on the one hand, true, on the other. The pleasure we take in the beautiful is a pleasure not through sight or hearing but through knowing. But knowing, in turn, can be a "knockout" like beauty. When beauty works on our heartstrings we are not deceived by its effect but by our own self-deception, and that is made possible by the fact that we feel most like ourselves curiously when we are looking at ourselves from the outside, as if an insight on our outlook. But again, outside looks easily become suspicions, and so we are motivated to trace our feelings to some other agent, whether subconscious or sublime.

At 300d, Socrates announces that many things are appearing forcefully to him and not to Hippias, which makes him feel as if Hippias might be forcing them onto him. The experience of the force of his own agency is causing him to feel as if he's divided from and so possessed by Hippias. In his longing to trace his distrust of his own agency (Hippias suggests that Socrates is not just *probably* but *actually* seeing amiss), he assumes that Hippias is the cause of the illusion. Socrates appears concerned that if Hippias does not agree, they cannot agree; but he also seems to be soliciting Hippias' premature agreement to demonstrate how much Hippias does not like conflict, and so, how much he does not want to be affected by Socrates. That comes out in the final move, where Socrates abstracts from pleasure through sight and hearing to ask about the both and each of their pleasure—"if I am just and you are just, are we both, too, and if both, also each, and similarly, if I am beautiful and you are, are we both too, and if both, also each?" (303b3–5). This fantasy relativism again plays on *heis* as a double for *eis*. Hippias treats relativity as if it were absolute, as if "both" were "and/or." Socrates further wonders, if Socrates and Hippias are two, then are both two, or if Socrates and Hippias are both one then is it necessary that two be one? This is horrible for Hippias because he doesn't want to be double and he doesn't want to be lumped in with Socrates. The experience of agreement will require both of these things. In our initial experience of the beautiful as the fitting that we come to doubt, we find the moment of beauty's truth expressed as the plot of beauty's deception. The beautiful is not unity but a wish for unity; the longing in it for its own unity is what attracts us to it and allows us to be relative to it. The argument has come indirectly to the realization that to be at a complete loss or to singularly agree in *logos* is to experience the effect of the beautiful. But in neither case could the experience be appreciated without division; whether Hippias likes it or not, he and Socrates are neither friends nor enemies but frenemies.

Perhaps a little rashly, Socrates concludes that sight and hearing are harmless pleasures, and therefore (this is even more forced) beneficial. This means to identify the beautiful and the good again, which he had already said was impossible. Hippias has had enough. He accuses Socrates of scraping and clipping speeches together, as opposed to being able to "put together a speech well and beautifully in a lawcourt or council chamber" (304a7–8). Socrates gives this reason for his failure: he has a daimonic fate—he vacillates, and then gets splattered with mud by sophists, and he's especially persecuted by a fellow who is closely related to him and lives in his house. This is apparently the sophist in Socrates. "Whenever, then, I enter into my own house and he hears me saying these things, he asks me if I'm not ashamed (ugly) in daring to converse about beautiful pursuits, when I'm so manifestly refuted about the beautiful that I don't even know what ever this very thing is" (304d4–8). Wouldn't Socrates be better off dead, wonders his roommate (e3)? "Splattering mud" is reminiscent of the passage in the *Republic* where Socrates speaks of sham philosophers who muddy true philosophers and give them a bad look (536c). But, it is all to the good. Socrates is helped along (benefited) by this impoverished condition. He seems to be building into the beautiful the teasing awareness not to take itself too seriously, lest it be deceived by the self-conscious reflection that made it possible. This self-appraisal hinges upon the otherness of his self from himself. Socrates-1 and Socrates-2 are a "both" that experiences something that each does not. Is there one Socrates that experiences something that neither Socrates-1 nor Socrates-2 experiences?[22]

In Socrates' own experience, pleasure arrives in experiencing the difficulty of the beautiful, and this is dependent on the experience of himself as coming from the outside, as frustrated by himself. This is also the sign that the beautiful and the good are inseparable. It begs the question: is discord necessary for an experience of harmony? If so, there would be no way to define the beautiful without defacing it. Beauty would need to be familiar with ugliness. Is beauty, then, mock self-reflection? The very thing that allows us to know ourselves seems to allow us to deceive ourselves. That we can be affected by beauty would then be a weakness only for those who prefer the enlightenment of darkness. Trite phrases like, "you're beautiful as you are" long to vindicate the self through the self; but self-affirmation has the character of self-division. Is there something shameful or ugly about that which is caused assuming the position of a cause? Is it an attempt to bury or refute your parents, to bite the hand that feeds you or to lash out against the very principle that made it possible for you to be at all?

This has something to do with the proverb with which the dialogue ends: beautiful things (*kala*) are difficult (*khalepa*).[23] Just before, Socrates says that he is afraid that Hippias is *khalepainein*, "becoming difficult" or even "angry" (302a1). There may be a link between the proverbial and the punitive; proverbs come across as lightly angry or reprimanding: "well, you know what *they* say." They present themselves as deceptively facile-looking laws, which seem to apply to multiple contexts. Their power comes from a presentation of unsourced agency, free from perspective. But this seeming ease of uncaused agency is really the sign of a difficulty. Proverbs pretend to give you access to the whole with no traceable authority and without reference to a context of particular experience. An oddball or misfit like Socrates does not seem initially to have any place in the world of such beautiful understandings.

But the structure of the dialogue has been deceptive from the start: the beautiful, singular Hippias stands against an ugly, double Socrates. The allure of beauty against a duplicitous audience is meant to answer the inquiry into the beautiful. Socrates' claim to be "torn" and to appeal to Hippias for unification (really, beautification) reveals that Hippias cannot be so complete as he professes. Hippias, on the other hand, is angry because Socrates wants to divide him. This is how the *Hippias Minor* opens, with a third party, Eudicus, asking why Socrates is silent in the face of Hippias' exhibition. But it will turn out that Eudicus wants Socrates to speak up because Eudicus himself has a conflict with his own father. The agreement of both with each is somehow indicative of the experience of beauty and its disillusion. To beautifully seek the truth of beauty there could be no agent behind the inquiry.

You

The first word of the *Hippias Minor* is "you." The second-person pronoun, stranded between the first and third, is neither entirely personal, like "I," nor entirely impersonal, like "he/she/it/one/they." These two are the poles of lonely selves. But you in the middle cannot be without reference to another. In the context of the dialogue, at first "you" seems to refer to Socrates. Eudicus wants him to give his opinion about whether Hippias should be praised or refuted, if something hasn't been said beautifully. But why does Eudicus care if Socrates remains silent? In Socrates' response, he reveals that Hippias holds Eudicus' father's view. Eudicus seems to be invested in Socrates' assessment of Hippias because he's interested in having Socrates assess his father.[24] "You" then actually means "me." And "Hippias" means Eudicus' father, "Apemantus." But we soon learn that Hippias is also representing what he takes to be Homer's view, and Homer's doubleness—as producing Achilles, on the one hand, and Odysseus, on the other—will be the subject of the dialogue. So in every way we encounter the duality of "you."[25]

"You" serves as an image for human perspective. And if beauty is in the eye of the beholder, the perspective of the eye is itself a beautification, and this serves to confirm beauty's injustice. Beauty sinks its talons in, but to be capable of being gripped is to invite the suspicion that something other than you is gripping you. The split self—signified again by the you in-between—is the condition both for morality and for beauty (*kalon* in both senses). Beauty divides us against ourselves in an experience of unabashed wholeness. Hippias was distinct for thinking that he was all alone, an "I" that needed no "you." But the experience of pleasure requires that we be the audience of our own actions. We experience ourselves as "you" to "me" and "you" to "you." This too is the perspective in which we wear clothes. The thought that there is some "I" that puts them on cannot be quite true.

What will be at stake in the *Hippias Minor* is a competition between Socrates and Hippias, which is really between Eudicus and his father, which is played out between Achilles, as an honest and true straight shooter versus Odysseus, a plotting man of many ways. Since Homer can only be like Odysseus insofar as he plays every one of his characters, Hippias' literary criticism in praise of Achilles only works if he allies himself with Homer's duplicity.

Socrates mentions he was afraid to ask this question during Hippias' speech because the crowd was great and "inside." But now that there are few (and outside?), he's willing to ask. If all of the selves here are doubling for other selves, inside also seems to refer to interior of the self. That is to say, we may look unified on the outside, but in fact our inner lives are multiple. Eudicus, in contrast, wonders not only why Socrates is quiet, but also why he doesn't now especially speak since "we" remain who contend (*anti-poieisthai*) to do philosophy. Eudicus presents the business of philosophy with a word whose components suggest the anti-poetic, if not literally then figuratively as eristic sport. We "philosophers" come in and un-poetically assess poetic claims with praise or blame. This simplistic view seems to be against the proverb: beautiful things are difficult. Yet Eudicus himself, in setting simplistic terms, is under the effect of the beautiful. The beautiful divides things cleanly, *e pluribus unum*. Beauty's cleanliness and morality's purity are shown to go together in this dialogue. Eudicus' name is important in this regard, because it means something like, "doing justice well," or perhaps, "righteous."

In the latter half, Socrates argues in favor of the inseparability of true and false (and so, in favor of Odysseus). This turns on the notion that the false, if they are *willing* liars (Hippias asserts that they *know* full well what they are doing) must be *capable*, and so, *good* at lying. This means they will have to be wise, at least with respect to deceit. But because of their skill, they will also be better at telling the truth, since the one who lies unwillingly might accidentally hit on the truth, and so, tell both truths and lies badly. The true and the false thus seem impossible to rend. Socrates exemplifies this with five examples (366cff.), the last of which is only implied: (1) being able to write down Socrates' name (perhaps a reference to Plato); (2) calculation; (3) geometry; (4) astronomy. In each case, it is the one who is skilled at knowing the correct answer who can also produce the false answer. The unlearned person, on the other hand, would be bad at being bad, and so, it is the good who must be bad, because only the good are good at being bad. Socrates collapses skill with motive. If you are unable to cook accurately, then you cannot be a bad cook because you'll fail at hitting badness with precision. It is only the good cook who can be evil.

A fifth example is implied by the sign of Hippias' enviable and extensive wisdom. Socrates says that he used to hear Hippias bragging in the marketplace by the banking tables,

> And you claimed that you once arrived at Olympia having[26] everything altogether which you had around your body as products of yourself. First, on the one hand, a ring—for you began from there—which you had on, had a product of yourself, inasmuch as you know how

> to carve rings, and another signet <had> your deed, and a scraper [or tiara] and an oil-flask, which you yourself manufactured. Next, you claimed that you yourself cut the leather for the sandals which you had on, and wove the cloak and tunic. And indeed, what seemed to everyone the most unusual and a demonstration of the greatest wisdom was when you claimed the belt of the tunic which you had on was such as the Persian ones in being very expensive, and that you yourself braided this.
>
> (368b2–c7)

Everything Hippias has made is a product of him. There is no discrepancy between inside and outside. What he "has" around his body "has" Hippias inside of it. His ring contains his *ergon*, "work," and so it is not only an ornament but the sign of Hippias' power. The effect shows the cause. In addition to two rings, Hippias carries around tools for cleaning off the surface of his body. This keeps away any residue of otherness or Hippian byproducts. Hippias also cut the leather for his sandals and wove his own cloak. Cutting and scraping precede weaving and putting together. Did Hippias make his own shuttle, too? Is he also the herdsman who sources the hides out of which his sandals are cut? By the end of the list, the task of composition has been completely absorbed into the product. The final item Hippias wears is a braided belt like the Persian ones in being very expensive (does its price refer to its look or its material?). The belt is both the "most unusual (most *atopos*)," "out-of-place," or "absurd" and the sign of the greatest wisdom. In the next section, Hippias is going to accuse Socrates of "braiding" speeches (369b8). Somehow Hippias' own braiding of a foreign belt avoids deceitful braiding, because it is apparently a true reproduction, even in its look of value. Hippias can imitate the Persian *way* to such an extent that his cultural appropriation appears germane; Hippias is a city unto himself, perfectly responsible in both action and reflection. Since he makes his adornments himself, even the things that cover him up will reveal him, as do the artifacts for doing away with accretions, which are also his and which he made. He is the inseparability of the true and false par excellence in one true image.

> And, in addition to these, <you claimed that> you came having poems, epics and tragedies and dithyrambs, and many speeches of every kind composed in prose. And, about the arts which I was just now speaking, <you claimed that> you arrived knowing in a way distinct from the rest, about rhythms and harmonies and rightness of letters, and in addition to these, quite a few others, as I seem to remember. And indeed, as seems

likely, I forgot your mnemonic device, in regard to which you suppose that you are most brilliant.

(368c8–d7)

In wearing his "own" compositions, Hippias "owns" them, too. He wears poetry (epics, tragedies, dithyrambs) and prose. He also knows "rhythms and harmonies and rightness of letters," and others that Socrates thinks he recalls. But he forgot (ironically) Hippias' ingenious mnemonic device. The movement is from what Hippias makes and literally wears to his showing himself by way of the capacity to make in general (even the copy of his own symbol appears self-contained, for he has and has on not just one signet ring but two). The mnemonic device shows that he knows the poems by heart, and so does not have to "have" these in the sense of "own" or "wear," but rather in the sense of "have it in his power." His exterior advertises his internal workings: he is "on brand." But what are the visible signs of his poetic abilities? In the *Ion* Socrates says that he envies the rhapsodes, for their bodies are always adorned and appear as beautiful as possible, while at the same time they busy themselves with "the best and most divine of the poets," that is, Homer (530b–c). Does Hippias carry scrolls as a prop to allude to the memory inside him? Or is he simply Homer incarnate?

Unlike the rhapsodes, Hippias does not engage in dialogic relay to demonstrate his poetic powers; he claims to have such powers individually, as if an Olympic athlete in answering questions never posed. He claims to be stronger than anyone else "at anything." It is not clear what this means. There were no contests in Q&A at the Olympics, and, Socrates comments, not even the athletes are so confident about their bodies as Hippias is about his thought. In running together his Olympic speeches with Olympic athleticism, Hippias runs together thought and action, just as he had claimed that Achilles' lies were honest because of his genuine conviction in their truth. In a perfect coincidence of intention and delivery, product and design, there is no room for lying, falsifying, and plotting. In the perfectly moral action, what looks good and is good are perfectly in harmony. Yet the motivation to do good and the motivation to look good then become hard to distinguish, and it is here that Socrates begins to forge his *wicked* argument in favor of the bad as good.

Looking Bad

But beforehand, Socrates reiterates similar apologetics to those at the end of the *Hippias Major*. He apologizes for his one wondrous good, which "saves" him—he is always tripped up by things and made to feel ignorant by those who are reputed among the Greeks to be wise. So, he vacillates: sometimes things seem one way, another time another way, and Socrates is confused about how things really are. He is not ashamed of this, but rather, gives thanks to those who teach him, and does not misattribute their wisdom to himself. This seems to be a smack at Hippias' outfit ("For I never yet denied that I learned something, making out (*poiein*) that the thing learned was my own discovery," 372c5–7). Socrates does not counterfeit his learning and pass it off as his own. Rather, he praises and thanks the designer. His current vacillation is over whether the unwilling are better than the willing. Right now, he's fallen into a swoon, that is, an unwilling state, in which the willing seem to be better than the unwilling. He again appeals to Eudicus in case Hippias is "not willing" to answer (373a). "Not willing" seems to mean something slightly different than unwilling. Someone may be not willing to do their homework. But they may also, while engaging in a stubborn refusal, unwillingly fall asleep. The end of the dialogue brings out the difference between being unwilling as being stubborn, and therefore as a sign of the will, and being unwilling as being in a swoon against your will. For the unwilling force of the argument will cause Hippias and Socrates to be unwilling to agree with it.

Socrates' great strength is this knowledge of his own weakness. He says he cannot be other than the sort he is: he has an unwilling trait of extreme willingness to become unwillingly possessed by the wisdom of others. But the acknowledgment of his own incapacity is a selective presentation of his inability to select otherwise. Speech as selecting seems to be tied to capability; the word *legein*, "to speak," literally means "to pick out" (to select letters and string them together). It is therefore interesting that Hippias, who is so good at remembering, keeps forgetting what is happening in the conversation (he had earlier either misremembered or selectively forgotten some of Homer's lines, 369c). If this is happening on a conscious level, Hippias would be a schemer like Odysseus, against his own argument in favor of Achilles. Socrates, on the other hand, thinks it is better to be a plotter—to be aware of your own poetry. His unwilling swoon is from another angle Plato's plan.

To justify his preference for self-conscious poets, Socrates introduces seventeen examples of willfully irreverent actors. These are agents who are invested in an intentional failure of their own agency. They show their expertise by showing how well they can perform badly. Baggy pants and a backwards cap: error turned divine plot. There will be no shortage of contemporary examples. In 2016, Vetements sent models down the runway with their blouse buttons askew and gaping. Brian Eno writes of "the newly discovered axis well-fitted ↔ badly fitted," in which clothes are "deliberately chosen to look completely wrong" (2020: 312–13). It will be the person who can give a masterful performance of screwing up their lines—Florence-Foster-Jenkins style—and afterwards says, "It was intentional" (Meryl Streep), who is or at least looks better than the one who is just a bad actor and can't perform the script.

Socrates takes as a starting point the fact that to be Odysseus, a man of many ways or fashions (*polytropos*),[27] entails having possibilities or options, and so being free to do well or badly. This is better than simply doing well or badly by accident. Where the adverbial character of the activity determines the character of the individual (well or badly → good or bad) it recedes into the adverbial character of the adverb—doing badly well. One now has to add to the epithet of Achilles, swift of foot, *intentionally* swift of foot.

1. Socrates' first example, the good racer (373c–d), turns on "running," expressed by the Greek participle *theôn*, which is identical in appearance to the genitive plural of "gods" (a pun made explicit in Socrates' etymology of *theos* at *Cratylus* 397d). The new prize in this race is not winning, but rather, achieving the self-mastery of not needing to win. This is the divine perspective that is going to turn the bad bad into the good bad. Goodness involves being *able* to act (*poiein*). The able person is therefore also the one who is better at intentionally failing to display their own authorship—at lying.[28] The race, however, already means you have a winner and a loser that conventionally defines who is better, outside of the subject who runs. This means that you are not running for the sake of displaying the character of running but because you are "making" yourself run, acting out running, *performing* a run. Given running badly, if it's willing, it's better; if it's unwilling, it's more wicked (and committing a bad and shameful thing, 373e4–5).

Ability now entails morality. But isn't it worse if you throw the race intentionally? Everyone thinks Achilles shouldn't throw the battle. Also, what if you are a bad runner but crafty enough to find a shortcut? It looks as if willingly throwing the race brings in a new reward and mode of running: not physical mastery of the racecourse but mental mastery of your desire to compete. When we wish to take the moral high road, and be the better person, it means ironically to adopt a godlike, neutral position above the race. Still, to be triumphant in morality depends on finding the race meaningful enough to reject.

2. The second example is wrestling (374a), and it is hard not to think of Ajax versus Odysseus. Odysseus is famous for winning in the contest of arms by beating Ajax with brains not brawn. Ajax is obviously stronger, but who is better again doesn't mean who is physically more able.

willing → acting / *poiein* / making → outcome

Socrates wants to say that no matter the outcome, even if it is a shameful/ugly product, the better man is the one who is willing and good at whatever he wills. The will is the locus of the good even if what the will produces is shameful. Socrates does not say anything about whether, when the intentionally ugly result is accomplished, it becomes beautiful, only that it is better. In any case, looking like a bad wrestler seems more intelligible, since bluffing requires competence. Odysseus, too, can bluff that he is a beggar, that he is "no one," and this is somehow the sign of his prowess.

3. The third example is "every other use of the body" (374a7)—which Hippias takes to mean physical strength (b4)—but the point of the prior two examples is that intellectual fortitude has already replaced physical strength.

4. The fourth example is "good form" or "carriage" (b5), sometimes translated as "gracefulness." Willingly bad form is a virtue, whereas if you just have bad form, and are graceless, it is wicked. But "carriage" might mean how you carry yourself or what you are carried in. Craft carriage, like craft cuisine, may have an ungraceful appearance, but this is the sign of a chef's intervention on behalf of nature's will.

5. The ambiguity is replicated in the fifth example, "voice" (c2), apparently detachable from body. *phônê* can mean "sound" or "what produces the sound." In either case, the sound is articulate, not mere utterance or noise.

6. The sixth example is "lame feet" (c7). Does this imply running badly? Is it an allusion to Oedipus or Hephaestus? Since feet can also mean metrical feet, foot notes,[29] whether it is better to have willingly or unwillingly lame feet seems to be asking whether it is better to be a tragic character who knows you are in a tragedy.

7. The seventh example, "dull sight" (d2-3), confirms that Oedipus versus Sophocles is Socrates' prime target.

8. The eighth example is "anything of yours and one account (*logos*) for all perception (*aisthêsis*)" (d6-9). All of the perceptions are interestingly double: sight/a sight; hearing/a hearing; taste/a taste; smell/a smell. *aisthêsis* is in its verbal form a deponent[30] activity: to use the senses is also to undergo sensations. As you actively perceive the world, the world also passively strikes you.

9. In the ninth example, Socrates moves to "organs" more generally—the community of tools (e3)—and so, from natural tools or bodily organs to artificial instruments. But what about the tool that is defectively built? You can imagine a rudder that is badly designed but piloted well by a skilled pilot.

Or even a well-designed rudder that makes a mediocre pilot steer better. Once you have an instrument, the functioning of the soul that is using the instrument is partially reliant on the tool. It is really the person who is able to transform a weak tool into a strength that we admire for being resilient. That seems to be the poet—the person who makes even sweat shorts look good. Does this mean poetry sees badly willingly, and so demonstrates its competence by way of beautifying atrocities?

Simmel offers this characterization of fashion at its best and worst: "Judging from the ugly and repugnant things that are sometimes in vogue, it would seem as though fashion were desirous of exhibiting its power by getting us to adopt the most atrocious things for its sake alone" (1904/1957: 544). Is the one who willingly steers the rudder badly also capable of composing tragic characters who are in the end unwilling to accept their own unwillingness? The comic poet can by the same turn make the good look bad.[31] This is exactly what Socrates is doing with the unjust agent. He makes everything a matter of whether the will is present, so that even if you were blind, if you were willingly blind this somehow rights your eyesight. Does that mean that the person born blind is wicked, whereas the one who gouges his eyes out is good?

At 374d7 Socrates moves to wicked things, a change from the trait of wickedness applying to the subject of the action. Now the willing doer of badly has become the doer of the wicked. If doing badly implies doing the wicked, then, does doing badly mean behaving as if you were the wicked? In this case it is again more wicked to be unwilling. But behaving unwilling is here a sign of the will. What is to prevent the one who is able to do badly from counterfeiting a swoon of unwillingness? He could behave as if what he does is unintentional (he can't help but be the sort he is), and so get away with it.

This argument cannot help but make the bad look good, and it was preceded by Socrates touting his own weakness as a strength. Socratic *sprezzatura* has made the bad over with good style. Instead of being a praise of wickedness, then, this seems to be an acknowledgment of the superiority of "looking good." Maybe it is not possible to seek good looks without some real goodness. Socrates and Hippias at least are unwilling to say that the good is a *mere* image.

10. The tenth example includes "the bow and lyre and flutes and altogether all the rest" (e5–6). Bow and lyre go together. There now seems to be a tool that serves another tool (is the bow the soul?).

11. The soul emerges explicitly in example eleven: "<Is it> better to possess a soul of a horse, with which willing someone will ride badly or with which

unwilling?" (375a1–2). That is, is it better to be in control of the soul of a horse or to let it control you? Or does this mean that you control the horse through the soul? Its soul or yours? Is this to possess the horse (Hippias?)? A reference to the equine imagery of the *Phaedrus*, where the self-motion of the soul is likened to a chariot pulled by two horses, seems plausible. When you become one with the object of your mastery, is there any longer a difference between you and the horse? The further you progress into active domination the more you would seem to obliterate the distinction between active and passive. It is as if Socrates is suggesting that the only way to be "good" is to know you are good, but once you know you are good, it is possible for you to employ this knowledge as a tool to "make" yourself good. That, in turn, means that you are forging yourself, and suddenly the distinction between unwilling and willing becomes strained.

Socrates subsequently alters the phrase to the "better soul of a horse," so that the betterness of riding badly willingly is now articulated as a betterness of soul, which is to say *not* that the activity is better when it is willing but that the soul of actor is better. But there is a very fine line between possessing the soul of the horse and being possessed by the horse. The more you become one with the horse the more the horse becomes you, and takes you over rather than you taking over it. The unbridled will looks as if it may be indistinguishable from nature's horsepower.

12. The twelfth example is the soul "of a dog or the rest of the animals" (a6–7)—one thinks about Socrates' oath "by the dog." Possessing animal souls seems to mean dominating creatures that are able to be reined in.

13. The thirteenth example is "the soul of a human archer" (a7–8). Is it better to unwillingly turn around and shoot your neighbor with an arrow as if you were possessed or to shoot with knowledge of what you are doing (e.g., Cambyses proving his sobriety to Prexaspes by shooting his son dead with an arrow, Hdt. 3.35)? Socrates has not identified the target, but the introduction of the "soul" has made evil archers unavoidable. It turns out that being a criminal without any agency is worse, because it is more inhuman. We are more intrigued by serial killers who seem rational than by homicidal maniacs. Only in a world where doing is *poiein* does punitive justice even make sense—you have to be in control of your having lost control, otherwise, you can't say, "you knew better." Morality seems to be utterly dependent on the fact that the bad is in theory the good. There is then a hopefulness that a bad person can be turned around, and this depends on a gloss over the fact that goodness is at least vicariously dependent on the "possibility" of badness.

14. The fourteenth example involves the "doctorly" art (and soul, b4–7); is it better to accidentally poison your patient or deliberately? The doctor's soul is better and more doctorly when it willfully poisons. But is such a soul also better at getting away with it? Does this soul make evil look good, when you think you're getting medicine but it is really arsenic? Do we admire the clever ruse, at least when we aren't the ones who have been poisoned? What began as intentional slipping on banana peels is now the ability to make intentional wickedness. That is, the person who was originally able to do badly willingly can now take on the image of wickedness willingly, as if it were a fashion, only wickedness here means *unintentionally* missing the mark. So the good are not only the bad, but good at appearing as if they only *accidentally* behaved badly: pleading insanity, self-defense, cultural constructs, faulty designers, god's willing, the causal casualty of billiard balls.

15. The fifteenth example is "the one [the soul?] more skilled in cithara-playing and flute-playing and all the rest of things in regard to both the arts and knowledges" (b7–c1). It turns out, as we expect, that it is better to deliberately play a bad tune.

16. The sixteenth example regards the souls of slaves—"But really, I suppose, at least with respect to the souls of slaves, we would rather possess the ones who willingly rather than unwillingly err and do evils, since they are better at these things" (c3–6). Given the previous examples, it is very unlikely that Socrates is alluding to the possession of actual slaves; rather he seems to mean the status of one's own soul as a slave. Is it better for the soul itself to be willingly or unwillingly in a passive state? Can a soul "possess" passivity? To begin to think means to admit possibility, which means to unwillingly admit freedom. When we try to acknowledge the agency of thinking, we end up with an unsavory conclusion: to highlight the willing over the end result leads Socrates and Hippias to become possessed by the argument against their will. Does this mean that the more you believe the soul to be free, the more chained you become?

17. The seventeenth example is justice. It would be uncanny (or canny, *deinon*) if "those doing injustice willing will be better than those unwilling" (375d3–4). Yet everything points to the notion that those who do injustice are more just when they know what they are doing (the just man must be all too familiar with injustice, *Rep.* 334aff.). Injustice is doing bad things, but it is the good person with the good soul (read: capable and knowledgeable) who does injustice, and so, justice, willing. Therefore, the good person is the same as the crook. Neither Socrates nor Hippias wants to concede this, especially since to argue it means to render the helpless wicked. And yet the argument makes agreement with it compulsory, which is to say unwilling.

Socrates' final remark is that, as he said, he vacillates. While for an amateur, that's fine, he finds it *deinon* that Hippias vacillates, too. The doubleness of *deinon* as canny and uncanny, terrifying and clever, haunts both the conclusion and the resolution. The argument had begun as a desire to articulate the will but it ends up as an unwilling articulation that both Socrates and Hippias are unwilling to believe. The sentiment—"I am unwilling to make anything but this conclusion but I am unwilling to believe it"—now renders *unwilling* the sign of the presence of the will.

Fashion's adverbial lilt contributes to the ambiguity here. There is something about the attack on fashion as complicit in some sort of immoral act that waits in the wings: is willingly bad fashion better than bad fashion that is unwilling? Does intentionally bad fashion look somehow smart, because it engages with fashion while also dismissing it with a smirk? Is this the mark of Plato's good design at fashioning Socrates looking bad?

The question of the *Hippias Minor* is whether we can call someone truly good without thinking of them as also capable of plotting. This means to ask whether we can conceive of a pure will that is not tailoring its actions to its circumstances. But Socrates has made it so that Mother Teresa's thoughtless goodness is equivalent to the unwilling wickedness of sheer evil. Socrates has thus rendered Hippias' seamless outfit the sign of either unwitting forgery or brainless design. Only the beautiful could facilitate a collapse between the knowledge of the good and the good. Yet, as an object of ambition, it might appear but can never be neutral. To be good and to know it introduces the possibility of disobedience. The good will can only here appear in a negative fashion by rejecting the appearance of its own unwillingness.

Philosophy and morality differ on this point. Morality must transform the good into the beautiful; philosophy, meanwhile, is on guard against the good that only "looks" good. Agency or motive enters in as a question. The disinvested investment of Socrates' seventeen examples requires the fundamental assumption of being responsible for one's actions, whether a bad outfit or bad behavior. In the final chapter, I will return to the question of fashion and its origins, which is to say to the possibility of postulating an agent behind fashion's designs. If it is true that we cannot remove our clothes, the moral person cannot admit it; the possibility of separating good and bad relies on the supposition that actors can be stripped of finery, and unveiled as their naked selves. On the other hand, like fashion, philosophy is unsure, and cannot be sure, of its own goodness. Errors teeter dangerously close to but are not the same as sins, while mastery of argument and outfit imply but do not require self-discipline. If a stitch comes undone or a question begged, philosophy and fashion are both tempted to say, "I meant to do that."

7
The Question of Fashion's Beginning

Though you may not be an old-fashioned girl,
you're still going to get dated
           —Elvis Costello & the Attractions, from "Girls Talk"

Marx begins *Der achtzehnte Brumaire des Louis Bonaparte* (*The Eighteenth Brumaire of Louis Bonaparte*, 1852) with these lines—"Hegel remarks somewhere that great world-historical facts and personages happen twice, so to speak. He forgot to add: Once as tragedy, another time as farce."

In what follows, Marx describes how human beings make their history with fabric dealt to them from "dead generations." During times of revolutionary crisis, they "anxiously conjure up into their service the spirits of the past, borrowing their names, battle cries, and costumes to perform a new world-historical scene in this time-honored disguise and with this borrowed language." History's necromantic revival is like Benjamin's tiger's leap: a mode of cultural advance. To be "hip" means to be mod, which is to say, *a la mode*, "in fashion," and so, to become aware of the now by having sprung out of it into the past. The now is apprehended only by thinking of it as a now that is now gone. Time's inevitable foreignness paves the way for the exoticism of old news. The hip are tragically hip. They make a farce of the present by invoking the wilderness of the once; to be on the fringe is to be in by being out. This liminal moment bears a similarity to Aristotle's argument about middle age and Socrates' refashioning of the good as the bad. Fashion's former affairs are indeed oddly philosophical. Fashions progress into "classics" as if they transcended particular eras and persons, occupying that prime moment of fleeting appropriateness in a forever sort of way. In this, fashion replicates the history it seems to dismantle. It "is capable of turning the ancient into the modern because its citations always have to remain incomplete" (Lehmann 2000: 1.6).

Among fifteenth-century humanists, there was a fascination with pagan texts and sculptures that "somehow 'cleared' the level of authorship" (Nagel and Wood 2010: 105–6). The past had become obscure only because it was perceived as distant enough to be imagined as a complete break from the present. Antique sculptures were rediscovered as if born from the very earth out of which they were reaped. Christianity helped this along by wiping away age with iconography; paganism returned as a cabinet of curiosities. Fashion's revolutions thus seem emblematic of thinking's, since thoughts, like fashion, appear to enter the mind from nowhere, and only thereafter to understand themselves as incomplete historical moments by virtue of trying to wrestle with their pastness as the symbol of the opacity of a present motion.

The fashion of traversing time in visual poetry, as if time were a mere costume, was also a fashion in ancient times. Lucretius, who was himself almost snuffed out by Christianity (until the Renaissance brought him back to life as a pagan idol), imagines that the politics of the Romans would benefit from a return to the clarity of the obscure Greeks. He borrows from an earlier author, Ennius, who channeled Greek epic in Latin verse. For Plato, Homer's historical significance was already a question. The rhapsodes had brought Homer into cultural consciousness by riffing on his lines for each new audience and generation. For the oral tradition, the futurity of the present could only be engaged in a constant refashioning of the past. One wonders, then, just how far back one can trace fashion; its ghost pops up unexpectedly in a plainclothes ideal of a *now once* that must've been *once now*.

In any case, neither fashion nor style plays by the rules. "Cool shirt."—"Where'd you get it?"—That is to say, rationalize the irrational appearance of your agency by justifying it in the source of cool. It makes a certain sense that certain academics who fancy themselves learned might bristle at the performative mockery of receding agency. Especially provocative is the way that fashionistas, as if philosophers, appear to discount historical context in favor of structural identities. The academic distrust of the untrained eye—symbolized, I think, by fashion's associations not just with sophists, but with "regular" people—seems to worry about what the popular diction of clothes *sans* proper pedigree might profess. Yet clothes seem to touch a philosophical nerve in everyone. They are right there on the person, teasing the depth that would grant meaning to life in spite of ephemerality.

Does this outfit make me look too dated or too fresh? Well, who really cares, they're *just* clothes. Or do clothes call to mind the just? Philosophy echoes, "just *just* clothes!" It sees its own reflection in fashion's egregious refashioning. "But when I looked into the mirror, I screamed, and my heart was shaken: for I saw not myself therein, but a devil's grimace and mocking laughter" (Nietzsche, *Thus Spoke Zarathustra*, Part 2, "The Child with the Mirror"). Philosophy would break through—perhaps smash through—the mirror if it could. To no avail, for it remains in time, and so, in fashion. Leisure and leisurewear are prime attempts to approximate in attitude and person the featureless sculpture of bygone ideals.

This is the idle idol: harnessing time's power for the exigency of the moment. But the contemporary was a look before it became the prey of modern tigers.

In Book 6 of the *Iliad* Diomedes meets Glaucus on the battlefield and wonders if he should kill him. Glaucus proceeds to precede: he traces his lineage back to the guest-friendship of Diomedes' grandfather, Oeneus, with Glaucus' grandfather, Bellerephon. This genealogy is "proof" that Glaucus and Diomedes are kindred spirits in the *now* by way of an appeal to the spirits of the *once*. Since their present enmity has been redefined by bygone equality, they can now swap outfits: gold armor for bronze—a bad deal, unless you consider the advantage of bronze armor in battle. Fashion historians tell a similar tale about fashion's upbringing. Fashion is said to arrive on the scene as early as the 1300s or as late as 1850 (see Preface, n. 20). Its specialness during these times lies in both the social conditions that pave the way for it—namely, the rise of the middle class—and in the emergence of an "aesthetic impulse toward significant distortion and creative tailoring (as opposed to creative draping and trimming)" (Hollander 1993: 17).

Hollander begins her masterful survey of the depiction of clothing through art history with the "natural" drapery found in fifth-century Greek sculpture "and nowhere else." There is something peculiar about this time in Greece. Classical drapery appears "natural," "graceful," as if it had a "buoyant lift" in solid marble. Attempts to reproduce it in wool and linen show that fabric cannot actually behave as it appears so naturally to do in these sculptures; "draped material, however naturalistic and random-looking, has not been copied faithfully from nature but *designed*" (8, my italics). During this period, a typical Greek household had the means to produce woolen garments from start to finish. Sculptors thus played the role of modern-day designers in depicting with unnatural materials the appearance of naturally moving fabric. Fabric was important in nude sculptures, too, where the naked body was highlighted against drapery (e.g., the cape of Apollo Belvedere); if cloth was completely absent, its absence was felt. According to Hollander, while drapery might seem like fashion, the idea of body as separable from cloth is a later development, and comes wrapped up not just in concealing but in obscuring and deforming the body. For Nagel and Wood, too, the late medieval period marks a critical transition. This is embodied in the secular fashion of paintings and the antiquarian lust for sculptures as art objects. Sculpture in particular seems to withstand time. It is helped along by the erosion of the paint on its surface, which fosters an enhanced impression of anonymity. Painting is stripped from the nude body, as fashion from clothes, creating an impossible nostalgia for antiquity as novelty. But the carved drapery remains.

Pappas finds a case for "ancient fashion" in extant accounts of variability and change in dress, and, importantly, the need to justify that changeability. His interest lies especially in Greek nudity as both natural and idealized. "There is a question here," writes Pappas, "about which direction one moves in after stripping: toward civilization and law or out into the frontier?" (2016: 81). Thucydides describes how the Athenians were first to set aside their arms in favor of a softer, more luxurious look (1.6). The Athenians "recently" retired this equipment (*skeuê*)—linen underwear and golden cicada clips—to adopt a more modest dress *es ton nun tropon*, "in accord with the current fashion." *tropos* means "turn" or "manner," while the word *skeuê* can mean both general attire and military outfit. The Athenians now put aside their former armor for a Free People look, and "this wardrobe representing democracy came not only from a foreign culture but from the one Greek culture that most opposed democracy" (Pappas 2016: 166). A Spartan innovation thus finds itself contingently appropriate to the Athenian image, and modesty the natural progression of their former autochthonous ornamentation.

The Spartans also set the fashion of exercising naked. Previously, the Greeks wore girdles even at the Olympics, a thing which "now" only the barbarians still do. The difference between Greek and non-Greek seems to turn on the interpretation of naked fashion; the Greeks no longer advertise their need for defense. The barbarian practice of wearing belts now appears uncivilized. That the Athenians adopted the Spartan outfit to express their democratic inclinations is no accidental formulation on Thucydides' part. "Having never known anything but the Same, Athens was, in nature and in origin, the polis at peace with itself. In other words the Polis" (Loraux 2000: 53). Such a polis that was *the* Polis could only begin to signify its sameness by an imperial conquest of every other polis. This movement—a tension between democratic and tyrannical impulses—is the subject of Thucydides' *History of the Peloponnesian War*. Its formulation in his beginning paragraphs in terms of changing fashions implies the inseparability of flux and stasis.

Where the looks of the past become more distant, they become both more static and more foreign, and their rejuvenation a form of conquest. But the city can never start from scratch, nor do citizens spring from its womb wearing native costumes. Foreign dress becomes native by being habitually worn, as the now traditional Japanese kimono was originally introduced from a style of Chinese court dress. At varying times, so-called Western fashion, too, understood as "free" fashion, appears as if it were an invading army. Myths that attribute a noncontingent status to dress appear to attempt to control history, and with it, the thought that the polis can be an original. In placing on par alternations of fashion and setting aside weapons, Thucydides implies that the Spartans and Athenians, though enemies, share a kindred fashion sense, as if dress were an armor that revealed cities and wars as contingent. The same thought lurks in another episode about a night battle at Syracuse. Even in the bright moonlight, the Athenians have difficulty telling friend from foe. Further confusion is caused when their watchword is compromised, and the similarity between the battle paeans on both sides makes it hard to tell who is who (7.44). In absence of clear indicators to differentiate insider from outsider, how does one adjudicate among the silhouettes of men? Invasion occurs through taking on the clothes and signals of the other; but clothes are already themselves other from the self, and their appropriation therefore almost *too* easy. If you want to make fun of someone, dress like them and act like them. Just be careful the impression isn't too exact, because there will then come to be very little difference between imitator and imitation— other and self, foreign and native … past and present? Nicias later gives this encouragement to the Athenian army, "Men are a city, not the walls or empty ships of men" (7.77). Nor do clothes make men, which makes one wonder if Athens' cosmopolitan nudity, by means of an absence of clothes, intended Athens to be the cosmos.

Entry into the democratic walls which are no walls can only be gathered by myths of priority. In the *Republic*'s perfectly just city this is the myth of the metals, which Demetra Kasimis argues "insinuates that an autochthonous designation is not so much the natural or stable effect of a biological fact as a fictional ideal that unevenly regulates the production of citizens" (2018: 102). Autochthony, in other words, is the clothes of blood and earth. It is mirrored in the mimesis of the democratic regime, where the *appropriate* tasks performed at the *appropriate* time are replaced by the leisure of free fashion, different threads embroidered in every which way. Kasimis's reading of mimesis in Book 8 is based on her interest in the status of metics in ancient Athens, but it also opens up a broader reading of democracy in which impersonation extends to the clothing of the "citizen" as such (106–8). Democracy's very principles stress the limits of democracy. Where everyone is strange it becomes difficult to spot a stranger. Democracy is the regime of every season and occasion, where clothing gets a bit too comfortable, and uncomfortable looks cannot help but pave the way for new suspicions.

To return to the parody of Athenian style in Aristophanes' *Knights*, the Sausage-seller's critical supplication to old man Demos is a pair of slippers and a tunic. Demos compliments this clothing as something not even Themistocles had thought of: Themistocles had moved Athens' port to the Piraeus, but that "to me appears no greater a discovery than this *chitôn*" (885–6). A *chitôn* is a tunic worn close to the body. In Hippocrates, it is used to mean "membrane." The "discovery" (which can also mean "invention," as our hackneyed word "original") of the *chitôn* suggests that even though Cleon, the leather-seller, had produced shoes by trade he had never yet understood them as *in fashion*. This is made even more dramatic by the fact that the garment itself is a foreign importation in common use (the word is Middle-Eastern in origin); fashion, like language, in shifting meanings out of the past, re-presents what is already there. What the Sausage-seller borrows and passes off as his own invention is not the garment and shoes themselves but the now-time of their wear. Later on in the play, Demos emerges rejuvenated with golden cicadas in his hair in the Athenian old style. It is hard not to think of Marx and Benjamin. As Demos is reincarnated into his older (younger?) self, the Sausage-seller announces, "I have boiled off the Demos for you and made him beautiful from ugly" (1321). Is this an aristocratic regression within the parody of Athenian democratic politics as "unprincipled, self-serving behavior" (Pappas 2020: 159)? Or is it a progressive appeal to democracy's roots?

There is a story in Herodotus that perplexes in a similar way. At 5.87–90 we learn about a battle between the Athenians and the Aeginetans and Argives. While the account of the conflict differs among them, one detail is shared: there was a single Athenian survivor, who, when he returned home, was stabbed to death by the wives of the other men with their dress pins. Where Athenian women had previously worn Dorian pinned robes, thereafter they were forced to wear Ionian sewn garments (actually, says Herodotus, they were originally Carian). Pappas argues that Thucydides inverts this story with his claim that the Athenians moved from Ionian to Dorian (Spartan) dress. The Argives and Aeginetans, on the other hand, enlarge their dress pins and even dedicate them to the shrine of the goddesses whose images were the subject of the dispute. While the Athenians are motivated by safety concerns, their rivals exaggerate the fashion of the vanquished in a devotional performance of their victory. Couldn't Herodotus, then, also have attributed the Athenian change to their subsequent humiliation? Being mocked in Dorian style by the Aeginatan caricature of Dorian dress, the Athenians would be forced to find an alternative mode against Athenian impersonators. This absurd feature of clothing ought to be underscored: clothes and thoughts are equally able to be worn and uttered by sham artists and copycats in what at first looks a mockery of the designer, but then becomes convincing enough to pass as rejuvenated truth. Fashion is contingency masquerading as necessity, but the greatest myth that surrounds it is that its apparent homage to contingency is separate from its longing for necessity.

About the Herodotus story, Pappas draws the following conclusion: "Without historical information everything done now seems natural and native. History shows how easily it could have been otherwise. One survivor more or less and wardrobe changes entirely" (163). So, too, what at first appears to be a "teleological narrative" in Thucydides about how the Athenians were once like barbarians but then ascended to democratic dress, now appears to emphasize the contingency of such dress having been imitated from those to whom they were most opposed. Pappas argues that this is taken further in the argument about nudity in Book 5 of Plato's *Republic*, which borrows the nudity narrative from Thucydides and extends it to the proposal that women, too, should exercise naked and at all ages. Socrates says this will appear ridiculous; it makes "the *telos* of equality into a philosophical joke," or "a joke at philosophy's expense," which Socrates counters with an anti-fashion stance: "looks matter to dress after all—another *way* of looking mind you, generating another *kind* of dress" (171). But there is a question that continues to press: why do we feel the need to justify changes in dress as if they were native to a rational process of self-definition? Is it merely to make ourselves less laughable and more serious? Is the stigma in philosophy against fashion all done up in its fear of seeming silly?

Fashion progresses, however ironically, toward the *perfect* age and the *perfect* outfit—even, in fashion photography, the *perfect* shot of the *perfect* look. It finds its idealized future in the incessant renewal of dead iterations. This is reflected in the myth of fashion's origin: a state in which fashion was once effortlessly absent or present without our having before noticed it. It is likewise the myth of the neutralized self that is shared by those who would pretend they are uninterested in fashion or content with old clothes (they are *so* over the present and stylishly stuck in the past). The longing to posit nudity seems to emanate from being enmeshed in clothing's folds. But while debates are had about "more important" things, fashion holds court in the tones and drapery of words, the ironing out of a conclusion, the hairiness of an unexpected insight, the fling of an ash tray. That the thought of fashion could be temporally lodged, as if only more recently did we progress beyond thoughtless modes, arriving not just in clothes but in style, seems ironically the result of fashion's wayward allure.

Fashion hits us like a flash of truth. It tantalizes the wearer with notions of burying the body, loosening conventions, and freeing us from time. But this sort of leisurewear—a more tongue-in-cheek version of philosophy's practice of dying and being dead—has within it a troublingly ideological seed. Spectator and actor break down in the activity of wearing clothes, as chorus and audience in a Greek tragedy. It is easy to imagine that "costumes" might impress those who see the wearer, and so, give the viewer and the wearer the impression that they are the impression they make. But time's passage asserts itself as a limit of fashion's leisurely freedom, for it must heed the occasion, even or especially in its adoration of a dusky, ageless prime.

Such is the vantage point coveted by clothes as a negative experience of the self. Where time would cease to have sway and our clothes could display some true self, we would live as naked shades in the deepest reaches of the cave. Philosophy, meanwhile, is best dressed in a negation of perception, which is to say in its sweeping rejection of fashion—a refusal to appear that is reminiscent of the philosopher's unwillingness to return to the shadows. The prisoners in the cave will laugh at the philosopher's enlightened looks.

Fashion arrives on the scene when we see not *that* things are but *how*—in what fashion—they are, which means *how* they appear. Where this adverbial sense becomes a noun for historical study, style becomes the newly elusive specter of fashion's attitude. Yet everything turns on the adverb being perceived as separable from the noun: the point at which the character trait inherent in the activity of the subject is mistranslated into a subject in its own right, as if one could pursue it independently of already being immersed in it. Modernity passes off this slight-of-hand as its own, but it was already there, where the wise in seeking wisdom confuse their own desire to know with the faraway image of wisdom. It thus becomes possible to divorce knowing from knowledge, which is to say that sophistry becomes possible. Philosophy and fashion are inseparable in the same mode, at least wherever you find human thinking.

You say with an air of depth, "It doesn't matter what you wear." You mean a cloaked imperative: "Don't be defined by the fashions of others." Convention-free leisure, alienated from its own intellectual attitude, mirrors philosophy's absurd styling when, having taken refuge in an academic suntan, it flees straight into the clutches of the fashion it longs to escape. Unfashioned thinking thinks the self out of thinking, so that nudity can only be the joke of intelligent despair. In the clothes and thoughts of others we helplessly corset our letters with some grammatical style, editing out the present moment as if it were a pastime. Fashion threatens to digress at any second, to sabotage our earnest efforts with its playful double entendre, since words are borne bursting at the seams. We ask for their conviction with banal ink and unseen tone, as if worshipping a colorless statue. Yet some muse giggles at us from a viewless view: "Time cannot catch *me*! I have arrived in the youthful bloom of an age-old argument."

Notes

Note to the Reader and Preface

1. In Greek, the addressee of these lines is feminine.
2. 607b5-6. "Socrates speaks of a quarrel between philosophy and poetry, not between philosophers and poets. This may well indicate that there will always be philosophers among the poets and poets among the philosophers" (Davis 2019: 4).
3. These two words are etymological relatives, and in some languages still identical. See, e.g., Carlyle 1836/2008: 28; Nagel 2004: 43–4 (also *habitus*).
4. The word "ascetic" has a similar doubleness. It comes from the Greek verb *askein*, which means, "to practice" or "to do in a routine way," but it carries the subsequent meaning, "to trick out." It can refer to the intricacy of the working and the intricacy of the work.
5. See Hanson 1990.
6. See, e.g., Pappas 2016: 21, 38, 130ff.
7. Ibid.: 20; Plato, *Protagoras* 316d.
8. See Lucretius, *De Rerum Natura* 1.934–50, cp. 3.191, 302, 891.
9. Diogenes Laertius, *Vitae* 10.120.
10. Here is Carlyle's earlier version of the same thought—Some styles are "lean," others are "pallid," there are "sham Metaphors, which overhanging that same Thought's Body (best naked), and deceptively bedizening ... may be called its false stuffings, superfluous show-cloaks" (1836/2008: 57). A similar claim that academic writing has unwittingly fallen prey to bad style is made by the proponents of "autotheory," albeit one that continues to be clothed in a pretentious moniker.
11. Aristotle, *Metaphysics* 7.5; cp. Aquinas, *On Being and Essence* 110.
12. Aristophanes, *Clouds* 340ff. Socrates has seen centaurs, leopards, and wolves in the clouds.
13. See Plato, *Republic* 452a–c. Cp. Pappas, 179ff.
14. Diogenes Laertius, *Vitae* I.34. For a redemption of Thales and the uselessness of philosophy, see Aristotle, *Politics* 1259a5–35, where philosophy appears to be able to use its abstraction for practical purposes. For his prediction of an eclipse, see Herodotus, *Histories* 1.74. Perhaps Thales is no airhead?
15. The phrase is from Pappas 2016: 142.
16. And the basic goes from the basic t-shirt to the basic bitch, the "Karen" to the "man-Karen." But not all t-shirts or Karens are basically alike.
17. Kosas's "Revealer Concealer" would be in Heidegger's compact.
18. *De rerum natura* 3.215ff.
19. See Gandhi's "Guide to London," and 1925–9/2018: 121–4.

20 Fashion's birthday is heralded as early as the 1300s or as late as 1850 (with the advent of individual designers in Paris). See, e.g., Wilson 2010: 18, 32; Lipovetsky 1994: 25–6; Nagel and Wood 2010: 388, n. 13; Hollander 1993: 17, 351–5; and Carnevali (2020: 25), who cites "individuality and originality" in clothing as key features of fashion's modernity.

Chapter 1

1 "Nature is fond of hiding herself" or "Nature likes to hide."
2 Plato, *Sophist* 216d. "For his part Plato would take an unamused satisfaction in learning that what is fashionable is called 'what is in'—how suitably he would take that phrase to fit what belongs in the cave's interior" (Pappas 2016: 168).
3 This is against Lipovetsky's characterization of fashion as running "counter to the spirit of growth and the development of mastery over nature" (1994: 24).
4 Aristotle, *De Anima* 422bff.
5 Merleau-Ponty expresses a similar thought: "There is an experience of the visible thing as pre-existing my vision, but this experience is not a fusion, a coincidence: because my eyes which see, my hands which touch, can also be seen and touched, because, therefore, in this sense they see and touch the visible, the tangible, from within, because our flesh lines and even envelops all the visible and tangible things with which nevertheless it is surrounded, the world and I are within one another, and there is no anteriority of the *percipere* to the *percipi*, there is simultaneity or even retardation" (1968: 122, trans. A. Lingis).
6 Both *haptein*, "touch," and *lambanein*, "grasp," have this ambiguity.
7 4.213–14. Cp. Pappas: "You cannot know the shape of your own body if you baffle it with pleats and pads. Lay hands on yourself and you will know something even when it is dark out" (2016: 222).
8 For the relationship between comfort, anti-dress code, and college, see Clemente 2014, esp. 56. For the insistence on wearing uncomfortable clothes, see Veblen 1899/1994: 60 and Simmel 1904/1957: 544.
9 Zebedee Talent has pushed back on this by more subtly undermining beauty ideals: not by showing different looks per se, but rather, using different looks to suggest how we might see differently.
10 The term is from Pappas 2016: 219.
11 Cp. Merleau-Ponty, "Like the flesh of the visible, speech ... is a relation to Being through a being, and, like it, it is narcissistic, eroticized, endowed with a natural magic that attracts the other significations into its web, as the body feels the world in feeling itself" (1968: 118). Perhaps of interest, too, are the remarks Olga Skorokhodova makes concerning seeing with her hands. Skorokhodova lost her hearing and sight as a child. In "How I Perceive the World around Me," she describes noticing that the hem

of a dress still contains the tacking. In seeing with her fingers she uses, "expressive hands," through which, she writes, "I can feel—to use the language of those who can see and hear, a 'lively, mobile face' or 'an intonation of voice'" (1972/1974: 11).
12 Rousseau 1781/1990: 59, ¶ 2.
13 Gen. 3:7, cp. 3:11 and 3:21.
14 I am grateful to Ronna Burger for this point.
15 5.1350–3, cp. 1.418, 6.42, 86–7. This is a reference to Lucretius' weaving of words and adornment of verses, which may also be lurking in the reference to papyrus sheets at 6.112.
16 *les moeurs*: "habits," "customs," "fashions."
17 A reference to Spartan nudity. See p. 182.
18 Plutarch, *Moralia* (*De capienda ex inimicis utilitate*) 2.
19 *textus* in Latin means "having been woven." See p. 91.
20 Here and on p. 51 translated by R. Louden and G. Zöller. In seeming contradiction to this stands the following line: "Where does the poetic license to now and then violate the laws of language, to which the orator is not entitled, come from? Presumably from the fact that the orator is not hindered by the law of form too much to express a great thought" (Kant 1798/2011: 7:249).
21 Heidegger 1950/2008: 142–203 ("The Origin of the Work of Art").
22 For more on the peasant shoes in fashion and art, see Bari 2019: 4–5 and Hollander 1993: 324.
23 "All forms of utilitarianism have to be refused through a refashioning of the human being through fashion" (Critchley 2011).
24 Pappas 2016: 212, 226; cp. 67.
25 It wasn't Francis Bacon who advocated stripping and beating nature's female character (see Pesic 1999), but Machiavelli. For his harsh advice about Lady Luck (*Fortuna*), see *The Prince*, Ch. 25.
26 Cp. Erasmus, *Ciceronianus*: "It is not great to speak like a grammarian, but it is divine to speak like Cicero."
27 O'Grady 2001.
28 *Phaedo* 99e.
29 In the *Phaedo*, however, Socrates tells his friends that he has turned to writing at the end of his life (60c–d).
30 276aff.
31 174a3–5.
32 Diog. Laert., *Vitae* 5.1.
33 Nagel and Wood 2010: 85–6; 93. See also Filarete, quoted in Nagel 2004: 47 and Nagel and Wood 2010: 93 (*Treatise on Architecture; Being the Treatise* by Antonio di Piero Averlino, known as Filarete, trans. J. R. Spencer, New Haven: Yale University Press, 1965).
34 See also Nagel 2004: 47, for similar sentiments in Leonardo da Vinci and Lodovico Dolce.
35 Baudelaire 1863/1995.

36 Barthes 1960/2013: 21. Barthes links historical costume to theatrical "roles," not so far removed from Nicolas de Larmessin II's grotesques, which depicted artisans in clothing that imitated their professions.
37 Salton 2017.
38 Rocamora and Smelik 2015: 28–9.
39 Trans. Harvey C. Mansfield with my italics in parentheses.
40 *curiali* suggests the Roman senate.
41 His statement of having "delivered" himself to them completely recalls the last line of *The Prince*, Ch. 13: "I submit myself entirely to these orders."
42 In Greek, *Historiai* means "Inquiries." I here read Herodotus' claims as philosophical curiosities rather than verifiable truths about the ancient Egyptians.
43 Benardete also notes other places in Book 2 where the same phrase is used: 86.2, 132.1, 170.1.
44 Trans. Caroline Alexander.
45 The Russian language *mat* gets its name from a bastardized form of "mother": it is made up entirely of curse words used to signify other words in all parts of speech, "a shadow-image of the Russian language as a whole" (Driezin and Priestly 1982: 233). Thank you to Marina Vitkin and Alexandre Gontchar for their help with this reference.
46 Nietzsche, trans. Kaufmann 1887/1989: 8. This is different apparently from grazing, which has connotations of divinity.
47 Plato, *Theaetetus* 150cff.
48 "Philosophy as the practice of dying and being dead precisely consists in the habituation to non-habituation" (Benardete 2000: 293, n. 2; *Phaedo* 64d).

Chapter 2

1 *Aeneid* 1.688–89; Servius Auctus, 688; Lucretius, 5.897–900; 1009–18.
2 This and subsequent *Bacchae* quotations are from Emily Wilson's translation with my changes in parentheses, unless otherwise noted.
3 Cp. Aristophanes, *Knights* 95–6.
4 290–6. The pun on Homer's name is also palpable.
5 Cp. New Testament, Phil. 2:7—"but he emptied himself taking the form (*morphê*) of a slave, coming to be in the likeness of human beings; and having been found in figure as if a human."
6 1.19.1. See also Lemoine 2020: 11–13.
7 Literally, "he would not be willing (*thelêsêi*) to put on a female (*thêlun*) outfit."
8 The difference between the prefixes of *gynaiko-morphos* and *thêlu-morphos* is that of noun versus adjective.
9 There are parallels in "Sumer and Akkad, where divine brides are given cosmic apparel" (West 1971: 53); the sense of the stars and planets as *kosmoi* is found in early cosmological accounts and later in authors

such as Aeschylus. See, e.g., *Agamemnon*, "night ... possessor of great *kosmoi*," 355–6.
10 Cp. Lucretius, *De Rerum Natura* 5.1418.
11 Pentheus is killed in the same place where Acteon met his end; Acteon was the son of Autonoë, one of Semele's other sisters (1291). He tried to watch Artemis bathe, but she saw him and transformed him into a stag. His own dogs then ripped him apart; hunter became hunted.
12 766–8; 701; 865–7.
13 Cp. Empedocles, Fragment 126, "clothing <them> in unfamiliar tunics of the flesh."
14 Weaving goes together with the absence of fire. They do not cook, but eat raw. When they invade villages to kidnap babies, the fire of the villagers does not touch them.
15 My literal translation.
16 "Spirits divine take many shapes (*morphai*) and many / are the unexpected actions of the gods. / Our predictions do not come to pass; / the god finds a way for what we don't expect. / This is what happened here today" (1388–92; *Helen* 1688–92).
17 It's tricky: in 2021, the brand "Dove" removed the word "normal" from their product ads, lest this allude to a norm.
18 *Republic* 449aff.
19 Cp. Nikulin 2017: 86.
20 This and subsequent translations from Euripides' *Helen* are Emily Wilson's with my changes in parentheses, unless otherwise noted.
21 Helen's name might come from *helenê*, "torch," *selenê*, "moon" (1366), or the verb *helein*, "to capture" or "take" (118). Helen is either shining like fire or the moon, or she is captive.
22 Cp. the poem "Helen's Burning" by Laura Riding.
23 Proteus has the same name as the shapeshifting god of the sea, Proteus. In the *Odyssey* (4.385ff.), Menelaus has to hang onto Proteus—when he stops shapeshifting he will tell Menelaus the way home.
24 Cp. Plato, *Phaedrus* 276a8-9, where writing is called the *eidôlon* of thought.
25 An interpolation.
26 The Hellenes are a pun on Helen, while Pelops gives us the Peloponnesians, where Sparta is.
27 See pp. 138–9.
28 See Muellner 2022.
29 In Book 24, Odysseus' father will be persuaded by his knowledge of the orchard (245ff.).
30 Cp. *Hippolytus* 925. And Bob Dylan, "Tangled Up in Blue," 1975.
31 Davis 2011: 108.
32 Literally, "with eyes (*opthalmois*)."
33 Davis 2011: 116.
34 See n. 21.

35 See Ch. 1, n. 11.
36 465. For the strange living presence of the dead Proteus who is entombed at the entrance to his palace, see Davis 2011: 110.
37 I have changed the first line of Wilson's translation, which reads, "Gods! It's a god to recognize one's love!"
38 Many thanks to my Vassar seminar, "Fashion & Its Enemies" (Spring 2020), for showing me that this is the same as the Spiderman meme, and to Hannah Maver for creating a version of the meme with Helen and Menelaus.
39 1185–92. See Davis 2011: 107, 120.
40 My literal translation.
41 The god Proteus has a daughter named Eidotheia. Theonoë is the daughter of a sea-nymph and related to Nereus.
42 The chorus is made up of captive Greek maidens, which suggests that either Theoclymenos has been out sacking towns or collecting any Greek that turns up on the shore; he is clearly worried that the Greeks will show up at his house to take Helen away. Helen tells Teucer that Theoclymenos kills all Greeks who come to Proteus' house (155).
43 Theonoë, appealing to her dead father as if he were a god, declares that "The mind of those who have died lives not but / it has immortal judgment (*gnômê*) falling into immortal ether" (1015, my translation).
44 Trans. Nina Kossman, reprinted in Kossman 2001: 213–14.
45 Davis cites Plato's *Republic* 332a–c as one occurrence of the definition of justice as helping friends and harming enemies.
46 1319–21. Strangely, Menelaus had called on Hades to help (967–73).
47 Also characterized by Jean Twenge as "i-Gen," or the "internet generation." The title of her book seems worth quoting in full—*iGen: Why Today's Super-Connected Kids Are Growing Up Less Rebellious, More Tolerant, Less Happy—and Completely Unprepared for Adulthood—and What That Means for the Rest of Us.*
48 Thank you to Brianna Benson, Lisa Deines, Allison Horack, Sarah Moskowitz, and Marlaine Reiner for their paramount knowledge of 1990s fashion and late-night conversation on the subject.
49 Plato, *Ion* 534d.
50 Pappas 2016: 24, 38, 224.
51 On Deleuze's folds, see Bari 2019: 36.
52 Here is a pretentious allusion to Kuhn's *The Structure of Scientific Revolutions*: the "tradition-bound" and "tradition-shattering" character of scientific progress seems mocked by fashion's similar framework. Cp., Heidegger's essay on the Anaximander Fragment, in which he argues that the history of Western philosophy is built on the illusion of borrowed origins. Metaphysics moves into its prime state when on its way into darkness it breaks into its own opacity. So, when words or fashions fracture into obscurity, the duskiness of our own understanding is primed to dawn

on us. The more obsolete or out-of-style something is, the riper it is for rebirth and redefinition. While this first seems to require a large span of time, it soon becomes clear that the opacity of history's dawn is a metaphor for the movement of thinking. See also my Ch. 7, in reference to the ideas of Benjamin and Marx.

53 See p. 171.
54 See p. 182.
55 Baudelaire went so far as to suggest that even if artifice claims to mimic the natural, this can only serve beauty, not nature (1863/1995: 31–4).
56 In his *Meditations on First Philosophy*, Descartes proposes the "brain in the vat" thought experiment in which he wonders if an evil demon is intentionally orchestrating his perception of the world.
57 Marx 1867/2017: 122. For the demonization of material objects in fetishism, see Stallybrass 1998.
58 Cp. Plato *Cratylus* 432b-c, "Would the following be two things—for example, Cratylus and an image of Cratylus, if one of <the> gods might not only make a likeness of your hue and figure just as the painters do, but also might make all the insides of the very sort that yours are, and give back to them softness and warmth, and put in them motion and soul and prudence of the very sort that are present in you, and in a word exactly all the things you have, he/she might establish others of the sort that are near you? Would such a thing then be a Cratylus and an image of Cratylus, or two Cratyluses?"
59 See *A Treatise concerning the Principles of Human Knowledge* (1710).
60 "According to ancient authors, Gyges was the first monarch to be called τύραννος, a term that indeed was believed to have a Lydian origin" (Arruzza 2019: 107). See also 107 n. 23 for the problem of Gyges' identity.
61 Cp. *Mabinogion* 2008, 159—"'Take this ring and put it on thy finger, with the stone inside thy hand; and close thy hand upon the stone. And as long as thou concealest it, it will conceal thee.'"
62 See Pl., *Rep.* 540c5.
63 Benardete translates *barbaros* as "Asia," meaning the greater region in which the Persian empire was situated. The word broadly indicates "that which is foreign to the Greek ear," and Strabo claimed it to be onomatopoeia for *bar-bar* (*Geographia* 14.2.28). It is often used specifically of Persians. But the Greeks were *barbaroi* themselves before they became the Greeks, as both Thucydides and Aeschylus suggest.
64 Translations of lines from Aeschylus' *Persians* are Seth Benardete's with my changes in parentheses, unless otherwise noted.
65 My translation.
66 The latter line is my translation.

Chapter 3

1. Corsets were originally worn by both men and women. For more on their deleterious effects and supposed benefits, see Ford 2021: 129–32.
2. See David 2015.
3. This section, especially the last two lines, owes much to a conversation with Nickolas Pappas.
4. Cp. Aristotle's characterization of plot (*mythos*), *Poetics* 1450b20ff and 1456b20ff.
5. "Thus Philolaus, the contemporary of Socrates, and the first to set forth, in writing, an extended exposition of Pythagorean doctrine, says concerning God, the author and governor of all things, that '"he is without variation, ever like himself and like no other, even as the number seven"' (Hadley 1873: 325). For other notions of a complete or perfect age, cp. Eph. 4:13. Christ is the *andra teleion*, the perfect man, and his age in this perfection is said in Ephesians to be the measure of an age of fullness.
6. The account that follows summarizes 2.12–14. *gêras* can also mean "age" more neutrally (as if its specificity as "aged" were implied by its appearance) or the skin a serpent casts off.
7. Trans. Walter Kaufmann. Preface to *On the Genealogy of Morals*.
8. This interesting meaning of the word, which has as its root, *nem-*, "to distribute" or "graze," may relate to the pipes played by shepherds—a profession that is often paired with poetry (e.g., in the opening of Hesiod's *Theogony*). It may also indicate a distribution of notes in a sequence. The young are caught up in the plot of life in this way. See p. 128.
9. This word is the same one that pointed to the ambiguity of the sense of touch in *De Anima*, where the *metaxu* was flesh. See p. 3.
10. In *The Reveries of a Solitary Walker*, Rousseau identifies age forty as a milestone after which he is as good as dead.
11. This metaphor is often used of erotic conquest, and its political and sexual connotations are of interest to the subject of fashion. Cp. Arruzza 2019: 154.
12. The line is missing the particle "per," which Michael Davis has suggested (in conversation) is a metaphor for the fuzz on Alcibiades' cheeks that reminds us of its prior absence. The references in Homer are "like to a boy prince / just getting a beard, for whom the bloom of youth is most graceful" (*Iliad* 24.347–8); and "like to a young man / just getting a beard, for whom the bloom of youth is most graceful" (*Odyssey* 10.278–9).
13. The Hermes in *Hadestown* (played by André de Shields) depicts him so well-aged "in his prime" that he is now the all-knowing narrator.
14. Blushing occurs seven times in six other Platonic dialogues—the *Lysis* (204b–c), the *Republic* (350d), the *Lovers* (134b), the *Protagoras* (312a), the *Charmides* (158c), and twice in the *Euthydemus* (275d and 297b). These are the six dialogues narrated by Socrates.

15 For the following section, I am grateful to conversations with Michael Davis, especially concerning Protagoras' claims to age.
16 See 328dff.
17 W.K.C. Guthrie conjectures about Protagoras' birthdate that "In Plato's *Protagoras*, before the company of Socrates, Prodicus, and Hippias, he states that he is old enough to be the father of any of them. This suggests a date of not later than 490 B.C." (1971: 262). This bizarrely requires taking Protagoras' words (done up by Plato) at face value.
18 Cp. also 320c, where the same language that was used for Alcibiades' bloom is used to describe Protagoras' manner: "'It seems, therefore, to me,' he declared, 'to be more gracious to speak a myth to you all.'"
19 Later on in the play, Cleon offers to change Demos' white hairs and make him young again (908).
20 Trans. Joe Sachs. The word "joke" is a rendering of *paizôn*, literally, "playing."
21 A neologism at Pl., *Euthyd*. 272e5.
22 That Socrates makes a distinction between Alcibiades' comely looks and his philosophical potential is clear from their conversation in Plato's *Symposium*.
23 Goth's influence is visible beyond the vampy subculture and hints of it in varying degrees are present in high fashion. See the exhibition catalog from *Gothic: Dark Glamour* (Steele 2007).
24 Something like Yolandi Visser. The turn in hip-hop to autotuned vocals and "baby" rapper names prefixed with "Lil" seems to represent a similar phenomenon, as does the fusion in rockabilly and psychobilly of the wholesome fifties with a menacing lilt. Never mind the cross between Buddhist nothingness and Satanic nihilism in the form of metal yoga, which seems to be enacting the irony of the band name Nirvana (thank you to Otto von Busch for enlightening me on this oxymoronic practice).
25 "Surprising" translates *daimonion*, literally, "daimonic"; "I am in doubt" is literally, "I am thinking both ways," or perhaps, "I'm thinking twice," or "of two minds."
26 They also die as a pair, but their striking is plural, as their hand is double (171–2).
27 But it depends on to whom you talk: cp. lines 206–7 and 257–8.
28 At line 192, Creon uses the word "brother" or "sibling" to refer to a decree he has made ("And here as brother to these principles / is my decree," trans. Frank Nisetich). In the first line of *Oedipus Rex*, Oedipus refers to the people as *tekna*, "children."
29 For a similar interpretation, see Butler 2000.
30 "I will lie dear with him, with a dear one, playing the rogue in a holy way" (74).
31 Literally, "swells," a pun on Oedipus' name.

32 Here and below (784-90) the translation is Frank Nisetich's.
33 See Plato, *Protagoras* 312e, cp. *Apology* 17b. The word in Greek is the neutral "man," really "human being," *anthrôpos*.
34 Ian Gilligan argues that agriculture was invented because of the need for clothing rather than food, though his separation of the two seems forced (2021).
35 See Thuc. 2.44.
36 Ambiguously, Polyneices or Ismene (see line 1, p. 76).
37 Consider, too, this description of Patroclus' helmet, "the hairs (plural) defiled with blood and dusts (plural)" (*Iliad* 16.796-7).
38 In Latin, the word for "dust," *pulvis*, gives us the word "pulverize." The English word "dust" comes from the Sanskrit root *dhu*, cognate to the Latin *fumus* and the Greek *thumos*. In English, we can use "dust" to mean cleaning off or dusting on; dusting a surface or dusting a cake. Putting on powder can do both: dusting off dampness by putting on dust. "To dust him" is mobspeak for killing someone: he bites the dust. But dust is not something you can sink your teeth into; it is like quicksand. See also p. 124.
39 155, 158, 395, 774, 1100, 1205.
40 Cp. *Republic* 536c, where Socrates says he spoke too intensely (*enteinein*), which doubles as "straining into meter," i.e., speaking too poetically. Poetry seems to be in the business of conflating seriousness and play. It is the same movement that Socrates' invocation of the Muses represents in Book 8 (545d8).
41 See also 1144-5 ("come with purifying *foot* / over Parnassian peak or booming strait," trans. Nisetich). "Lead an empty man *ekpodôn* (out of the way)" (1339; cp. 1324); "for briefest <is> best for evils at the feet (*podes*)" (1327); 985, *orthopodos*, of Cleopatra.
42 Cp. 269, where the guards are too sheepish to tell Creon the body has been buried. They nod their heads *en pedon*, "at the ground" (or "at their feet").
43 Echoed by Hanson 1990: 115—"Clothes, in their intrinsic and yet always breakable relation to our embodied life, can seem a *memento mori*."
44 For vintage fashion as a way of achieving individuality amidst a sea of clones, see Clark and Palmer 2005: 197-214.
45 I owe all of my knowledge of Tiktok to Eden Tijerina and Mark Allen.
46 See the "Stratford" handbag of the 1950s, featuring the works of Shakespeare (British Pathé). See also Hippias, p. 171.
47 Cp. Andromache at 22.440.
48 See, e.g., Aristophanes, *Clouds* 545.
49 A comment said by Barrow in a conversation with me about the history of hairdressing.
50 The word comes from the Latin *texere*, "to weave," which is related to the word "text." While I will not treat the rich world of linguistic weaving here, I point the reader to two books—one concerning letters as woven—R. Woodard, *The Textualization of the Greek Alphabet*, 2014—and

the other concerns weaving as metaphor, G. Fanfani, M. Harlow, M.L. Nosch (eds.), *Spinning Fates and the Song of the Loom: The Use of Textiles, Clothing and Cloth Production as Metaphor, Symbol and Narrative Device in Greek and Latin Literature*, 2016.
51 Cp. *Protagoras* 321b.
52 I am grateful to Brian Seitz for this thought.
53 Plut., *Lyc.* 22.1.
54 See Caravaggio's *Medusa*—a depiction of the Gorgon on a shield (Uffizi Gallery, Florence).
55 Ears of corn are referred to as "beard hair," e.g., Vergil, *Georgics* 1.8.
56 There is another word *eudoxa*, which refers to "good opinion."
57 See p. 42, 45, and the word *dokêsis*.
58 Cp. Xenophon, *Cyropaedeia* 1.17.
59 Coates 2021.

Chapter 4

1   My translation of this line is inspired by Muellner 2022.
2   Cp. Miller 2009: 8.
3   See Butler 1990: 24, quoted in Rocamora and Smelik 2015: 287–8. I continue to use the pronoun "he" to follow the Dandy's literary appearances in Barbey but not in fact.
4   Frame 2009: 739–40.
5   Cp. Lehmann 2000: 1.6.
6   Kelly 2005: xiv.
7   The same passage appears slightly revised ("historicism" is replaced with "chronological complacency") in Nagel and Wood 2010: 91.
8   See Simmel 1904/1957: 543.
9   See p. 22.
10 Diog. Laert., *Vitae* 8.2.73.
11 I allude both to the concept of revolutionary suicide in Newton 1973/2009: 5, and to Foucault's "style of existence" that manifests "the concrete possibility and the evident value of an *other* life, which is the true life" (Foucault 1984/2011: 184, trans. Graham Burchell).
12 For an image of protestors for racial justice, June 14, 2020 in Columbia, South Carolina wearing their "Sunday best" in homage to activists of the past, see Ford 2021: 240, image 13.
13 For other stories about the Congolese dandies in France, see also, e.g., Daniel Biyaoula, *Agonies* and *L'Impasse*.
14 Its language is a fusion of Lari (a dialect of Brazzaville), French, and Lingala. Again, see Makouezi 1970.

15 I owe a thank you to Branden Kosch for making me aware of this short film, and to Rose Callahan and Natty Adams for their insight on the dandy fashion scenes throughout the world.

16 See also Mbembe as quoted in Thomas 2003: "In the postcolony, magnificence and the desire to shine are not the prerogative only of those who command. The people also want to be 'honored,' to 'shine,' and to take part in celebrations .... in their desire for a certain majesty, the masses join in the madness and clothe themselves in cheap imitations of power to reproduce its epistemology" (103).

17 "The *sape*d body, which has become a sort of *social skin* (Turner 1980: 112), is not only an egotistical surface that allows the *sapeur* to define the boundaries that separate him from the Other, but also serves as a defined social territory that distinguishes one group, the *sapeurs*, from the rest of society" (Gondola 1999: 26). Gondola is also the author of *Tropical Cowboys: Westerns, Violence, and Masculinity in Kinshasa*—about the emergence of another interesting subculture in Kinshasa that models itself after the Hollywood trope of the "American cowboy."

18 Literally, a macaroni—in Italian, this word means "blockhead" and also refers to a shape of pasta that was later fashionized by the Macaroni Club in England in the eighteenth century. The term "macaroni" was used as a slang term for "in fashion," like *a la mode*.

19 *Dark Princess* weaves together aesthetics, romance, and race, and Du Bois considered it his "favorite" work (see *Dusk of Dawn: An Essay toward an Autobiography of a Race Concept*, 270).

20 The term was coined by Flügel; see, e.g., Wilson 2010: 29 and Lipovetsky 1994: 27.

21 This word for "wool" only occurs in the Ionic form, *eiros*, but it is from *eros*—a close homonym for *erôs*.

22 See p. 77.

23 See, for example, Judith Thurman on Ann Lowe, 2021.

24 See Baudelaire 1863/1995: 27.

25 Queen, "Killer Queen," 1973.

26 Tac., *Ann.* 1.41, but cp. Suet., *Calig.* 9.

27 "Breeches" have the same root—they are a garment *broken*, breached, into two legs.

28 See Adorno 1981: 127–8, cited in Bernstein 2021. Thank you to Jay Bernstein for a conversation about this.

29 1.2, "*exutoque Lepido.*" The same metaphor of stripping (power) is used in Col. 3:9–12.

30 Plato, *Protagoras* 320d; 322c. See also n. 34.

31 See Plato, *Republic* 8–9 for the account of regime change in terms of sons rebelling against fathers.

32 See Pappas 2016: 92–100.

33 From the Vassar College Archives, Photo Album No. 270, VC, 1924, Jeanne (Russell) Janish. I owe this reference to Emma Iadanza.
34 Plato, *Phaedrus* 264c, "every *logos* must be set up, like a living being, with a body of its own, so as not to be headless or footless, but to have a middle and extremities, fitting to one another and written to/in the whole." For the various meanings of *logos*, see n. 39.
35 This word might also be translated "compulsory." Cp. *Protagoras* 321c–322a. The *genos* of human beings remains "unadorned" (*akosmêton*); it is only after Prometheus steals fire that human beings acquire clothing.
36 "… all human societies that exchange goods use money" (Arruzza 2019: 167).
37 In Book 10, the couch is used as an example to illustrate the remove of an idea (597a; Benardete 1992: 215).
38 Chantraine 1968/2009: 826.
39 A nebulous Greek word that can mean "speech," "argument," "account," "word," or even "sense."
40 *Republic* 517a, cp. *Theaetetus* 172c4–6.
41 This section on the carnival would not have appeared if not for the suggestion of Dmitri Nikulin.
42 Athenaeus, *Deipnosophistae* 220B; Diog. Laert., *Vitae* 6.8.
43 Cp. Wölfflin: "How people like to move and carry themselves is expressed above all in costume, and it is not difficult to show that architecture corresponds to the costume of its period" (quoted in Nagel 2004: n. 5).
44 In order of appearance, song titles are: The Beatles, "A Day in the Life," 1967; Bowie, "Young Americans," 1975; Grandmaster Flash & the Furious Five, "The Message," 1982.
45 Originally written by Charles Fox and Norman Gimbel in conjunction with and first sung by Lori Lieberman (who was inspired by Don McClean), "Killing Me Softly with His Song" was made famous by Roberta Flack and The Fugees. Barry Lam inspired this riff.
46 See also Future's "Codeine Crazy" and Lil Uzi Vert, "XO Tour Llif3." Thanks to Edward Dioguardi for his insight into hip-hop's transformation from its 1990s heyday.
47 From an interview on *Genius*, "Pop Smoke, 'Welcome to the Party,' Official Lyrics & Meaning."
48 Dr. Dre ft. Snoop Dogg, "Still D.R.E.," 1999.
49 See also Nirvana, "Something in the Way," 1991.
50 In order of appearance, song titles evoked in this paragraph are: Richard Hell, "Blank Generation," 1976; Tom Waits, "Misery Is a River of the World," 2003; Nas ft. Lauryn Hill, 1996; Bowie, "Time," 1973; and Eminem, "Rap God," 2013—Marshall Mathers as Napoleon?

Chapter 5

1 "Nothing that he has touched has he not adorned."
2 Cp. Matt. 6:25–30; 22:10–11.
3 For a scathing critique of the affected commonness of normcore style, see Zaleski 2014. For a strange parallel to normcore in medieval forgery, see Nagel 2004: 51.
4 This kind of satirical doubleness eventually ruined Carlyle's career. In 1849 he published, "An Occasional Discourse on the Negro Question," and reactions were split over whether this was only a thin veil for Carlyle's own racist views or a lofty critique of racism, the latter making use of a Swiftean irony. For further reading, see Kinser 2012.
5 Perhaps the real solution to this quandary was not German idealism but quantum physics.
6 "Not only all common Speech, but Science, Poetry itself is no other, if thou consider it, than a right *Naming*" (68; this seems to be a reference to Plato's *Cratylus*).
7 The pun in Oedipus' name on *oida* ("know") and *pôs* ("somewhere"or "where") seems important to cite, even if it wasn't on Carlyle's mind.
8 About this book Nietzsche said of Carlyle that he was "an English atheist who makes it a point of honor not to be one" (quoted in the Introduction, xxviii, from *Twilight of the Idols*, 521).
9 Cp. Plato, *Protagoras* 322a.
10 Carlyle, and Nietzsche and Rousseau too, would have loved that paper is now being made out of elephant dung and cow manure. Because they are already partially digested, these forms of shit contain high quantities of cellulose, and require less processing than wood to turn into paper. Rabelais' Gargantua, on the other hand, knew that the best toilet paper was a live goose.
11 See Aristotle, *De Interpretatione* 16.3–4.
12 "Oh, ho, ho, ho, ho! What the devil is this? Do you call this ordure, ejection, excrement, evacuation, *dejecta*, fecal matter, *egesta, copros, scatos,* dung, crap, turds? Not at all, not at all: it is but the fruit of the shittim tree, 'Selah! Let us drink' (Book 4, Chapter 67)" (Rabelais' *Gargantua* quoted in Bakhtin 1968/1984: 175).
13 Trans. Sarah Ruden.
14 The translations of the *Iliad* throughout this section are Caroline Alexander's, unless otherwise noted.
15 When Odysseus later meets Achilles in the underworld in the *Odyssey*, Achilles seems to regret this thought that shades imitate life—so go his famous lines, "I'd want to be the laborer of another, a man without lot for whom there's not much livelihood, than to rule over all the dead who've wasted away" (11.490–1, my translation).

16 If there is an allusion to winter, it appears to be very brief—"The lions break in on this as though to prevent the world of the shield from being too perfect" (Taplin 1980: 9).
17 There are also six instances of *polydaidalos*, all of which seem to refer to inanimate objects or humans whose parentage is not directly divine—3.358, of Hector's breastplate; 4.136, of Menelaus' breastplate; 7.252 of Hector's breastplate; 11.32 of Menelaus' shield; 23.743 of prizes at the funeral games; 24.597 of a chair Achilles sits on.
18 At 5.60, Harmon can make *daidala* because Pallas Athena loved him; at 14.179 *daidala* is used of Hera's robe that Athena decorated; at 18.400 *daidala* jewelry and hair accessories are forged by Hephaestus.
19 In a reimagining of the shield (www.theshieldofachilles.net), Katharine Vail renders this in bright red enameling, but while blue enamel is mentioned in the description, red is not.
20 My translation and italics.
21 Cp. Plato, *Phaedo* 108d–115a.
22 "Here—somewhat altered, for we are dealing with a subtle poet not a crude emblematist—here we have the *Iliad* and its belligerent deities" (Taplin 1980: 6).
23 *cholos* means "gall," "bile," "bitter anger," as in *melancholia*, "black bile."

Chapter 6

1 A version of this section first appeared as a standalone essay in *Public Seminar*, February 2, 2021.
2 In Aristophanes' *Birds*, Socrates becomes a verb: "Before you built this city, at that time altogether all human beings were mad for Sparta, letting their hair grow long, fasting, being filthy, Socratizing, and carrying little sticks" (1280–3).
3 This insight about the comical reality of starter pack memes came from Olivia Lynch, one of my Sarah Lawrence students in 2017.
4 Baudelaire 1855/1868.
5 In a short piece, "Do My Lies Say Anything about Fashion?" Otto von Busch notes the irony of blaming fashion for its illusions, when much of the lying happens "around fashion," which is to say, lying about whether or not one has succumbed to fashion's illusions (2020).
6 "Major" and "Minor" refer to the respective lengths of the texts; sometimes these dialogues are referred to as "Greater" and "Lesser."
7 See Sweet 1987: 340.
8 When we meet Eudicus again, we learn that his apparent flattery of Hippias is actually a wish to have Socrates refute him, since Hippias holds the same views as Eudicus' father.
9 Cp. *Protagoras* 314c.

10   150 minas is about 15,000 times the 1 drachma day-laborer's wage.
11   Cp. *Protagoras* 313b-c.
12   For this, see 286a and *Hippias Minor* 368e.
13   Thuc. 2.13.5.
14   Cp. *Euthydemus* 304b, where Socrates suggests to Euthydemus and Dionysodorus that they should charge money—perhaps a sign of his second thoughts?
15   Thank you to my Vassar seminar "Do Looks Matter?" (Spring 2019) for showing me that this evil twinning, which will ultimately be representative of beauty itself, is Socrates as Kermit and evil Kermit.
16   A little more than four gallons.
17   Heraclitus 82.
18   The only play of Aristophanes that does not have a pot is the *Clouds*. See Benardete 1984: xxx.
19   In the response, Socrates-2 tells Socrates-1 that once again he is asking about the *kallos* ("beauty") itself—in this instance using the noun (also used at 289b2-5, where it appears "to be only one fine thing among many." David Konstan takes this to be "short-circuiting the kind of adjectival response that has been offered so far" (2014: 117-18).
20   297d; "Pleasantly spoken, Hippias," says Socrates at 300c.
21   See, e.g., 297eff. for *eidenai* and *hora*; in the context the latter means "Look," as in, "See here" or "Look with your mind (observe)."
22   Skeptics about whether Plato had a concept of intellectual unity might consider this passage on both and each, in conjunction with 296d8 ("our soul"). The use of the first-person plural for the singular, especially in Socrates' case, is not so strange, but the strategic use of it where Socrates has divided himself in half and allied himself with Hippias is interesting.
23   Socrates uses another proverb at 301c4-6: "Our affairs, Hippias, accord not with what one wishes, as humans say on occasion, speaking proverbially, but with the power one has."
24   Also mentioned at *Hippias Major* 286a.
25   I first translated the *Hippias Minor* in conversation with Michael Davis, and there is no telling whose thoughts are whose. For Davis's remarks on the dialogue, see 2019: Chapters 8-10.
26   The words "have," "hold," "had," and "contained" in this paragraph are all the Greek verb *echein*.
27   In the *Odyssey polymêtis* occurs sixty-eight times; it only occurs eighteen times in the *Iliad*, and all of them are of Odysseus. Odysseus is only called *polytropos* twice in the *Od.* (and never in the *Il.*). See Davis 2019: 212, n. 13. That Hippias has seized on *polytropos* as Odysseus' defining feature makes it clear that he hasn't read past the first line of Homer's epic.
28   All misinterpretations of Platonic error seem to be critiqued in this portrait of good bad acting.

29   *pâda* in Sanskrit has the same double meaning.
30   A verb that uses a middle voice form to express the active voice. In Greek the middle voice is something different from either "I bear" (active) or "I am borne" (passive)—it is something more like, "I bear the burden." Certain verbs are middle in their active sense, and *aisthanesthai*, "to perceive," is one of them.
31   Cp. Aristotle, *Poetics* 1452bff.

Bibliography

Adorno, T. W. (1981), "Freudian Theory and the Pattern of Fascist Propaganda," in A. Arato and E. Gephardt (eds.), *The Essential Frankfurt School Reader*, 118-37, New York: Continuum.
Aeschylus (1991), *Aeschylus II*, David Grene and Richmond Lattimore (eds.), Chicago: The University of Chicago Press.
Aeschylus, Sophocles, Euripides (2016), *The Greek Plays: Sixteen Plays by Aeschylus, Sophocles, and Euripides*, Mary R. Lefkowitz and James S. Romm (eds.), New York: Modern Library.
Allhoff, F. (2011), *Fashion: Philosophy for Everyone*, J. Wolfendale and J. Kennett (eds.), Malden, MA: Wiley.
Aoki, S. (2001), *Fruits*, New York: Phaidon Press.
Arendt, H. (1998), *The Human Condition*, 2nd edn, Chicago: University of Chicago Press.
Arruzza, C. (2019), *A Wolf in the City*, New York, NY: Oxford University Press.
Bakhtin, M. (1984), *Rabelais and His World*, Helene Iswolsky (trans.), Indiana University Press.
Baldwin, J. (2008), "Nothing Personal," republished in *Contributions in Black Studies*: Vol. 6, Article 5.
Bancroft, A. (2012), *Fashion and Psychoanalysis: Styling the Self*, London: I.B. Tauris.
Barbey d'Aurevilly, J-A. (1988), *Dandyism*, Douglas Ainslie (trans.), New York: PAJ Publications.
Bari, S. (2017), "Austerity Chic, What We Wear in the Underfunded University," *Chronicle of Higher Education*.
Bari, S. (2019), *Dressed: The Secret Life of Clothes*, London: Jonathan Cape.
Barthes, R. (2013), *The Language of Fashion*, English edn, A. Stafford (trans.), M. Carter (ed.), London: Bloomsbury Academic.
Baudelaire, C. (1868), "Exposition Universelle," in *Curiosités esthétiques*, vol. II, 211-44, Michel Lévy frères: Oeuvres complètes de Charles Baudelaire.
Baudelaire, C. (1995), *The Painter of Modern Life and Other Essays*, 2nd edn, J. Mayne (trans.), Art & Letters, London: Phaidon.
Bell, Q. (1948), *On Human Finery*, London: The Hogarth Press Ltd.
Benardete, S. (1984), *The Being of the Beautiful: Plato's Theaetetus, Sophist, and Statesman*, University of Chicago Press.
Benardete, S. (1992), *Socrates' Second Sailing*, University of Chicago Press.
Benardete, S. (1999), *Sacred Transgressions*, South Bend: St. Augustine's Press.
Benardete, S. (2000), Ronna Burger and Michael Davis (eds.) "On Plato's Phaedo" in *The Argument of the Action*, 277-96, University of Chicago Press.
Benardete, S. (2009), *Herodotean Inquiries*, South Bend: St. Augustine's Press.
Benjamin, W. (1980), "Über den Begriff der Geschichte," in *Gesammelte Schriften*, 692-704, Frankfurt: Suhrkamp.

Benjamin, W. (2002), *The Arcades Project*, 1st paperback edn, H. Eiland and K. McLaughlin (trans.), Cambridge, MA: The Belknap Press of Harvard University Press.
Bentham, J. (2011), *The Panopticon Writings*, M. Božovič (ed.), London: Verso.
Bernstein, J. (2021), "Enlivenment, Love, and the Aesthetics of Violence: *Fight Club* in the Age of Trump," in *Metacinema: The Form and Content of Filmic Reference and Reflexivity*, D. LoRocca (ed.), Oxford: Oxford University Press.
Blaszczyk, R. L. (2006), "Styling Synthetics: DuPont's Marketing of Fabrics and Fashion in Postwar America," *Business History Review*, 80(3).
Boardman, J. (1996), *Greek Art*, London: Thames Hudson.
Bolton, A., A. McQueen, S. Frankel, T. Blanks and S. Sundsbø (2011), *Alexander McQueen: Savage Beauty*, distributed by Yale University Press, New York: Metropolitan Museum of Art.
Bolton, A. and H. Koda (2012), *Schiaparelli & Prada: Impossible Conversations*, New York: The Metropolitan Museum of Art.
Bowie, D. (1971), "Oh! You Pretty Things" [Song], *Hunky Dory*.
Bowie, D. (1973), "Time" [Song], *Aladdin Sane*.
Bowie, D. (1975), "Young Americans" [Song], *Young Americans*.
Brodesser-Akner, T. (2015), "Iris Apfel Doesn't Do Normcore," *The New York Times Magazine*, April 9.
Butler, J. (1990), *Gender Trouble: Feminism and the Subversion of Identity*, New York, London: Routledge.
Butler, J. (2000), *Antigone's Claim*, New York: Columbia University Press.
Callahan, R. and N. Adams (2013), *I Am Dandy: The Return of the Elegant Gentleman*, Berlin: Die Gestalten Verlag.
Callahan, R. and N. Adams (2017), *We Are Dandy: The Elegant Gentleman around the World*, Berlin: Die Gestalten Verlag.
Carlyle, T. (2008), *Sartor Resartus*, K. McSweeney and P. Sabor (eds.), Oxford: Oxford University Press.
Carnevali, B. (2020), *Social Appearances: A Philosophy of Prestige and Display*, Z. Hanafi, (trans.), New York: Columbia University Press.
Carson, A. (1995), "Shoes: An Essay on How Plato's 'Symposium' Begins," *The Iowa Review*, Spring-Summer, 25 (2): 47–51.
Cassirer, E. (1962), *An Essay on Man: An Introduction to a Philosophy of Human Culture*, New Haven, CT: Yale University Press.
Castiglione, B. (1901), *The Book of the Courtier*, L. E. Opdycke (trans.), New York: Charles Scribner's Sons.
Chang, E. (2005), "A Chronicle of Changing Clothes," in *Written on Water*, A. F. Jones (trans.), New York: Columbia University Press.
Chantraine, P. (1968-1980), *Dictionnaire etymologique de la langue grecque: histoire des mots*, Paris: Klincksieck.
Cixous, H. (1994), "Sonia Rykiel in Translation," D. Jenson (trans.), in *On Fashion*, S. Benstock and S. Ferriss (eds.), 95–99, New Jersey: Rutgers University Press.
Clark, H. and A. Palmer (2004), *Old Clothes, New Looks: Second Hand Fashion*, Oxford: Berg.

Clemente, D. (2014), *Dress Casual: How College Students Redefined American Style*, Chapel Hill, NC: University of North Carolina Press.

Coates, H. (2021), "This Divisive Hair Trend Was the Most Popular Look at the Golden Globes 2021," *Vogue Magazine*, March 1.

Cobain, K. (1991), "Something in the Way" [Song], *Nevermind*, Nirvana.

Commeford, T., T. Morello, Z. De La Rocha and B. Wilk (1992), "Take the Power Back" [Song], *Rage against the Machine*, Rage Against the Machine.

Costello, E. (1979), "Girls Talk" [Song], *Repeat When Necessary*, Elvis Costello & the Attractions.

Critchley, S. (2011), "The One True Philosophy of Clothes," *A Magazine* (#9).

Critchley, S. (2020), *Notes on Suicide*, 2nd edn, London: Fitzcarraldo Editions.

Critchley, S. (2021), *Bald: 35 Philosophical Short Cuts*, New Haven, CT: Yale University Press.

Crowley, J. E. (2010), *The Invention of Comfort: Sensibilities and Design in Early Modern Britain and Early America*, Baltimore and London: Johns Hopkins University Press.

Cunningham, B. (2018), *Fashion Climbing: A Memoir with Photographs*, New York: Penguin Press.

David, A. M. (2015), *Fashion Victims: The Dangers of Dress Past and Present*, New York: Bloomsbury Visual Arts.

Davies, Sioned, ed. (2008), *The Mabinogion*, Oxford World's Classics, Oxford; New York: Oxford University Press.

Davis, M. (2011), *The Soul of the Greeks: An Inquiry*, Chicago: University of Chicago Press.

Davis, M. (2019), *The Music of Reason: Rousseau, Nietzsche, Plato*, Philadelphia: University of Pennsylvania Press.

de Beauvoir, S. (2011), *The Second Sex*, Constance Borde and Sheila Malovany-Chevallier (trans.), New York: Random House.

de Quincey, T. (1873), *Last Days of Immanuel Kant, and Other Writings*, Boston: Shepard and Gill.

Descartes, R. (1996), *Meditations on First Philosophy*, J. Cottingham, (ed.), Cambridge: Cambridge University Press.

Dreizin, F. and T. Priestly (1982), "A Systematic Approach to Russian Obscene Language," *Russian Linguistics*, 6 (2) (February): 233–49.

Du Bois, W. E. B. (1995), *Dark Princess: A Romance*, Jackson, MS: Banner Books.

Du Bois, W. E. B. (2007), *Dusk of Dawn: An Essay toward an Autobiography of a Race Concept*, in The Oxford W.E.B. Du Bois Reader, New York: Oxford University Press.

Dylan, B. (1975), "Tangled Up in Blue" [Song], *Blood on The Tracks*.

Eno, B. (2020), *A Year with Swollen Appendices: Brian Eno's Diary*. Faber & Faber Limited.

Entwistle, J. (2000), *The Fashioned Body*, Cambridge: Polity Press.

Epstein, J. (1985), "Reflections of an Academic Dandy," *Gentleman's Quarterly*, 44–49, (October).

Fanfani, G., Harlow, M., and Nosch, M.L., eds., (2016), *Spinning Fates and the Song of the Loom: The Use of Textiles, Clothing and Cloth Production as Metaphor, Symbol and Narrative Device in Greek and Latin Literature*, Oxford: Oxford Books Limited.

Fitzgerald, F. S. (2009), "Bernice Bobs Her Hair," in *Flappers and Philosophers*, 131–62, New York: Vintage.

Fletcher, E., M. Mel, C. Chase and S. Robinson (1982), "The Message" [Song], *The Message* Grandmaster Flash and the Furious Five.

Ford, R. T. (2021), *Dress Codes: How the Laws of Fashion Made History*, New York: Simon & Schuster.

Foucault, M. (2011), "29 February, 1984: Second Hour," in *Courage of Truth*, Frédéric Gros, François Ewald, Alessandro Fontana, Arnold I. Davidson (eds.), Graham Burchell (trans.), 23–32, London: Picador.

Fox, C. and N. Gimbel (1972), "Killing Me Softly with His Song" [Song], Lori Lieberman; *Killing Me Softly*, Roberta Flack; and *The Score*, The Fugees.

Fox, G. P. (1871), *Fashion: The Power That Influences the World: The Philosophy of Ancient and Modern Dress and Fashion*, New York: American News Company.

Frame, D. (2009), *Hippota Nestor*, Washington, DC: Center for Hellenic Studies.

Freud, S. (1959), *On Transience*, Vol. 5 of *Collected Papers*, J. Strachey (ed.), New York: Basic Books.

Frías de la Parra, F., dir. (2019), *I'm No Longer Here* [Film].

Gadamer, H-G. (1994), *Heidegger's Ways*, New York: State University of New York Press.

Gadamer, H-G. (2013), *Truth and Method*, London: Bloomsbury Academic.

Gandalou, J. D. (1989), *Dandies à Bacongo: Le culte de l'élégance dans la société congolaise Contemporaine*, Paris: l'Harmattan.

Gandhi, M. (2018), *An Autobiography or The Story of My Experiments with Truth*, New Haven: Yale University Press.

Gilligan, I. (2021), "The Clothing Revolution," *Aeon*, May 13.

Gondola, C. D. (April 1999), "Dream and Drama: The Search for Elegance among Congolese Youth," *African Studies Review*, 42 (1): 23–48.

Gossetti-Murrayjohn, A. (2006), "Sappho as the Tenth Muse in Hellenistic Epigram," *Arethusa*, 39 (1) (Winter): 21–45.

Grewal, G. (2021), "Bernie's Mittens," *Public Seminar*, February 2.

Guthrie, W. K. C. (2014), *Sophists*, Cambridge: Cambridge University Press.

Hadley, J. (1873), *Essays Philological and Critical*, New York: Holt & Williams.

Hanson, K. (1990), "Dressing down Dressing up—The Philosophic Fear of Fashion," *Hypatia*, 5 (2): 107–21.

Heidegger, M. (1950), *Holzwege*, Frankfurt: Klostermann.

Heidegger, M. (2008), *Basic Writings: From Being and Time* (1927) to *The Task of Thinking* (1964), D. F. Krell (ed.), New York: Harper Perennial Modern Thought.

Hell, R. (1976), "Blank Generation" [Song], *Another World*, Richard Hell & the Voidoids.

Hellenic Culture Organization S.A. (2004) *Ptychoseis = Folds + Pleats: Drapery from Ancient Greek Dress to 21*st *Century Fashion*, Peloponnesian Folklore Foundation.
Heti, S. et al. (2014), M. Mann (ed.), "The Surfer Is Nothing without the Wave," in *Women in Clothes*, 187–89, New York: Penguin Press.
Hollander, A. (1993), *Seeing Through Clothes*, Berkeley: University of California Press.
Homer (2015), *Iliad*, C. Alexander (trans.), New York: Ecco Press.
Horwell, V. (2016), "Bill Cunningham Obituary," *The Guardian*, June 27.
Jackson, B., Loblack, A. (2020), "Dior" [Song], *Meet the Woo*, Pop Smoke.
Jean, W., Hill, L., Michel, P. (1996), "Family Business" [Song], *The Score*, The Fugees.
Jones, N., S. Barnes, J. Olivier, K. Walkers (1996), "If I Ruled the World (Imagine That)" [Song], *It Was Written*, Nas ft. Lauryn Hill.
Judah, C. (2019), "Observer Picture Archive: My Clothes and I," *The Guardian*, March 17.
Kadyrova, N., dir. (2015), *The Congo Dandies: Living in Poverty and Spending a Fortune to Look Like a Million Dollars*, [Documentary] USA: Janson Media.
Kant, I. (2011), *Anthropology, History, and Education*, R. Louden and G. Zöller (trans.), New York: Cambridge University Press.
Kasimis, D. (2018), *The Perpetual Immigrant and the Limits of Athenian Democracy*, Cambridge: Cambridge University Press.
Keller, G. (2011), *Kleider Machen Leute*, (2005), Frankfurt am Main: Suhrkamp.
Kelly, I. (2005), *Beau Brummell: The Ultimate Dandy*, Hodder and Stoughton.
Kinser, B. E. (2012), "Fearful Symmetry: Hypocrisy and Bigotry in Thomas Carlyle's 'Occasional Discourse[s] on the Negro Question,'" *Studies in the Literary Imagination*, 45 (1) (Spring): 139–65.
Klein, W., dir. (1966), *Who Are You, Polly Maggoo?* [Film] France: Delpire Productions.
Konstan, D. (2014), *Beauty: The Fortunes of an Ancient Greek Idea*, New York: Oxford University Press.
Kossman, N. (2001), *Gods and Mortals: Modern Poems on Classical Myths*, Oxford; New York: Oxford University Press.
Kuhn, T. S. (1996), *The Structure of Scientific Revolutions*, 3rd edn, Chicago, IL: University of Chicago Press.
Lagerfeld, K., J. Napias and P. Mauriès (2013), *The World according to Karl: The Wit and Wisdom of Karl Lagerfeld*, London: Thames & Hudson.
Lehmann, U. (2000), *Tigersprung: Fashion in Modernity*, Cambridge, MA: MIT Press.
Lehmann, U. (2018), *Fashion and Materialism*. Edinburgh: Edinburgh University Press.
Lemoine, R. (2020), *Plato's Caves: The Liberating Sting of Cultural Diversity*, New York, NY: Oxford University Press.
Lennon, J. and P. McCartney (1967), "A Day in the Life" [Song], *Sgt. Pepper's Lonely Hearts Club Band*, The Beatles.

Leopardi, G. (1982), "Dialogo della Moda e della Morte," *Operette Morali*, Milano: Mursia.
Levi, P. (2008), *Survival in Auschwitz: If This Is a Man*, Stuart Woolf (trans.), New York: Orion Press.
Lidz, F. (2020), "Here Lies the Skull of Pliny the Elder, Maybe," *The New York Times*, February 14.
Lipovetsky, G. (1994), *The Empire of Fashion*, C. Porter (trans.), Princeton, NJ: Princeton University Press.
Loos, A. (1998), *Ornament and Crime: Selected Essays*, Riverside, CA: Ariadne Press.
Loraux, N. (2000), *Born of the Earth*, Ithaca, NY: Cornell University Press.
Lorde, A. (2017), *A Burst of Light: And Other Essays*, Newburyport: Dover Publications.
Mabanckou, A. (2012), *Black Bazaar*, London: Serpent's Tail.
Machiavelli, N. (1985), *The Prince*, H. C. Mansfield (trans.), Chicago: University of Chicago Press.
Makouezi, E. G. (1970), *Dictionnaire de la SAPE*, Paris: Publibook.
Mann, T. (1989), *Death in Venice, and Seven Other Stories*, H. T. Lowe-Porter (trans.), 1st Vintage International (ed.), New York: Vintage Books.
Martin, P. M. (1996), *Leisure and Society in Colonial Brazzaville*, Cambridge: Cambridge University Press.
Marx, K. (2016), *Der achtzehnte Brumaire des Louis Bonaparte*, Hofenberg.
Marx, K. (2018), *Capital*, London: Lawrence & Wishart.
Mathers, M., J. Bass, L. Resto, S. King (2002), "White America" [Song], *The Eminem Show*, Eminem.
Mathers, M. et al. (2013), "Rap God" [Song], *The Marshall Mathers LP 2*, Eminem.
Matteucci, G. and S. Marino (2017), *Philosophical Perspectives on Fashion*, London; New York: Bloomsbury Academic.
Mbembe, A. (2001), *On the Postcolony*, Berkeley: University of California Press.
McAleer, G. J., *Veneration and Refinement: The Ethics of Fashion*, http://www.ethicsoffashion.com/.
Meichtry, S. (2006), "Does the Pope Wear Prada?," *Wall Street Journal*, April 25.
Mercury, F. (1973), "Killer Queen" [Song], *Sheer Heart Attack*, Queen.
Merleau-Ponty, M. (1968), *The Visible and the Invisible*, C. Lefort (ed.), and A. Lingis (trans.), Evanston: Northwestern University Press.
Miller, J. I. (2005), "Fashion and Democratic Relationships," *Polity*, 37 (1): 3–23.
Miller, M. L. (2009), *Slaves to Fashion: Black Dandyism and the Styling of Black Diasporic Identity*, Durham: Duke University Press.
Muellner, L. (2022), "On Plato Not Misquoting Homer and What's 'New' at *Republic* 424b-c," in G. Grewal (ed.), *Poetic (Mis)quotations in Plato*, *Classics@*, 22. Center for Hellenic Studies.
Munns, J. and P. Richards (1999), *The Clothes That Wear Us: Essays on Dressing and Transgressing in Eighteenth-century Culture*, Newark: University of Delaware Press.

Nagel, A. (2004), "Fashion and the Now-Time of Renaissance Art," *RES: Anthropology and Aesthetics*, 46: 32–52.

Nagel, A. and C. Wood (2010), *Anachronic Renaissance*, Zone Books.

Nagy, G. (2009), *Hesiod and the Ancient Biographical Traditions*, Center for Washington, DC: Hellenic Studies.

Nails, D. (2002), *People of Plato: A Prosopography of Plato and Other Socratics*, Indianapolis: Hackett Publishing.

Nanda, B. R. (1996), *Mahatma Gandhi: A Biography*, Delhi: Oxford University Press.

Newton, H. P. (2009), *Revolutionary Suicide*, Penguin classics deluxe edn, New York: Penguin Books.

Nietzsche, F. W. (1954), "Twilight of the Idols," in *The Portable Nietzsche*, W. Kaufmann (ed. and trans.), New York: Viking Press.

Nietzsche, F. W. (1967), *On the Genealogy of Morals*, W. Kaufmann (trans.), New York: Random House.

Nietzsche, F. W. (1989), *Beyond Good and Evil: Prelude to a Philosophy of the Future*, W. Kaufmann (trans.), New York: Vintage Books - Random House.

Nikulin, D. V. (2017), *The Concept of History*, London; New York: Bloomsbury Academic.

O'Grady, J. (2001), "Elizabeth Anscombe," *The Guardian*, January 10.

Padilla Peralta, D. (2015), "From Damocles to Socrates: The Classics in/of Hip-Hop," *Eidolon*, June 8.

Pappas, N. (2016), *The Philosopher's New Clothes: The Theaetetus, the Academy, and Philosophy's Turn against Fashion*, London: Routledge.

Pappas, N. (2020), *Plato's Exceptional City, Love, and Philosopher*, London: Routledge.

Pesic, P. (1999), "Wrestling with Proteus: Francis Bacon and the 'Torture' of Nature," *Isis*, 90 (1): 81–94.

Piaf, É. (1996), "Le Brun et le Blond" [Song], *1936–1945*, vol 2.

Picon, A. (2013), *Ornament: The Politics of Architecture and Subjectivity*, West Sussex, UK: John Wiley & Sons Ltd.

Pitman, J. (2003), *On Blondes*, London: Bloomsbury.

Plato (1987), *Greater Hippias*, in *The Roots of Political Philosophy: Ten Forgotten Socratic Dialogues*, D. R. Sweet (trans.), Ithaca: Cornell University Press.

Plato (2008), *Plato's Gorgias and Aristotle's Rhetoric*, J. Sachs (trans.), Focus.

Plato (2018), *Phaedo*, G. Grewal (trans.), Center for Hellenic Studies. https://chs.harvard.edu/primary-source/platos-phaedo-trans-gwenda-lin-grewal/.

Plato (2022), *Euthydemus*, in *Thinking of Death in Plato's Euthydemus: A Close Reading and New Translation*, G. Grewal (trans.), Oxford: Oxford University Press.

The Rational Dress Society (January 1889), *The Rational Dress Society's Gazette*, London: The Rational Dress Society.

Rocamora, A. and A. Smelik (2015), *Thinking through Fashion: A Guide to Key Theorists*, London: I.B. Tauris.

Rousseau, J-J. (1969), *First & Second Discourses*, R. Masters (ed.), J. Masters (trans.), New York: Bedford/St. Martin's.

Rousseau, J-J. (1990), *Essai sur l'origine des langues*, Gallimard.

Rousseau, J-J. (1992), *The Reveries of a Solitary Walker*, C. E. Butterworth (trans.), Indianapolis: Hackett.

Salton, M. (2017), "Is Santa a Psychedelic Mushroom?," *The New York Times*, December 21.

Savage, J. (1992), *England's Dreaming: Anarchy, Sex Pistols, Punk Rock, and Beyond*, New York: St. Martin's Press.

Scapp, R. and B. Seitz (2010), *Fashion Statements: On Style, Appearance, and Reality*, New York: Palgrave Macmillan.

Scarry, E. (2013), *On Beauty and Being Just*, Princeton, NJ: Princeton University Press.

Simmel, G. (1957), "Fashion," *American Journal of Sociology*, 62 (6), 541–58.

Simon, C. (1972), "You're So Vain" [Song], *No Secrets*.

Skorokhodova, O. (1974), "How I Perceive the World around Me," *The UNESCO Courier*, March.

Snyder, J. M. (1980), *Puns and Poetry in Lucretius' De Rerum Natura*, Amsterdam: Grüner.

Stallybrass, P. (1998), "Marx's Coat." In *Border Fetishisms: Material Objects in Unstable Spaces*, 183–207, New York: Routledge.

Steele, V. (1991), "The F-Word," *Lingua Franca*.

Steele, V. (2007), *Gothic: Dark Glamour*, New Haven, CT: Yale University Press.

Steele, V. (2011), *Daphne Guinness*, New Haven, CT: Yale University Press.

Steinkopf-Frank, H. R. (2017), "La Sape: Tracing the History and Future of the Congos' Well-Dressed Men," [unpublished bachelor's thesis], University of Oregon Clark Honors College.

Stevens, W. (1990), *The Palm at the End of the Mind*, New York: Vintage Books.

Svendsen, L. (2006), *Fashion: A Philosophy*, London: Reaktion Books.

Taplin, O. (1980), "The Shield of Achilles within the 'Iliad,'" *Greece & Rome*, 27 (1) (April): 1–21.

Taylor P. (2016), *Black Is Beautiful: A Philosophy of Black Aesthetics*, Hoboken: John Wiley & Sons.

Thomas, D. (2003), "Fashion Matters: 'La Sape' and Vestimentary Codes in Transnational Contexts and Urban Diasporas," *MLN*, 118 (4): 947–73.

Thompson, D. (2018), "Everything You Wear Is Athleisure," *The Atlantic*, October 28.

Thurman, J. (2021), "Ann Lowe's Barrier-Breaking Mid-century Couture," *New Yorker*, March 29.

Twenge, J. (2017), *I-Gen: Why Today's Super-Connected Kids Are Growing Up Less Rebellious, More Tolerant, Less Happy and Completely Unprepared for Adulthood and What That Means for the Rest of Us*, New York: Simon & Schuster.

Vail, K., *The Shield of Achilles*, foreword J. Arieti, www.theshieldofachilles.net.

Vassar College (1924), *Scrapbooks: Vassar College Endowment Fund*, Photo Album No. 270, VC, Jeanne (Russell) Janish, Poughkeepsie, NY: Vassar College.
Veblen, T. (1994), *The Theory of the Leisure Class*, New York: Dover Publications.
Vergil (2008), *Aeneid*, S. Ruden (trans.), New Haven, CT: Yale University Press.
von Busch, O. (2018), "Inclusive Fashion—an Oxymoron—or a Possibility for Sustainable Fashion?," *Fashion Practice*, 10 (3): 311–27.
von Busch, O. (2020), "Do My Lies Say Anything about Fashion?," *Public Seminar*, February 11.
von Busch, O. (2020), *The Psychopolitics of Fashion: Conflict and Courage under the Current State of Fashion*, London: Bloomsbury Publishing.
Waits, T. (2002), "Misery Is a River of the World" [Song], *Blood Money*.
Wesselmann, K. (2011), *Mythical Structures in Herodotus' Histories*, Washington, DC: Center for Hellenic Studies.
West, M. L. (1971), *Early Greek Philosophy and the Orient*, Oxford: Clarendon Press.
Whistler, J. (1967), *The Gentle Art of Making Enemies*, New York: Dover Publications.
Wieczorek, A. (2013), *Die Macht der Toga: Dresscode im Römischen Weltreich*, Regensburg: Schnell & Steiner.
Williams, A. (2014), "The New Normal," *The New York Times*. 2 April.
Wilson, E. (2010), *Adorned in Dreams: Fashion and Modernity*, London: I.B. Tauris.
Wölfflin, H., M. Selzer and H. Wölfflin (2017), *Prolegomena to a Psychology of Architecture*, Colorado Springs: KeepAhead Books.
Woodard, R. D. (2014), *The Textualization of the Greek Alphabet*, Cambridge: Cambridge University Press.
Woolf, V. (1989), "The New Dress," in *The Complete Shorter Fiction of Virginia Woolf*, Mariner Books.
Worthy, A. L. (2012–21), *Hitler Wears Hermes* [Album], Westside Gunn.
Wu-Tang Clan (1996), "Triumph" [Song], *Wu-Tang Forever*, Wu-Tang Clan.
Young, A., S. Carter, M. Bradford and S. Storch (1999), "Still D.R.E." [Song], *The Chronic 2001*, Dr. Dre ft. Snoop Dogg.
Zaleski, L. (2014), "10 Reasons You, Normcore Guy, Are an Idiot," *GQ*, February 27. https://www.gq.com/story/normcore-fashion-is-for-idiots
Zanker, P. (1995), *The Mask of Socrates: The Image of the Intellectual in Antiquity*, A. Shapiro (trans.), Berkeley: University of California Press.
Zhi, L. (2016), *A Book to Burn and a Book to Keep (Hidden)*, R. Handler-Spitz, P. C. Lee and H. Saussy (ed. and trans.), New York: Columbia University Press.
Zimmer, A. L. (2019), "The Logic of the Mask: Nietzsche's Depth as Surface," *The Agonist: A Nietzsche Circle Journal*, XII (1): 22–31.

Index

academia (Academy) xiii, xvi–ii, 9, 10, 39, 52, 99, 100, 116
academic (style) xii–iii, 1, 13, 16, 17, 52, 86, 87, 90, 94, 100, 123, 128, 130, 150, 180, 186, 187n10
Achilles 49, 68, 88, 97, 120, 127, 155, 158, 168, 171–3, 200n15
-shield of 142–6
Adam, *see also* Eve 7–9, 20, 135
adornment xvi, 7, 18, 27, 34, 61, 72, 75, 118, 156, 170
Adorno, T. W. 114
Aeneas 142
Aeschylus 128
-*Persians* 61
aesthetics 110, 127, 147
Agamemnon 44, 48, 88, 120
age, *see also* aging xix–xx, 19, 40, 51, 64–72, 85–7, 91, 180, 185, 186
-of bloom 68–71, 186
-middle age 17, 65, 67, 68, 179
-of midlife crisis 64, 69
-old age 21, 65, 67, 68, 70, 194n6
-of prime, *see* prime
-of youth 23, 64–7, 68, 69, 70, 71, 73, 74, 75, 80, 88, 91, 95, 115, 127, 155, 184, 186
agency 6, 19, 50, 58, 135, 165, 167, 172, 176, 177, 178, 180
agent 85, 165, 168, 172, 175, 178
aging, *see also* age xx, 24, 64, 71, 72, 75, 87, 91
-anti-aging 64, 66, 70, 71, 73, 74, 76
Ajax 43, 173
Alcibiades 28, 68, 69, 71, 102, 107, 114, 123, 194n12
Alighieri, Dante 22
American (fashion) xviii, 3, 4, 16, 29, 37–8, 41, 74, 109, 112, 115, 125–7

anonymity 29, 39, 55, 60, 149, 181
Anscombe, G.E.M. 15
anti-aging, *see* aging
anti-fashion 51, 72, 101, 149–50, 163, 185
Antigone (Sophocles) 64, 73, 76–85, 87, 128
antinomian 9, 30, 35, 106
Aphrodite 28, 31, 42, 43, 49, 50, 89, 90, 97, 142, 160
Apollo 31, 127, 143, 181
apparent xv, 26, 44, 75, 143, 148, 162, 163, 164, 184
appearance xvii, xx, xxii–iii, 1–2, 9, 15, 23, 40–3, 48, 50–1, 56, 58, 67, 70, 72, 75, 110, 114, 118, 121, 143, 148, 150, 160, 163–5, 174, 178, 180, 181
aprons 26, 137
Arendt, H. 17, 40
argument (as style) xv, 21, 52, 72, 74, 94, 99, 118, 129, 130, 139, 140, 141, 154, 163–4, 166, 171, 172, 175, 177, 178, 186
Ariadne 94, 144
aristocratic (fashion) 56, 104, 106, 115, 184
Aristophanes 28
-*Birds* 201n2
-*Clouds* xvii, 90 (196n48), 202n18
-*Knights* 38, 70, 161, 183
Aristotle xvii, 18, 74, 118, 157
-*De Anima* 3
-*Metaphysics* 90
-*Nicomachean Ethics* 95
-*Poetics* 147, 194n4
-*Politics* 118, 121
-*Rhetoric* 64, 65–8, 70, 179
armor xiii, 7, 48, 49, 85–90, 106, 120, 143, 145, 181, 182, 183

art 9, 10, 13–19, 32, 70, 126, 128, 131, 140, 149, 156, 170, 177, 181
Artemis 92, 191n11
Athena 42, 43, 88, 96, 112, 120, 142, 144, 157–61
Athens xii, 28, 32, 53, 60, 102, 107, 150, 152, 154, 157, 160, 182, 183
athleisure xix, 4, 37, 56, 115–16
autochthony 36, 85, 183

Bacchae, *see* Euripides
Bacchus, *see also* Dionysus 33, 36, 50
bad, *see also* evil xviii, 44, 46, 53, 87, 113, 161–9, 171–8, 179
   -fashion xv, 21, 26, 27, 39, 71, 97, 178, 187n10
bald, *see also* hair xiii, 90, 91
Baldwin, J. 4, 65
barbarian (Greek *barbaros*) 10, 43, 182, 185, 193n63
Barbey d' Aurevilly, J-A. 100–8, 115, 124
Barthes, R. 20, 189n36
basic xix, xx, 2, 12, 20, 75, 114, 118, 187n16
Baudelaire, C. 19, 68, 109, 149, 151, 152, 193n55
beard 11, 68, 94, 95, 194n12, 197n55
beautiful, *see also* beauty xxii, 16, 24, 25, 34, 41, 66, 67, 72, 82, 88, 90, 91, 92, 94, 105, 106, 107, 110, 116, 119, 129, 137, 147–69, 171, 174, 178, 184
beauty xx, xxii, 3, 12, 16, 18, 37, 39, 41–3, 47, 49, 57, 64, 66, 71, 75, 88–9, 92, 96, 108, 112, 140–1, 147–9, 151–5, 158–60, 162–8, 202n19
Benedict XVI ("Prada Pope") 131
Benjamin, W. xxiii, 104, 106, 125, 179, 184
Bentham, J. 12
black 17, 53, 132
   -dress (LBD) 20, 87
   -and goth, *see* goth

   -hair dye 91, 96
   -for mourning 47
   -tie 24
   -turtlenecks 17
blond, *see* hair
blood 13, 18, 35, 73, 78, 82, 84–5, 86, 91, 97, 103, 108, 131, 142, 143, 144, 183
blush xxii, 5, 24–5, 69, 71, 74, 194n14
bob (hairstyle), *see* hair
body xxi, xxii, 5–8, 34, 36–8, 40–1, 46, 48, 56–7, 59, 60–1, 64–5, 72–3, 75, 80, 88, 90, 92, 94, 99, 103, 106, 111, 113, 115–16, 131, 133, 136, 138–43, 169–70, 174, 181, 188n7, 199n34
   -and death 23–5, 29, 77, 79, 82, 85–7, 185
Bowie, D. 100, 127, 130
braid 32, 91, 94, 170
brand 52, 54, 55, 92, 131, 132, 171
britches (also *breeches*) 106, 138, 198n27
Brummell, G. B. "Beau" 18, 100–8, 115, 124
bullshit, *see also* shit 26, 134, 137
burial xx, 24, 48, 76–9, 82–5, 162
button 52, 57, 122, 151, 172

Cadmus 31–2, 35–6
Caesar 14, 103
Candaules 56
Carlyle, T. 25–6, 133–6, 138
carnival 122–3
cave xii, 37, 41, 42, 52, 66, 72, 83, 85, 112, 122, 186, 188n2
celebrity 10, 38, 101, 108
Chanel 37, 132
Chanel, Coco 56
Chang, Eileen 117
character xvii, xx, 16, 28, 32, 34, 36, 38, 41, 65–7, 73, 76, 82, 85, 92, 94, 119, 126, 132, 134,

139, 141, 142, 160, 167, 168, 173–5, 186
chitôn 183–4
choker 87
chorus 30, 32, 35–6, 46, 48–50, 70, 76–84, 130, 185
Christ, see Jesus
Christianity 127, 180
Cicero 14
Civil Rights Movement, see also protest 109–10
civilization 8, 10, 35, 121, 137, 182
Cixous, Hélène 6
classic (style) xix, 24, 149, 152, 179
cloak 14, 45, 58, 87, 112, 116, 117, 119, 120, 124, 144, 170
 -of invisibility 53
 -as a metaphor xvi, 49, 53, 55, 74, 90, 113, 119, 121, 155
cloth xxii, 6, 13, 29, 48–9, 61, 79, 112, 124, 131–5, 181
clothed xx, 3–4, 8–9, 21, 24, 35, 38–9, 54, 58, 72, 74, 100, 136, 138
Clotho xxii, 44, 138–9, 141–2, 146
coat 7, 11, 20, 55, 80, 91–3, 135, 148
color xvi, 12, 16, 17, 30, 70, 85, 87, 91, 95–7, 102, 119, 132, 136, 144, 186
comfortable xix–xx, 3–6, 11, 12, 21, 40, 54, 62, 116, 138, 148, 150, 183
comical 29, 37, 102, 114, 127, 143, 146, 150, 151, 160–1, 175
concealment xx, xxii, xxiv, 11, 24, 35, 77–9, 83
consumption 111, 147, 150, 152
contingency xiii, xx, xxiv, 2–3, 121, 149, 182–5
convention 3, 27, 35, 36, 38, 54, 59, 70, 95, 102, 104, 115, 185–6
conventional xix, xxii, 5, 11, 34, 52, 66, 93, 156, 173
corpse xii, 23–5, 57, 77, 79, 82–5, 143, 147, 148

corset xv, 4, 6, 15, 63, 116–17, 186
cosmos, see also kosmos xvii, xxiv, 113, 142, 144, 183
Cunningham, Bill 53, 161
Cupid, see also Eros 30, 58
custom, see also costume xv, xxiii, 18, 35, 63, 66, 97–9, 110, 120, 127, 135
cut (of hair and clothing) 21, 24, 47, 91, 93–8, 111, 132, 136, 148

Daedalus 143–4, 155
daidalon 139, 144, 201n17, n18
Dandy 90, 99–116, 122–5, 150
dandyism 100–6, 109, 124
 -Black dandyism 109
 -in Brazzaville and Kinshasa 111–12
de Beauvoir, S. 53
dead, see also death xii, xxi, 22–4, 41, 45–6, 52, 55, 57, 63, 72–80, 85, 94, 97, 105, 126, 137, 155, 166, 179, 185
death, see also dead xxi, 5–6, 8, 21–4, 29, 41, 76–85, 113, 143–6
 and fashion xxi, 21, 63–4, 72–4, 85, 87, 91–3, 108, 146
deception 8, 139, 165–6
deinon 81–2, 84, 90, 145, 177–8
Delilah 112
 -and Samson 94
demagogue 38, 113
Demeter 31, 44, 49–50, 139
democracy, democratic xix, 5, 38, 40, 51, 53–6, 60, 62, 70, 115, 119, 127, 161, 182–4
Demos (character) 38, 161, 183–4, 195n19
denim, see also jean 85–7, 110
Descartes, R. 11, 54
design xix, 5, 33, 55, 59, 61, 85–6, 111, 113, 117, 171, 178
designer 5, 13, 16, 20, 25, 50, 86, 88, 117, 137, 151, 161, 164, 172, 177, 181, 184

devil 26, 29, 57, 125, 133, 138, 180
Diogenes the Cynic 14, 87
Diogenes Teufelsdröckh, see Teufelsdröckh
Diomedes (and Glaucus) 181
Dionysus 30–6, 42, 94
Dior, Christian 123, 129, 132
diva, see also icon, idol 88, 131
divine xvi, 10, 22, 26, 30, 32, 35, 42–3, 47, 51, 57–8, 65, 79, 88–90, 97, 105, 107, 123, 131, 133, 145–6, 171–3
divinity 22, 31, 35–6, 69, 88, 134, 143, 190n46
doxa 36, 93
drapery 54, 152, 181, 185
dress 2, 12, 20, 32, 52–5, 59–61, 75, 87, 89, 109–11, 116–17, 124, 126–7, 130, 138, 140–1, 160–2, 182–5
  -codes 5, 39–40, 94, 106, 109, 115, 122, 128
  -as *kosmos* 33–7
dressing down 52–4, 100, 120
dressing up xv, 16, 17, 22, 27, 30, 53, 54, 111, 120, 149
Du Bois, W. E. B. 112
dust 79, 81–5, 196n38

eccentric 17, 33, 59, 71, 105, 141
Eden, Garden of 2, 8, 10, 11, 55, 136
effortless xix, 4, 54, 58, 148–9, 153, 185
Egyptian fashion (ancient) 10, 23–4, 41, 44–5, 48, 94, 113, 158
eidôlon 41–6, 142, 191n24
elegance 53, 101, 103, 105, 108, 110, 140, 148
elite 2, 101, 132
elitist 37, 59, 133, 151
embroidery 55, 61, 89, 114, 119–21, 129, 139–40, 185
Empedocles xvii, 108, 191n13
enlightenment 9, 117, 167
Eno, Brian xii, 95–6, 172
Epicurus xvii, 16

equality 39, 54, 181, 185
Er (myth of) xxii, 65, 139
Eros, *erôs* 81, 85, 114, 198n21
error 74, 93, 151, 153, 172, 178
esprit 101–2, 107, 125
Euripides 128
  -*Bacchae* 30–7
  -*Helen* 41–51, 54–5, 191n21, n26
Eve, see also Adam 7–9, 20, 96, 112
evil, see also bad 54, 73, 76, 80, 154, 157–8, 160, 164, 169, 176–8
excess 1, 2, 12, 67, 87, 101, 118, 149, 165
explicit speech, see profanity
eye 4, 11, 18, 24, 39, 49, 71, 84, 145, 175, 188n5
  -makeup 73, 87, 127
  -of recognition 6–8, 11, 45–6, 56–7, 60, 108, 135, 138, 147–5, 152, 160–1, 164, 168, 180
eyebrows, brow(s), see hair

fabric xxi, 5–7, 11, 29, 36, 37, 48, 54, 63, 79, 85–91, 115, 119, 132, 137–8, 144, 146, 179, 181
false 42, 45, 48, 74, 77, 97, 107, 139, 140, 143, 153, 169–70
fascism 114, 147
fashion industry 36, 64, 71, 147
fashion sense 1–5, 6–7, 11, 183
fashioning xv, 40, 72, 114, 120, 128, 141, 178–80
fashionista xvii, 52, 86, 145, 149, 180
fate
  -as a goddess xxii, 139
  -and time 66, 88, 97, 102, 105, 142–6
  -and tragedy 43–4, 49, 51, 76, 78, 80, 82, 85, 155, 166
faux 11, 36, 87, 91, 123, 132
feminine 32, 34, 36, 71, 112–13, 119, 158
femininity 17, 32–4, 97, 112
fig leaves 7–8, 24–6, 91

fit
- of clothes and words 2, 5, 6, 29, 38, 39, 41, 44, 54, 56, 60, 64, 103, 106, 116–17, 130, 141, 160, 163–6
- of physique 80, 116

flag xxii, 48, 79, 82, 85, 103, 106, 114
flesh 3, 29, 35, 38, 40–1, 86, 136, 139, 191n13
folds 7, 48–9, 55, 61, 122, 185, 192n51
foreign 7, 33, 43, 61, 70–2, 95, 104–7, 110, 130, 136, 153, 156–7, 170, 182–4
foreigner 10, 32–3, 100, 104
form, *see also* shape 12, 23, 31, 33, 36, 41, 56, 58, 80, 92, 94, 111, 145, 174
France 93, 103–5, 108, 111
freedom 2, 4–6, 16, 25, 54, 60, 86, 109, 177, 185
French (language) 100, 101, 103, 104, 107
French Revolution 87, 104, 126
Freud, S. 40, 126, 128
fur, *see* hair

Gadamer, H. G. xvii, 17
Gaia, *Gê* 34, 44
Gandhi, M. xxii, 18
Gen Z 50, 87, 95
general, *see also* particular 26, 34, 103–4, 115, 133–4, 145
Genesis 7, 14, 136
German idealism 17, 26, 133–4
ghost xxii, 43, 51, 54, 58, 61, 85, 180
Glaucus, *see* Diomedes
glory 50, 82, 88, 93, 112, 129, 142
glove 86, 88, 103
god, gods 12, 97, 130
- in ancient Greece 9–10, 31–7, 43–9, 55, 61, 68, 79, 81–2, 88, 93, 114, 119–21, 127, 142–6, 158–61, 173, 177, 184
- in Christianity 7

- in Egypt 23–4, 158
- of fashion xxii, 18, 85, 111, 126
- wish to be a xix, 10, 28, 50–1, 57–9, 105, 108, 124, 131–9

gold, golden 8, 28, 43, 53–4, 86, 108, 119, 131, 144, 156, 160–1, 181–2, 184
good 12, 116–17, 155–6, 162, 169, 171–9
- and beautiful 67, 91, 129, 147, 164–7
- fashion 71, 80, 130, 150, 152
- intentions 54, 150
- looks xvii, xviii, 1–2, 14, 18, 28, 39, 53, 87, 101, 109, 114, 175

goth (style) xix, 64, 73, 80, 82, 85, 87, 136, 195n23
grace 103, 105–9, 139, 174, 181
grave 50, 76, 79, 82, 84, 122–3, 162
Greek xii–xiv, 19, 43–4, 48–9, 61, 65, 68, 88–9, 98, 116, 126, 141, 153, 172, 180–2
- language 41, 76, 92, 173, 203n30
- tragedy, *see also* tragedy 64, 73, 87, 185

Gucci teeth xix, 163
Gyges 56–9
gym clothes, *see* athleisure
gymnos 33, 61

habit xv, 5, 14, 21, 53, 55, 93, 110, 132, 187n3
Hades 33, 41, 43–4, 50, 69, 74, 76, 81–2, 85, 142
hair, *see also* nails 1, 11, 18, 24, 32, 35, 47, 53, 88–98, 100, 116–18, 120, 132, 184, 201n2
- blond, blonde 95–6
- bob 95–6
- curls 19, 94, 96
- eyebrows 88, 93, 95
- fur 73, 91, 92, 127, 137
- parting 95
- pelt 11, 91

Hanson, K. 7, 52, 196n43

harmony 35, 139, 167, 171
hat xv, xxiii, 28, 90, 100, 106, 115, 124, 126, 160
Hebe, *hêbê* 68
Hector 25, 88, 90, 143
Hegel, G.W.F. 134, 179
Heidegger, M. 12–13, 17, 73, 192n52
Helen (character) 28, 41, 89, 112, 148
Helen (play), *see* Euripides
Hephaestus 142–3, 145, 174
Hera 31, 41–3, 49, 142–3
Heraclitus xx, 1, 59, 159
Hermes 48–9, 68–9, 72, 94, 114, 125
Herodotus 23–4, 56–7, 60, 92–3, 113, 176, 184
Hesiod 119, 126, 140, 194n8
hip-hop (and rap) 127–30, 195n24
Hippias of Elis 111, 151–78
Hippodamus of Miletus 118
hipster xix, 12, 54, 110, 120
history xxiii, 18–19, 39, 51, 56, 74, 91, 101–5, 112, 121, 152, 179, 181–4
Hollander, A. 19, 131, 181
holy 26, 97, 105, 111, 126, 131, 133, 136–8
Homer 28, 39, 41, 68–9, 83, 102, 134, 168, 171–2, 180
 -*Iliad* 25, 28, 68, 88–9, 97, 112, 142–45, 155, 181
 -*Odyssey* 99, 112
honesty 11, 26, 31, 34, 101, 133, 136, 153, 155
Horace 97–8
human 4–6, 14, 34–6, 39, 43, 45, 53, 59, 65, 85–90, 94, 113, 149, 160, 168, 186, 190n5, 196n33, 199n35
 -beings 7–12, 28–32, 41, 56, 61, 63, 70, 73, 81, 99, 101, 114–15, 121, 135–9, 141–5, 159, 179
 -body 34–6, 79, 133, 137
 -clothes xvii–xx, xxiv, 18–19, 24, 73–4

Hume, D. 132
hygiene 6, 153

icon, see also *idol* xxii, 18, 28, 41, 51, 64, 74, 88, 145
iconography 19, 51, 148, 180
ideal 5, 37, 40, 47, 116, 158, 165, 180, 183
identity xix, xxi, 2, 5, 28, 30–1, 34, 40, 44–8, 52, 55–6, 92, 105, 106, 114, 153–4
idol 21, 37, 41, 52, 71, 94, 102, 112–13, 180–1
ignorance 9, 10, 15, 27–8, 67, 69–71, 74, 109, 118, 136–8, 150, 153, 163
Iliad, see Homer
illusion 5, 35, 36, 43, 46, 54, 70, 75, 80, 85, 153, 163, 165, 168
image 3, 4, 8, 13, 15, 18, 22, 23, 34, 43–6, 48–9, 56, 61, 85, 88, 144–5, 170, 175, 193n58
imitation 12, 16, 18, 20, 23, 41, 47, 51, 54, 66, 81, 109–10, 130, 183
immaterial, *see also* material xxi, 41, 138
incest 58, 66, 73, 82
individual xii, 6, 12, 19, 46, 54, 59–60, 92, 110, 116, 122, 150, 163, 173
individuality 5, 37, 40, 55, 115, 188n20
investment xviii, 24–8, 137, 178
invisibility xxii, 21, 29, 37, 39, 53, 56–8, 60, 112, 148
irony 11, 87, 107, 109, 136, 151

jean, *see also* denim xix, xx, 54, 89, 95
Jesus 86, 129, 133, 194n5
jewelry 23, 25, 34, 86, 131, 201n18
justice 39, 49, 58, 74, 77, 109, 118, 120–2, 151, 168, 169, 176–7

kairos 118–19
kalos 116, 143, 148, 152, 156, 162, 165, 167–8
-*kalos kagathos* 67, 152
-*khalepa ta kala* (proverb) 148, 167
Kant, I. 12–13, 51, 126, 189n20
knowledge xxi, 9–10, 14, 22, 45, 69–72, 85, 100, 111–12, 123, 163, 172, 176–8, 186
-of ignorance 10, 15, 27, 67, 69, 71, 74
- *see also* self-knowledge
kosmein 92, 114, 160
kosmos, see also cosmos xvi, 33–4, 36–7, 55, 61, 72, 112, 114, 118–9, 142, 153, 190n9

Lagerfeld, Karl 37, 56, 99, 123, 132, 151–2, 158
language 2, 7, 9–11, 81, 87, 107, 110, 113, 124, 129–30, 136, 179, 184
laughter 18, 58, 66, 109, 122–3, 135, 155, 162, 180
law xxi, 4, 12, 21, 34, 35, 49, 54, 66, 77, 81, 92, 97, 102, 106, 109–10, 116, 122, 156–7, 165, 167, 182
leather 14, 16, 119, 138, 170, 184
leisure xvii, 26–7, 117–20, 152, 154, 180, 183, 186
leisurewear xxii, 37, 52, 70, 115–16, 180, 185
Leopardi, G. 63–4
Levi, P. 5–6
logos 47, 49, 94, 118, 121, 139, 166, 174, 199n39
Loos, A. 151, 158
Lucretius xxi, 3, 8, 11, 15, 25, 69, 180
luxury 54, 104, 115, 119, 163, 182
lying 31–2, 152, 169, 171, 173, 201n5

Machiavelli, N. 21–2, 34, 103–5, 131, 132
madness 1, 32–4, 81
maenad 30, 32–6, 57
maiden 32, 98, 144, 158–60
makeup 24, 160
manners 33, 105, 107, 147
Marsyas 123, 127
Marx, K. xxiii, 20, 55, 179, 184
masculine 32–3, 71, 112
mask 29–30, 37, 93, 122–3, 150
material, *see also* immaterial xxi, xxiv, 6, 22, 24, 48, 65, 86, 111, 122–3, 132, 136, 138, 145, 162, 170, 181
materiality xxi, 123, 132, 138
McQueen, Alexander 74, 85–6, 124, 160
medieval xvii, 18–19, 122–3, 132, 181
memento mori 80, 85
Menelaus 42–9, 89, 143
mere xvi, 5–6, 15, 18, 23, 38, 41, 49, 51, 71, 77, 88, 91, 98, 114, 132, 135, 140, 148, 152, 163, 175, 180
Merleau-Ponty, M. 188n5, n11
metaphor 5, 8, 22, 24, 35, 48, 78, 81, 83–4, 134, 136–8, 145, 152, 187n10
mirror xvii, 15, 34, 56, 59, 60, 134, 149, 160, 180
mockery 74–5, 85, 106, 109, 122–3, 132, 150, 160–3, 167, 180, 184
mode xii, xv–xvii, 99, 101–2, 107, 109, 115, 173, 179, 186, 198n18
model 105, 126, 156, 158–9
modernity xii, xxiii, 19, 113, 149, 179, 186, 188n20
moment xx, xxiii, 2, 11, 19, 28, 45, 70, 73–5, 110, 116, 118–19, 148–9, 166, 179, 180–1, 186

money 53, 66, 97, 120, 154, 156–7, 160, 162
monk 131–2
moral xiii, 2, 9, 37, 104, 134, 165, 171, 173, 178
morality 2, 152, 168–9, 173, 176, 178
morphê 32, 34, 42, 49, 191n16
mummy 23–4, 105
The Muses xii, 50, 107, 112, 127, 139–40, 156, 196
music 26, 66, 99, 128–30

Nagel, A. xix, xxiii, 18, 104, 129
 –and Wood, C. 19, 87, 179, 181
nails, *see also* hair 91–3, 97–8
name (as clothing) 34, 42, 47–8, 52, 55, 111, 114, 134–6, 155, 179
natural xix, 8, 11, 33, 36, 53–4, 57, 59, 61, 70, 90–3, 96–8, 105, 116, 119, 149, 174, 181–4
nature 11, 14–15, 35–6, 47, 55, 59, 61, 87, 93, 95, 119, 121, 129, 181
 –"state of nature" 8–10, 137
neutral xviii, 14, 16–17, 27, 55, 57, 72, 75, 95, 108, 159, 164, 173, 178, 185
Nietzsche, F. W. xvii, 16, 27, 34, 66, 68, 96, 128, 131, 132, 180
noble lie 59, 100
nomos 35–6, 48, 66, 81, 92, 99, 129
normal xviii–xxi, 33–4, 52, 54, 151, 191n17
normcore xix–xxi, 40, 51–5, 132
nothing xix, xxiv, 26, 44, 49, 54, 58, 63, 107, 113, 124, 133, 140, 157–8
nude xix, 7, 9, 14, 23, 27, 64, 73, 79, 137, 181
nudity xv, 5–6, 8, 11, 14, 22, 25–8, 33, 39, 52, 54, 56, 58–9, 80, 95, 138, 182–3, 185–6
nun 60, 131–2

obscure 24, 29, 36, 93, 100, 108, 124, 134–5, 138, 179–80
Odysseus 44–5, 65, 68–9, 95, 155, 168–9, 172–4
Odyssey, see Homer
Oedipus 26, 73, 76–8, 82, 84, 130, 174
original 7, 21, 50–1, 74, 91, 103–6, 124, 129, 139, 150, 182, 184
ornament 9, 11, 14, 23, 52, 170, 182
outerwear 3, 8, 12, 21, 49
Ovid 10, 22

pagan 123, 179–80
pain 4, 21–2, 31, 76, 78, 85, 97, 147, 153
paint, painting 2, 12–13, 18–19, 55, 74, 99, 119, 127, 129, 151–2, 181
pandemic 29, 150
Pappas, N. xiii, xvi, xviii, xix, 6, 39, 58–9, 137, 182, 184–5
Paris (character) 28, 41–3, 49–50, 89–90
Paris (city) 37, 59, 147, 188n20
parricide 58, 66
particular xix–xxi, 18, 34, 41, 48, 54, 75, 83, 92–3, 101–2, 106, 134, 141, 145, 158, 162, 179
patriotism 53, 79, 82, 84
Peloponnesian War 154, 182
Pelops 44, 138–9, 141, 191n26
perception xvi, xviii, 3, 8, 54–5, 57, 174, 186
personality 7, 52, 92, 106
phantom 5, 8, 14, 30, 33, 41–51, 54–5
pharmakon 30–1
phenomenology 100, 138
Phidias 157, 160–1, 163–4
philosophy xiii–xviii, xx, xxiv, 1–2, 13–16, 22, 26, 27–8, 32, 52, 55, 71–2, 75, 108, 111–12, 133, 141, 151, 157, 169, 178, 180, 185–6

Pindar 138–40
Plato xii, xvii, 14, 16, 27, 52, 102, 112, 127, 150, 163, 172, 178, 180, 202n22
 -Academy of xvi, 52
 -*Cratylus* 193n58, 200n6
 -*Epistulae* 16
 -*Euthydemus* 71–2
 -*Euthyphro* 129
 -*Gorgias* 72
 -*Hippias Major* 148, 152–68
 -*Hippias Minor* 152, 167, 168–78
 -*Ion* 171
 -*Parmenides* 91
 -*Phaedo* xvii, 30, 94, 113
 -*Phaedrus* 15, 160, 176, 199n34
 -*Protagoras* 9, 53, 68–72, 114, 155
 -*Republic* xv, xviii, 39, 41, 55–8, 69, 90, 114, 118–22, 128, 139, 166, 183, 185
 -*Sophist* 113
 -*Statesman* 113
 -*Symposium* xxiii, 16, 72, 107, 123
 -*Theaetetus* xvi, xviii, 14, 46, 72, 116
 -*Timaeus* 92
pleasure 53, 77–8, 93, 95, 113, 137, 152, 164–8
Pliny the Elder 23, 152
poetry xv–xviii, 22, 26, 28, 30, 38–9, 41, 61, 77–8, 81, 83–4, 96, 98, 100, 107, 119, 121, 125, 128, 130, 137, 141–2, 144–5, 171–2, 175, 180, 196n40
politics 50, 108, 112, 118, 121, 126, 155, 180, 184
prime, *see also* age 64–5, 67–9, 72–3, 75, 81, 121, 179–80, 185
profanity 25–6, 128, 131, 137, 190n45
Prometheus 9–10, 12, 20, 114, 199n35
prose xvii, 16–17, 52, 141, 170–1
protest (style) 87, 95, 103, 109–10, 116–17, 125, 127, 129
punk 30–1, 73, 95, 110–11, 124–5

rap, *see* hip-hop
real xvii, xxii, 21–2, 27, 41–6, 48, 50–1, 113, 149–53, 162–4
reality xviii, 1, 7, 11, 15, 22, 34–7, 38–9, 43, 81, 83, 85, 136, 148–9, 153, 163–4
rebel 21, 39, 59, 79, 102–3, 106–10
red 20, 87, 110, 131–2
reflection xviii, 3, 8, 15–16, 32, 36, 39, 46, 56, 60, 75, 83, 97, 126, 128, 143, 164, 167, 170, 180
relativism 15, 70, 166
Renaissance, renaissance xxiii, 18, 20, 51, 131, 180
revolution xxiii, 103–4, 126, 179–80
rhythm 51, 78, 96, 99, 102, 128–30, 170–1
ritual 1, 3, 20, 22, 74, 75, 105, 122, 132, 138, 153
Rome 10, 55, 92, 96, 103–4
rose xii–iv, 107
 -colored glasses 12
Rousseau, J-J. 8–11, 13, 68
runway 2, 18, 27, 123, 126, 138, 160, 172

Samson, *see* Delilah
la Sape 110–11
sapeur, sapeuse 110, 112, 198n17
Sappho xii, 107, 147
satire 52, 100, 126, 133–4
sculpture 19, 116, 179–81
seeing xviii, 3, 13, 15, 19, 22, 32, 35, 40, 46, 49, 51, 56–7, 99, 152, 165, 188n11
self xx, xxi–ii, 2–3, 5–7, 11, 14, 21, 23, 27, 30, 40, 52, 54–6, 64–6, 74–5, 80, 82, 87, 121, 127, 135–6, 138, 141, 163, 167–9, 183–6
self-expression 11, 74
self-knowledge 126
self-reflection xxii, 7, 8, 60, 149, 163, 167

selfie 39, 51
sex 93, 100, 113
-act of 25, 31, 66, 71, 122, 165
Shakespeare, W. 29, 43, 87, 134
shame 7, 25, 55, 116, 136
shape 23, 32–8, 49, 58, 80, 91, 97, 139, 141, 160
shapeless 33, 34, 36–8, 58, 60, 115
shit, *see also* bullshit 25–6, 133, 137–8, 200n10, n12
shoes 5, 12–13, 16, 17, 23, 108, 114, 117, 118–20, 131, 153, 162–3, 184
sight 3, 45–6, 148, 153, 162, 165–6, 174
Simmel, G. 52, 175
simulacrum 8, 15, 83, 138
skin xx, 2, 4, 6–7, 8, 11, 35, 40, 85, 91, 134, 136, 138, 139, 160
social media 28, 38–40, 55, 57, 62, 148
Socrates 15–16, 116, 127–9
-and Alcibiades 68–72, 102, 107, 114, 123–4, 195n22
-death of, *see* death xiii, 10, 30, 53, 75, 94, 150
-and the kallipolis 39, 58–9, 118–21, 130, 185
-and looking bad 169–78
-and ugliness xvii–xviii, 16, 27–8, 41, 90–1, 152–69
Solon 64, 130
sophist xvi, 27–8, 33, 53, 69, 71, 107, 111–13, 123, 141, 156, 166, 180
sophistry 1, 38, 53, 65, 70, 111–12, 186
soul xxi, xxiv, 4, 8, 36, 46, 58, 64–7, 72, 76–7, 79, 84, 92, 111, 113–14, 118, 121, 131–3, 136, 138, 139, 141–2, 175–7
Sparta 42, 46, 107, 154, 156–7, 163, 165, 191, 201
Spartan (style) 53, 92, 102, 156–7, 182–4
sprezzatura 14, 54, 100, 175
Steele, V. 16, 53, 86, 147

stripping xvii–iii, 14, 58, 114, 121, 182
style xv, xix, 19–20, 39, 56, 90, 96, 99, 101, 109–10, 117–18, 129–30, 175, 180, 185, 186
suit 17, 20, 21, 25, 27, 40, 55, 111, 112, 114–16, 118, 123, 125, 136, 138, 140
sumptuary laws 109
surface xviii, xxii–iii, 1, 2, 6–8, 10, 18, 23, 26, 55, 123, 132, 135, 138, 148, 150–2, 170
sweatpants 4, 37–9, 40, 41, 52, 54–7, 60, 62, 175
symbol xxii, 12, 24, 36, 46, 55, 83–4, 114, 125, 127, 143, 171, 180

Tacitus 114
tailor, tailoring xvi, 28, 60, 62, 103, 113, 119, 133–5, 141
Tantalus 44, 138–9, 162
tattoo 2, 73, 80, 93
Teufelsdröckh 26, 133–6
text 11, 91, 96, 103, 108, 136, 196n50
textile 11, 32, 91, 93
Thales xviii, 14, 154, 187n14
Theseus 32, 94
Thoth 10
Thucydides 53, 71, 120, 182, 184–5
thumos 66, 68, 84, 124, 196n38
tie xxii, 16, 17, 24, 38, 40, 92, 106, 110, 117
tiger's leap (German *Tigersprung*) xxiii, 87, 104, 106, 125, 179
time, *see also* leisure xxiii–iv, 2, 5, 18–19, 22, 24, 37, 44, 64–5, 69–70, 74–5, 91, 98, 104, 108, 113, 115, 116, 122, 126, 137, 138, 142, 145, 180, 184–6
touch 2–3, 6–7, 15, 97, 162
tragedy, tragic xii, 29–30, 36–7, 38, 43, 64, 66, 73–4, 76, 78–9, 83, 98, 133, 143, 145, 174–5, 179, 185

Index

transcendence 14, 22, 27, 35, 40, 51, 75, 133, 135, 148, 179
transcendental ego 74
translation (and fashion) xxiii, 7, 107
trend xx, 19, 21, 50–2, 56, 98, 111
Trojan War 43, 48–9
tropos 120, 182
truth xv, xvii, xxiii, 1, 10, 14–18, 22, 25, 27, 30, 33–4, 36, 39, 56, 67, 75, 93, 107, 109, 111, 123, 138, 141, 147–9, 151, 153, 155, 158, 163, 166, 168–9, 171, 184–5
turban 97
tweed 16, 53
tyranny 3, 17, 54, 62, 105, 113

ugly xvii, 16, 27, 66, 91, 92, 97, 116, 117, 140, 148–9, 153, 157, 159, 161, 165–7, 174–5, 184
uniform xx, 4, 5, 15, 28, 60, 104, 106, 140, 150–1
utilitarian 12–13, 18, 20, 148, 162–3

van Gogh, Vincent 12–13
vanity xvi, xviii, 1, 4, 11–12, 18, 28, 100–1, 105, 150
Venus, *see also* Aphrodite 30, 142
vestment (Latin *vestis*) xviii, 8, 11, 14, 23–8, 52, 92, 134, 138
vintage xxiii, 14, 21, 59, 86, 141
virtue 29, 33, 37, 57–9, 99, 111, 115, 123, 152, 156, 174
vulgar xiii, xv, 2, 25, 56, 107, 128, 134

war 5, 8, 43, 48, 61, 82, 86, 89, 90, 95, 106, 124, 125, 127, 142–5
152, 154
weapons 35, 107, 128, 182
weaving 8, 40, 89, 112–13, 136, 170, 189n15, 191n14, 196n50
white xxi, 18, 20, 43, 73, 115, 132, 136, 195n19
whole, *see also part* xv, xix, 32, 34, 35, 76, 118, 121–2, 133–6, 144–5, 148, 153–4, 160–2, 167, 199n34
Wilde, O. 52, 124, 126
wit xvii, 66, 100–2, 106–9, 151
wool 28, 89, 91–2, 113, 119, 133, 150, 181, 198n21
Woolf, V. 59–60
words (as fashion) xvi, 2, 7–11, 15, 22, 26, 35, 52, 53, 57, 72, 74, 80, 87, 91, 101–3, 106, 108, 111, 118, 120–1, 122, 124, 128–9, 136–7, 140–1, 147, 184, 186
wrinkles 23, 52, 58, 71, 90, 107

Xerxes 61

you 18, 39, 44, 46, 54, 55, 64, 163, 168
youth, *see* age

Zeus 10, 30–4, 36, 42–3, 48–50, 58, 61, 68, 72, 76, 88, 96, 100, 112, 142, 145

223

www.ingramcontent.com/pod-product-compliance
Lightning Source LLC
Chambersburg PA
CBHW051809230426
4367ZCB00012B/2665